SHAKESPEARE
THE THEATRE-POET

ROBERT HAPGOOD

CLARENDON PRESS · OXFORD
1988

Oxford University Press, Walton Street, Oxford OX2 6DP
Oxford New York Toronto
Delhi Bombay Calcutta Madras Karachi
Petaling Jaya Singapore Hong Kong Tokyo
Nairobi Dar es Salaam Cape Town
Melbourne Auckland
and associated companies in
Berlin Ibadan

Oxford is a trade mark of Oxford University Press

Published in the United States
by Oxford University Press, USA

British Library Cataloguing in Publication Data
Hapgood, Robert
Shakespeare the theatre-poet.
1. Drama in English. Shakespeare, William, 1564–1616.
Critical studies
I. Title
822.3'3
ISBN 0–19–812990–4

Library of Congress Cataloging in Publication Data
Hapgood, Robert.
Shakespeare the theatre-poet / Robert Hapgood.
p. cm. Includes index.
1. Shakespeare, William, 1564–1616—Criticism
and interpretation. I. Title.
822.3'3—dc19 PR2976.H29 1988 88–10206
ISBN 0–19–812990–4

Typeset by Hope Services
Printed in Great Britain by
Biddles Ltd.
Guildford and King's Lynn

TO MARILYN

Preface

MANY prefaces to books on Shakespeare begin with an apology, explaining why, despite the shelves of books already written on the subject, still another is justified. I make no such apology here. This book was written not despite but to a large degree because of this previous body of commentary, for its very size, diversity, and contradictoriness are prime evidence of the chief feature of Shakespeare's art with which I will be trying to come to terms: his extraordinary openness to interpretation. When to these published interpretations are added those of the innumerable productions I have seen and of the hundreds of university students I have taught, the reader will understand the need I have felt—after thirty-five years of professional engagement with Shakespeare's plays—to work out in my own mind what can be said for sure about them and what cannot. What reliable guidance *does* Shakespeare give his interpreters?

This perennial question is made timely by recent general tendencies that resist or minimize or appropriate or take for granted the role of the creating writer in favour of the interpreting critic or performer or the responding audience. Some go so far as to assert the essential absence of the writer from his work, thus freeing its interpreters to make of it what they will. When such free renderings are done with genius, they should be welcomed as such. As Oscar Wilde saw, a critic can be an artist. Alas, few are. Most often, it is the creator of the work who is the genius. Certainly this is true where Shakespeare is concerned. Those engaged in the enactment of his plays and their reception make their indispensable contributions to them, of course. I will be much concerned with defining the nature of their involvement. Yet the balance needs to be kept true. This book was in part prompted by my neo-conservative desire—in a time of deconstruction—to reassert the primacy of the writer's creative presence.

This desire was sharpened by my intense exposure recently to Eastern drama—chiefly to that of Japan but also that of China, Bali, Java, and India. For two and a half years I revelled in 'total theatre' of the very highest sort, a dazzling combination of all the performing arts that made Western theatre seem tame and timid by comparison. The experience widened my dramatic horizons in ways that have contributed positively and radically to this book, which—as will be explained in Chapter 1—aspires to do for Shakespearian drama what Japanese and Indian theatre-aesthetics have done for Noh and Sanskrit drama. Yet this exposure also had a negative effect. I came to see that in one crucial way much of Eastern 'total theatre' is not as total as it seemed at first. It is largely anonymous, its stories often coming from traditional sources, its dialogue often being improvised. It is drama without a dramatist, and when the initial excitements had passed, I began to miss the sense of a single, original, master-hand in control. I found myself much preferring the exceptions to the Eastern rule—Noh, the classic puppet love-tragedies of Chikamatsu, the Javanese shadow-puppets—and, to my surprise, actively disliking kabuki, which in the service of star actors and their fans high-handedly rewrites, truncates, and otherwise dismembers its playwrights' scripts. My Eastern exposure thus made me realize how remarkable in the context of world theatre our Western playwrights are and how highly their presence should be valued, Shakespeare's in particular.

The aim of this book, therefore, is to come fully to terms with Shakespeare's openness to interpretation while respecting the primacy of his creative guidance.

This book was begun on a fellowship from the American Council of Learned Societies and completed on a Faculty Scholar's grant from the University of New Hampshire, whose Central University Research Fund supported the word-processing of the manuscript. I am grateful for this support.

All quotations are from *The Complete Works of Shakespeare*, edited by Stanley Wells and Gary Taylor (Clarendon Press, Oxford, 1986).

Chapter 6 on *Hamlet* reworks articles previously published in *The Tulane Drama Review* (Summer 1965), 132–45, and in *Perspectives on Hamlet* (Lewisburg, 1975), 29–47. Permission to draw upon these publications has been graciously extended.

Some of the ideas guiding the whole book were first sketched in a paper given to the Shakespeare Association of Japan. Various parts were presented at a seminar of the World Shakespeare Congress in West Berlin, the Royal Shakespeare Theatre Summer School at Stratford-upon-Avon, the Boston Area Shakespearians, and the Tuesday at One and Graduate Colloquium series at the University of New Hampshire.

Joseph A. Bryant, jun., Andrew Gurr, Marvin Rosenberg, James Siemon, and Stanley Wells have read and helpfully commented on parts of the manuscript. Monica Bethe was my mentor in Noh. Kim

Scott Walwyn and Alice M. Park of the Oxford University Press have been exemplary editors.

   This book is dedicated to my wife, who was more help with it than she thinks.

R.H.

Contents

Illustrations

I

Shakespeare the Theatre-Poet

SHAKESPEARE the theatre-poet is a maker of theatre-events. Elizabethans invariably called the author of a play a 'poet', in the Greek sense of 'maker'. I call Shakespeare a 'theatre-poet' in that sense: he *makes* theatre. In using the term I am not thus referring to the fact that he wrote most of his dialogue in the form of verse. The 'theatre' in 'theatre-poet' refers to what is now commonly called a 'theatre-event', the coming together of players and playgoers to imagine the world outlined in the playwright's script, complete with characters, plot, dialogue, and atmosphere.[1]

Obviously the making of a theatre-event is a collaborative act. The playwright, the players, and the playgoers comprise a performance-ensemble, to which each makes a distinctive and necessary contribution. It is a partnership within which each participant has a considerable degree of autonomy. Accordingly, the theatre-event that occurs at a given performance will to a large degree vary not only with the script but with the individuals involved, whether on the stage or in the auditorium.

Even so, Shakespeare does provide invaluable guidance for the event that occurs when one of his texts is performed. Given their due, his texts function not only as scripts but as scenarios for the workings of the performance-ensemble. The players, in suiting their actions to the playwright's words, must make a host of choices; Shakespeare the theatre-poet guides these choices. The playgoers must not only assist the playwright and players in imagining a world but respond to the result; Shakespeare the theatre-poet guides these responses. His creativity thus extends not only to outlining make-believe worlds (as

[1] The term 'theatre-poet' is not in common use. In a narrower sense than mine, it was used in setting the theme of the 1970 International Conference in Stratford-upon-Avon concerning 'Shakespeare the Theatre Poet'. Its focus there was on Shakespeare's mastery of spoken language as a theatrical instrument. In a wider sense than mine, Francis Fergusson in *The Idea of a Theater* (Princeton, 1949) adapted Cocteau's idea of substituting for 'poetry in the theatre' a 'poetry *of* the theatre', in which 'scenes are integrated like the words of a poem' (p. 166). Fergusson extends the term to encompass 'modes of action and awareness associated in our time with poetry in the widest sense, and in other periods with myth, ritual, and traditional (as opposed to machine-made) popular art' (p. 195).

playwright) but (as theatre-poet) to guiding their enactment and reception.

Shakespeare has also of course been regarded as a dramatist whose works become dramas when interpreted by readers. In this case, the reader's contribution to the partnership combines the actor's function of (imaginatively) embodying the text and the playgoer's function of bearing witness to the result. The collaborative 'event' occurs in the study or library, not the theatre. Still, the guidance provided by Shakespeare's theatre-poetry applies to what takes place in the theatre of the mind as well as to actual performance.

Although the distinctive emphasis of this book is on Shakespeare's theatre-poetry, it will necessarily be much concerned with his work as a playwright. It will indeed seek to define the role that Shakespeare as theatre-poet assigns himself as playwright within the performance-ensemble and to explore the ways in which his concerns with the encompassing theatre-event enter into his choices as a playwright.

Clearly Shakespeare's presence as a theatre-poet is of a special sort. The presence of a novelist is usually overt and audible. Whether or not we are addressed directly as 'dear reader', we can hear the narrator's voice. Often it will be quite personal and distinctive, a voice to which we can warm as to that of a friend. Shakespeare's presence is much less overt. The voice to be heard in his texts is more like that of a wonderfully gifted and resourceful colleague, quietly offering wise guidance to fellow participants as they work with him in enacting a play. The guidance he provides is rarely simple or directive. Many times it is not even clear. Usually it offers players and playgoers alike a rich choice of options for interpretation and response, within generously wide limits. It is the aim of this book to sense this presence, listen for this voice, discern these guidelines.

It has long been recognized that Shakespeare's texts project a double awareness: of an imagined world and of the theatrical situation that encompasses it. Recall the beginning of Olivier's film of *Henry V*, in which the camera slowly pans across Elizabethan London and descends to show the Globe Theatre where a performance of *Henry V* is in progress—complete with a signboard naming the scene, a boy-actress in the tiring-room, a rowdy audience, and other picturesque features of the period. In these ways we are made very conscious of the theatrical conditions of Elizabethan London. In the same spirit, scholarly commentators who have emphasized this double awareness have mostly stressed Shakespeare's immediate Elizabethan circumstances and his habit of building stage directions into his lines.[2] It is only beginning to be realized that his texts provide scenarios for theatre-events that occur whenever and wherever they are performed. Again, there is nothing new about recognizing that such encounters between participants in the performance-ensemble are an important part of our dramatic experience, that—for example—the live interplay between actor and audience is a key part of what distinguishes legitimate theatre from film. Such interplay has been understood, in its most obvious form: the rapport or lack of it between a particular performer and a particular audience on a particular day, the result of the special circumstances of a given performance when—say—an actor is in especially good or bad form and an audience in an especially good or bad humour.

This rapport has usually been seen as a spontaneous interaction between actor and audience in which the author is at most a silent partner and which is only partially under any one person's control, that person being the director. Much of what I am calling theatre-poetry has been regarded as the special province of the director. The director, however, is concerned with finding what 'works' in particular circumstances. The theatre-poet's guidance applies whatever the circumstances.

I am not concerned with the *vicarious* experiences that all members of the performance-ensemble share. It is a commonplace that the playwright must imagine himself into the shoes of his characters, that the actors must create the inner as well as the outer lives of their assigned roles, that the spectators must join in the make-believe, or at least suspend disbelief towards the characters the playwright has conceived and the players embodied. In the very process of thus mutually imagining a make-believe world, its participants also experience a *direct* kind of involvement. As the playwright writes his script and adapts his sources to his purposes, he is obliged to make certain choices, as are the actors in the process of rehearsal. And in their responses to a performance playgoers must laugh or weep, welcome or deplore what they are witnessing. As theatre-poet Shakespeare guides these direct involvements. Through his text he defines their general frame of reference, poses the problems, specifies the alternatives, places the emphases. If his cues are heeded, he largely

---

[2] Bernard Beckerman, *Shakespeare at the Globe* (New York, 1962); Ann Pasternak Slater, *Shakespeare the Director* (Totowa, 1982); Alan Dessen, *Elizabethan Conventions and Modern Interpreters* (Cambridge, 1984); David Bevington, *Action is Eloquence: Language of Gesture* (Harvard, 1984).

determines, through what happens in *Hamlet*, what happens *at* its performance.

In many instances Shakespeare's audience must face problems and make choices that are analogous to those that his characters experience. Of course, there are large areas where there is no such overlap. Do we feel ambition at *Macbeth*? Not much, I would say, if at all. But we do experience the tug towards forbidden knowledge that draws Macbeth on. And the way Macbeth deals with these experiences conditions our own responses. The pity Prospero learns to feel for others in the last act of *The Tempest* prepares us to pity him in the epilogue.

In making their interpretative choices, actors, too, often share a common experience with the characters they are playing. Morris Carnovsky, for example, reports his experience in performing King Lear:

It is appropriate that Lear became a test of my own life's work, for that word 'test' is the very touchstone of the play . . . As I waited offstage for my first entrance, what was going through my mind, both as actor and as the character, was something like this: 'I must discover for myself *what I am*: I must test myself against whatever ultimate values there are in life, by the extreme course of deliberately dividing up my kingdom, of surrendering all the visible appurtenances and evidences of royalty and facing up to whatever may result from that action.

And for Carnovsky this process of discovery continued through to the end:

At the conclusion of *Lear* I love that moment with Edgar: 'Do you see this? . . . Look there . . . Look there.' The word is *look*. We can say that the whole interpenetration with a role like Lear is a series of fits and starts of discovery, as if the actor is exclaiming with startled, new-found vision, 'how about *this*! and this! Look at *this*! My God, and *this*!'[3]

Very likely Shakespeare found the writing of *King Lear* a similar process of testing and discovery.

For in his work as playwright Shakespeare seems often to be caught up in the same distinctive processes that drive his characters. In *Shakespeare's Mediated Vision* (Amherst, 1976) Richard Fly sees a number of the plays as reflecting in their imagined worlds the very artistic problems that the playwright was facing in writing them.[4] On

---

[3] Morris Carnovsky, 'The Eye of the Storm: On Playing King Lear', *Shakespeare Quarterly*, 28 (1977), 147, 150.

[4] See also Lionel Abel, *Metatheatre* (New York, 1963); James L. Calderwood, *To Be and Not to Be* (New York, 1983), and earlier books.

the other hand, it seems to me as likely that Shakespeare entered into his imagined world so completely that his creative choices reflected *its* characteristics, and that the influence was thus reciprocal. Carnovsky's word 'interpenetration' is again apt. For the most part, the capacity for such imaginative immersion is one of Shakespeare's greatest strengths, as will be illustrated in later chapters. At times, however, the quality of his art may be diminished by the imaginary company he keeps. When he named the recruits in *2 Henry IV* Mouldy and Bullcalf and Feeble, he was not above playing straight-man to Falstaff, setting up too easy one-liners for his by then tired comedian. To Mouldy Falstaff says: ''Tis the more time thou wert used', a joke so heavy-handed that even Shallow gets it: 'Things that are mouldy lack use. Very singular good, in faith, well said, Sir John, very well said' (3. 2. 107–9).

For another example, consider *Measure for Measure*, whose characters have a remarkable proclivity for substitution: the Duke substitutes Angelo for himself as ruler, the Provost substitutes Ragozine's head for Claudio's, the Friar substitutes Mariana for Isabella in Angelo's bed.[5] The playwright engages in the same sort of activity, both in detail and in the large. In 4. 2, at the very moment when Mariana is losing her maidenhead (it having been substituted for Isabella's), the Provost talks first with Pompey and Abhorson about the beheading of Claudio and Barnardine and then with the Friar about substituting the one head for the other. Thus the playwright substitutes talk of the loss and switching of male heads for showing the loss of a substitute maidenhead. In addition to the implicit structural pun, Shakespeare throws in references to a 'woman's head' in the dialogue and to 'snatches'.

In overall structure, too, the playwright makes a basic substitution. In all of the source versions, the final mating is between the equivalents of Angelo and Isabella. After awakening our expectations of the same from their first interview, Shakespeare in the event substitutes a different mate for each, thus achieving a more or less happy ending for his finale. If we in the audience are as willing as the citizens of Vienna to substitute the facsimile for the real thing, we too can enjoy the happy ending as such. Many spectators, however, have not been willing to enter so completely into the imagined world of this play. Shakespeare the theatre-poet may try to engage all the

---

[5] For a more extensive survey see Nancy S. Leonard, 'Substitution in Shakespeare's Problem Plays', *English Literary Renaissance*, 9 (1979), 281–301.

participants in the performance-ensemble in the same kind of activity, but he does not always succeed.

Although each of the participants in the performance-ensemble is essential, it is upon Shakespeare as theatre-poet, the maker of the whole theatre-event, that I wish to focus. One might expect to find aid in this matter from the field of 'performance theory', a branch of dramatic criticism concerned with the event that occurs when a play is performed. In fact, however, the theatre-poet's share has been consistently slighted by current performance theorists, most of whom are themselves performers. My book is designed to help to fill this gap. Since in this respect I hope to contribute to performance theory, I should like to say something further about its main outlines, which may well be unfamiliar to many readers.

'Performance theory' is a new term, coined by Richard Schechner, for a recently revived approach to drama whose origins are very old.[6] In the East, the fullest major document is India's *Natyasastra*, which is thought to have been codified sometime during the first centuries on either side of the birth of Christ.[7] The other major Eastern contribution is Zeami's writing about the secrets of Japanese Noh, which survives from the fourteenth and fifteenth centuries AD.[8] They are very different works. The Indian compilation is elaborately systematic; the Japanese, more personal and glancing. The Indian image of theatre-poetry is of *rasa* (taste), the Japanese of *hana* (flower).[9] Yet they are alike in being fully inclusive in their treatment of the theatre-event, giving due attention to each of the participants in the performance-ensemble and their interrelations. For both *rasa* and *hana* depend upon the contributions of all. Zeami writes:

What is called 'opening the eyes' refers to the moment in a Noh play when the deep sensations inherent in the play are suddenly experienced in one moment of profound exchange. When their 'eyes are opened,' the spectators receive this extraordinary impression through the aesthetic qualities related to dance and movement. This moment arises from the manifestation of the artistic and spiritual power of the actor. It may seem that such a moment may bear no relation to the drama as actually composed, but in fact this visual impression

---

[6] Richard Schechner, *Essays on Performance Theory 1970–6* (New York, 1977) and *Between Theater and Anthropology* (Philadelphia, 1985).

[7] Bharata Muni, *The Natyasastra*, trans. M. Ghosh (Calcutta, 1961–7).

[8] Zeami, *On the Art of the Noh Drama*, trans. J. T. Rimer, M. Yamazaki (Princeton, 1984).

[9] Schechner, *Between Theater and Anthropology*, 143–8. Typically, Schechner leaves the playwright out of account.

of superb skill could not come about if the actual moment for its realization had not been planned for in the play itself. The one composing the text must consider with extreme care where to place the moment when the actor's visual movements can create this effect. (pp. 158–9)

Thus each participant in the theatre-event contributes to 'opening the eyes'.

Western efforts in this field have been less inclusive, and have concentrated instead on some one of the participants or relationships. Aristotle's *Poetics* (written in the fourth century BC) is the first and greatest such work, focusing as it does on Aristotle's responses as a spectator to the Greek tragedies that he had read or seen performed and his analysis of the features in them which produce those responses. He largely leaves out of account, however, the contributions of the actors, a neglect which has been furthered through subsequent centuries by the inclination among his academic followers to make an artificial distinction between 'drama as literature' and 'drama as theatre'.

This neglect of the performer is true even of the two academic critics who are the most important forebears of current performance theorists, Francis Fergusson in *The Idea of a Theater* and Eric Bentley in *The Playwright as Thinker* (New York, 1967) and other books. Both have a keen awareness of the whole event that occurs when a play is performed. For Fergusson the theatre-event for playwright, player, and playgoer alike is fundamentally determined by the prevailing 'idea of a theatre' of their time. He sees the theatre as a social institution, whose image of man has progressively disintegrated through the ages. Once whole—in the times of the ancient Greeks and Dante—this image has in successive periods been fractured into smaller and smaller pieces, and the dramas written for these theatres have accordingly become partial and fragmentary. He assumes that the deterioration he finds in the theatre considered as a social institution is paralleled by a deterioration in the artistic worth of the drama written for it. As brilliant as is his study of *Hamlet* and the Globe Theatre, he does not thus know quite what to make of Shakespeare, whose mastery he fully appreciates yet whose theatre, none the less, he sees as poised between the old and the modern. His theory does not allow for the possibility that drama might thrive at the moment when traditional understandings are still current enough to be a real factor in a play, yet are beginning to go to pieces.

Nor in his emphasis on 'tradition' does Fergusson give sufficient importance to the 'individual talent' of the dramatists who put their own impress on the 'idea of a theatre' they inherited. This last is what

Bentley's books supply, especially for playwrights of the nineteenth and twentieth centuries. (He has a blind spot where Shakespeare is concerned.) Between them, Fergusson and Bentley provide the best account to date of the playwright's contribution to the theatre-event.

Since both Fergusson and Bentley have had practical experience in the theatre, it is surprising that neither gives due weight in his theories to the relationship between the playwright and the performers. That has been the focus of Harley Granville-Barker and his many followers. Like Granville-Barker, himself a playwright and director, some have looked at the texts as if they were scripts for a production they were about to do.[10] Others, such as A. C. Sprague, have drawn on theatre history to comment critically on the actual treatment the playwright has already received at the hands of his actors.[11] Few such studies, however, have included the audience as a factor.[12]

The audience has, however, come in for its share of attention. Kenneth Burke's remarkable essay, 'Antony in Behalf of the Play', anticipated the present concern with 'reader response'. In it he imagines that Antony, instead of delivering a funeral oration, addresses the off-stage audience, revealing the methods of Shakespeare's theatre-poetry:

> My Elizabethan audience, under the guise of facing a Roman mob I confront you at a most complicated moment. As a matter of fact, up to this point in our play you have been treated most outrageously. It can honestly be said that, in no major particular, have you been granted those clear and simple responses to which, as customers, you might feel yourselves entitled. Instead your author has kept you in as vacillating a condition as this very Roman mob you have been watching with so little respect. I doubt if he distinguishes between the two of you . . .[13]

He then goes on to reveal wittily just how 'our Great Demagogue continues to manipulate your minds'. Like Burke, subsequent commentators have assumed a very passive sort of audience whose

[10] Harley Granville-Barker, *Prefaces to Shakespeare*, 4 vols. (Princeton, 1946–63) and *More Prefaces to Shakespeare* (Princeton, 1974); J. L. Styan, *Shakespeare's Stagecraft* (Cambridge, 1967). Their treatment of Shakespeare's text as a guide to performance is limited by their pre-selection of single lines of interpretation (persuasive though they may be) rather than acknowledging the multiple options that Shakespeare leaves open.

[11] A. C. Sprague, *Shakespeare and the Actors* (Harvard, 1944) and *Shakespearian Players and Performances* (Harvard, 1953). See also Carol Carlisle, *Shakespeare from the Greenroom* (Chapel Hill, NC, 1969).

[12] A notable instance is John Russell Brown, 'Playing for Laughs in the Last Plays', in his *Shakespeare's Plays in Performance* (New York, 1967).

[13] Kenneth Burke, 'Antony in Behalf of the Play', in his *The Philosophy of Literary Form*, 3rd edn. (Berkeley, 1973), 329–43.

responses can be mechanically 'manipulated' (to use the term habitually applied to the process). And again like him, they have concentrated on the audience's relation to the author while neglecting the mediating actor.[14]

There has thus been a genuine need for attention to what happens in a theatre between an actor and an audience. A number of recent books, mostly written by actors or directors, have provided helpful insights into this relationship. For example, in *The Presence of the Actor* (New York, 1972) Joseph Chaikin asks, 'Should the audience be addressed as fools or saints?' (p. 140). He advises actors secretly to 'dedicate' a performance to some specific kind of ideal audience—to Martin Luther King, all prisoners, 'fire itself', or some other person or force with which they can make a 'living contact . . . as though an electric wire was running between you' and thereby 'call on something in another which is also alive in yourself'. He has found that the actual audience will then—without realizing it—join in the dedication: 'if what I pick is representative of what I feel is in each person in the audience, as well as being specific and subjective to me, then I don't have to turn away from the audience, but the audience makes the dedication possible' (pp. 143–4).

As here, those who have placed the face-to-face encounter between actor and audience at the heart of the theatre-event have tended to leave the playwright out of account. In *The Theatrical Event* (Middletown, Conn., 1975), David Cole, for example, defines drama by analogy with shamanism in a way that in effect leaves the playwright out of consideration altogether. Similarly, in *The Actor's Freedom* (New York, 1975) Michael Goldman has developed a whole theory of drama from the idea that 'the forms of drama all flow from the confrontation that takes place between any actor and his

[14] See, e.g., E. A. J. Honigmann, *Shakespeare: Seven Tragedies: The Dramatist's Manipulation of Response* (New York, 1976) and Jean E. Howard, *Shakespeare's Art of Orchestration: Stage Technique and Audience Response* (Urbana-Champaign, Ill., 1984). Howard allows for a freer response in 'Shakespeare's Creation of a Fit Audience for *The Tempest*', in *Shakespeare: Contemporary Critical Approaches*, ed. H. Garvin (Lewisburg, 1980), 142–53; here she commendably brings out the trust that Shakespeare places in his audience. An outstanding exception is Thomas Whitaker, *Fields of Play in Modern Drama* (Princeton, 1977). Ch. 2, 'Playing the Player', is especially congenial to my own approach. In it he finds a 'spontaneous reciprocity, inherent mutuality' between actor and spectator and calls attention to meaningful analogies (and contradictions) between the 'performed action' implied in the play-text and the 'action of performance' that occurs when it is enacted and witnessed. See also my article, 'Shakespeare and the Included Spectator', in *Reinterpretations of Elizabethan Drama*, ed. N. Rabkin (New York, 1969), 117–36.

audience; plays are best understood as ways of intensifying that confrontation and charging it with meaning' (p. 3). There is truth to Goldman's formulation, and it brings out a factor that has been neglected; but surely it is not the whole truth.[15] One wonders about the imagined world of the play. Isn't that the main thing to which a spectator responds at a performance? And what about the playwright? Doesn't he too have a role in the 'confrontation'? May he not himself, through his text, 'dedicate' his play to a particular kind of audience-response—and to a particular kind of acting as well? If Chaikin as an actor can address 'fire itself' as audience, does not the Chorus of *Henry V* invoke a 'muse of fire' for the whole performance?[16]

Michael Pennington provides another example. Discussing the role of Hamlet as he performed it, he shows an admirable feeling for the theatre-poetry of the suspenseful moment at which Hamlet seems about to stab Claudius:

A man with a sword comes upon his enemy, whom he has sworn to destroy, at prayer. The promised act of revenge can at this point be performed with relatively little difficulty—indeed with no greater fear of discovery than that of the praying man on an earlier occasion when he destroyed his enemy in an orchard. With exultation the armed man approaches his victim and raises his sword.

At this point we stop and see where we are. There is no question in the mind of the spectator but that the sword will certainly come down on the neck of the praying man with all the fury with which it was raised. There is also no question in the mind of the armed man but that he will now do the deed—no question at all. Most oddly of all, in the mind of the actor personifying the man with the sword there is a momentary certainty that tonight will be different, and that his colleague on the floor is about to suffer a severe and unexpected injury.

The alarming question arises: who is actually in charge? If the actor himself is in doubt, then who is masterminding the event and guiding us towards the next action? Everyone waits, the spectators, the two men, the two actors playing the two men, all held for a moment on the same edge, holding the same breath.[17]

[15] Where Shakespeare is concerned Goldman's practice is sounder than his theory. He gives the playwright his due as a key participant in the theatre event in *Shakespeare and the Energies of Drama* (Princeton, 1972) and *Acting and Action in Shakespearean Tragedy* (Princeton, 1985).

[16] Keir Elam, *The Semiotics of Drama* (London, 1980), recognizes the importance of both 'the theatrical or *performance text*' and 'the written or *dramatic text*'. But he analyses them separately, in his conclusion looking to the future for the 'united enterprise' that would combine the two. My book, in its own way, seeks to make that combination.

[17] Michael Pennington, 'Hamlet', in *Players of Shakespeare* (Cambridge, 1985), 128.

1. Michael Pennington as Hamlet (1980).

Who is 'in charge'? Pennington doesn't say, yet the answer to his 'alarming question' seems to me clear. Who else but Shakespeare the theatre-poet? He has pre-imagined this eye-opening moment of suspense for the character, spectator, and actor. Perhaps he felt it himself before, as playwright, making the crucial choice against the deed.

Such testimonies concerning the relationship between the actor and the audience thus help to fill out one's overall understanding of the theatre-event but are not themselves a balanced view of it. The same may be said of the other studies discussed. Taken singly, they seem partial. Taken together, they suggest the value of an approach as inclusive as the Eastern models, one which would give due attention to all of the participants in the performance-ensemble and their relationships with one another.

The modern work that has so far come closest to this inclusiveness is Peter Brook's *The Empty Space* (London, 1968). In addition to his concern with the actor, he is acutely mindful of the playwright's contribution to the theatre-event (especially that of Shakespeare) and of the involvement of the spectator. But his primary emphasis is on the role of the director. Indeed, his book is more than anything else an attack on the 'deadly' conventional theatre and a manifesto for certain new approaches to performance. My emphasis, on the other hand, is on Shakespeare, especially upon the ways in which—as theatre-poet—he guides the workings of the performance-ensemble to produce the distinctive kind of rapport that best suits a given play. By studying this rapport (my word for *hana* or *rasa*) in a variety of plays, I seek to make a start towards doing for Shakespearian drama in performance what Zeami in his treatises did for Noh and the *Natyasastra* did for Sanskrit drama.

Zeami was, of course, writing about the theatre-poetry of Noh with the direct and all-inclusive authority of a great playwright, a star performer, and a very discerning contemporary spectator, acutely aware of both his own responses and those of his noble patrons. Shakespeare's theatre-poetry, on the other hand, can be known only through a process of interpretation. And the more one learns about this process from the accumulated experience of centuries of interpreters, the more one comes to see its difficulties.

There was a time, not so long ago, when scholarly discussion proceeded as if there were one right reading for each play. Interpreters might well differ about what this reading was, but there was a common assumption that, when the disagreements had been argued out and the gaps filled in, the true and full meaning would emerge. Similarly, it was felt that, if they only would, actors could 'do Shakespeare straight' in 'true-to-score' fashion.

Those days are well past. It is generally acknowledged that Shakespeare's texts permit many different yet valid interpretations. Indeed, the pendulum has tended to swing to the other extreme, from

excessive authoritarianism among interpreters to excessive latitudi-
narianism. It now seems that 'anything goes'.

The swing is to be seen in one of the major efforts of Shakespearian
commentary of our time, in which Marvin Rosenberg is devoting
a book to each of the four tragedies A. C. Bradley studied in
Shakespearean Tragedy (1904). The first, *The Masks of Othello*
(Berkeley, 1961), makes clear its adherence to the older approach in its
subtitle: 'The Search for the Identity of Othello, Iago, and Desdemona
by Three Centuries of Actors and Critics.' He writes as though for
each of the three characters there is only one basic 'identity' that will
work in the theatre and he has discovered it. The most recent book in
the series, *The Masks of Macbeth* (Berkeley, 1978), has swung to an
almost indiscriminate acceptance of multiple readings of the play.[18]

From the Age of Bradley in which Shakespeare's text was read as if
it were a novel by George Eliot and then the Age of Wilson Knight in
which the text was read as if it were a visionary poem by T. S. Eliot,
we have entered the Age of the Casebook, in which a variety of writers
consider various aspects of the play from a variety of perspectives, and
the text is treated as if it were *The Sound and the Fury* or the film
Rashomon. In the theatre, directors have often not even tried for a full
or balanced rendering of a text but rather offered a 'version' of it.
Charles Marowitz summed up a common attitude when he called one
of his productions not *Macbeth* but '*A* Macbeth'.

Stephen Booth's effort to provide the reader with every possible
Elizabethan reading of each Shakespearian sonnet, without indicating
preferences, is another case in point.[19] He rightly decries the necessity
that earlier interpreters of Shakespeare have felt to make 'either/or'
choices. Yet to go on, as he does, to extol a 'both/and' approach in its
stead can be no less misleading if overdone. There is a vast middle
ground between the two. At an extreme, critical tolerance can mask a
failure of nerve, an unwillingness to say: 'this is more likely than
that', 'this is given greater emphasis than that', 'this is more central or
better balanced than that'. For Shakespeare's texts do permit such
discriminations. They do not provide hard and fast directions for their
own interpretation, but they do provide guidelines, do set limits to the
latitudes they allow. Hence, although no single reading is definitive,
some are downright wrong and among the rest some are in certain
repects to be preferred to others.

Exploration of this middle ground will provide fresh challenges to

---

[18] Rosenberg's intervening study, *The Masks of King Lear* (Berkeley, 1972),
seems to me to strike a sound balance between the two extremes.

[19] Stephen Booth, *Shakespeare's Sonnets* (New Haven, 1977).

Shakespeare's interpreters. Although it will involve a degree of self-regulation in observing Shakespearian limits (wise judgement is after all a part of his genius), it also opens invitingly on the fertile plenitude of his creativity. When his intention is regarded not as a single line but as a locus or spectrum of options, interpreters may concern themselves not merely with selecting a single 'reading' of a text but with charting and weighing the range of options that he has built into it.

Such options apply not only to the imagined world of Shakespeare's plays but to the theatre-events that occur when they are performed. For, as will be discussed in later chapters, Shakespeare's theatre-poetry allows opportunities for choice to all of the participants in the performance-ensemble. His texts reflect the options he chose as a playwright reshaping his sources and those that he offers his players and his playgoers. As a kind of prelude, the next chapter looks in detail at the performance-ensemble in the two plays in which Shakespeare was most explicit about its workings: *Henry V* and *A Midsummer Night's Dream*.

2

The Performance-Ensemble:
Henry V and *A Midsummer Night's Dream*

O for a muse of fire, that would ascend
The brightest heaven of invention:
A kingdom for a stage, princes to act,
And monarchs to behold the swelling scene.

So, at the beginning of *Henry V*, the Chorus dreams of his ideal
theatre for the play to come. The key word is 'fire'. Like fire, his dream
reaches irrepressibly upward and outward. It swells. Its playhouse
expands from a wooden O to kingdom-sized proportions; its actors
and spectators are raised to the highest ranks of nobility; and beyond
that its presiding Muse is exalted to divine heights. Only then may
the dream-theatre do justice to the swelling scene the Chorus heralds;
only 'then should the warlike Harry, like himself, / Assume the port
of Mars'.

The Chorus's impulse to dream not only of an imagined world but
of an ideal theatrical situation for its performance is one that
Shakespeare shared. Implied in each of his texts is the kind of
performance-ensemble best suited to its enactment and reception,
creating the distinctive rapport among playwright, players, and
playgoers that is best suited to its imagined world. In *Henry V* and to a
lesser degree in *A Midsummer Night's Dream*, these implications are
made most clear. They can thus provide special help for understanding the performance-ensemble in texts which are less explicit.

The Chorus's concerns with expansiveness and ennoblement deserve
extended treatment. Even though they are important preoccupations
of the text, they have not as yet been emphasized in thematic analyses
of *Henry V*. Furthermore, they are key impulses in the workings of the
performance-ensemble.

Obviously a 'swelling scene' is apropos to a play about territorial
expansion. Before the prologue is over, the Chorus will have included
in his purview not merely one kingdom but two, and before the play is
over Henry will rule them both. Henry's expansiveness, moreover,
goes beyond acquisition of land and subjects. At each stage of his

career he seeks to secure and build a distinctive sense of community. Before his departure to France, this community is a conventional hierarchical one, by which government through division of labour united by common purpose and consent may bring the society to 'congree', like the honeybee:

> For government, though high and low and lower,
> Put into parts, doth keep in one consent,
> Congreeing in a full and natural close,
> Like music.   (1. 2. 180–3)

Once in France with his army Henry seeks a brotherhood in blood and death. After Agincourt, Henry emphasizes a family of royalty, where his match with Kate is held together not only by dynastic interest but by love and—despite the barriers of language and national custom—mutual understanding.

Often, the impulse towards expansion works hand-in-hand with that towards elevation and ennoblement. Henry's consistent method is to promote the appropriate community by himself temporarily descending to a lower status. He submits to the guidance of his bishops and military advisers before announcing his decision to launch the French campaign. On the eve of Agincourt he goes in the disguise of a common soldier among his men and prays to God for help. After his victory he assumes the role of a bluff, inarticulate soldier in his wooing of Kate. In each case, his temporary descent helps to build a sense of community that results in his eventually gaining the upper hand.

It is thus that King Henry rises to be ruler of France as well as England and moreover to become the mirror of all Christian kings. He raises others as well. This is the recurring theme of his exhortations to his soldiers. At first he is very class-conscious. In his 'Once more unto the breach, dear friends' speech the King discriminates between the nobility and the yeomen. He exhorts 'you noblest English, / Whose blood is fet from fathers of war-proof!' to 'Be copy now to men of grosser blood, / And teach them how to war.' He then addresses 'you, good yeomen', and urges them to prove themselves 'worth your breeding':

> For there is none of you so mean and base
> That hath not noble lustre in your eyes.   (3. 1. 29–30)

Those who are mean and base are thus complimented but in a qualified way.

In the King's St Crispian's Day speech, his embrace is warmer. It is a

fellowship in death he offers ('We would not die in that man's
company / That fears his fellowship to die with us'):

> We few, we happy few, we band of brothers.
> For he today that sheds his blood with me
> Shall be my brother; be he ne'er so vile,
> This day shall gentle his condition.   (4. 3. 60–3)

His awareness of prior 'vileness' (low birth) is still present and
expressed, but nobility and yeomanry are no longer addressed
separately. When he went among his men the night before, according
to the Chorus, he called them 'brothers, friends, and countrymen'. In
practice, however, his fellow-feeling runs into difficulties, as when—
after his dispute with Williams—Bates must intervene: 'Be friends,
you English fools, be friends.'

It is in battle and death that the 'band of brothers' reaches its
practical fulfilment. Its apotheosis would seem to come in the
account of the deaths of Suffolk and York, where an exalting
community in death reaches an ultimate. After kissing the bloody
gashes on dead Suffolk's face, York cried aloud for Suffolk to tarry:

> 'My soul shall thine keep company to heaven.
> Tarry, sweet soul, for mine, then fly abreast,
> As in this glorious and well-foughten field
> We kept together in our chivalry'   (4. 6. 16–19)

Not only did York see their souls flying abreast to heaven, but at the
moment of his death on earth:

> over Suffolk's neck
> He threw his wounded arm, and kissed his lips,
> And so espoused to death, with blood he sealed
> A testament of noble-ending love.   (ll. 24–7)

One senses a straining for effect at this point, as though in reaching its
ultimate the glorification of an elevating espousal in death revealed
something sick or anti-life about it. Is it significant that at the end of
this scene Henry first gives his order to kill the prisoners? Is there
something morbid about his later response to the names of the noble
French dead? 'Here was a royal fellowship of death!'

The twin impulses towards ennoblement and community are
presented in various comic perspectives. They are given a debased
prelude by Nim and Pistol (2. 1). At first they quarrel, but Bardolph
intervenes: 'Come, shall I make you two friends? We must to France
together . . .' Thanks to his intercession Nim settles for the promise of

a 'noble' coin in payment of the eight shillings he won from Pistol at betting, plus liquor:

> And friendship shall combine, and brotherhood.
> I'll live by Nim, and Nim shall live by me.

Pistol's promise of future payment is backed up by his claim that 'I shall sutler be / Unto the camp, and profits will accrue'. Thus Nim is to be 'ennobled' by the war-effort! He and Bardolph go on to become 'sworn brothers in filching' (3. 2. 44).

The French nobles claim their exaltation before they have won it. (3. 7). In their pre-battle boasting, the Dauphin's celebration of his *'cheval volant*, the Pegasus' is an unwitting parody of the play's impulses toward elevation ('he trots the air . . . he is pure air and fire') and ennoblement ('It is the prince of palfreys. His neigh is like the bidding of a monarch'). His extravagance is undercut by its self-aggrandizement ('When I bestride him, I soar . . . It is a beast for Perseus') and by Constable's put-down: 'it is a most absolute and excellent horse.' The two then go on to develop the idea that, as the Dauphin puts it, 'my horse is my mistress'—thus contributing to the community theme. Again, as with Suffolk and York's espousal to death, a mating metaphor is used—this time with a bawdy turn.

The inability of the French to tell true nobility from false is reflected in the French soldier (4. 4) who mistakes Pistol for *'le gentilhomme de bon qualité'* and surrenders to him accordingly, promising him 'two hundred crowns'. Throughout the play, the frequent talk of 'nobles' and 'crowns' provides an intriguing monetary analogy to the theme of ennoblement.

Not all of the English are able to rise to Henry's vision. The three traitors betray their noble 'worthiness' for the sake of 'a few light crowns'. Although Bardolph echoes the King's fight-talk ('On, on, on, on, on! to the breach, to the breach!'), his repetitions exaggerate and in effect parody what is already extravagant in the King's ringing words. Nim's response is 'Pray thee corporal, stay', to which Pistol and the Boy readily agree. Only Fluellen's style of exhortation serves to drive them on; unimpressed by Pistol's repeated raising of the captain's rank to that of 'great Duke', Fluellen insists: 'Up to the breaches, you dogs!' He incites them to greater effort by accusing them of being less than they are rather than, like Henry, seeking to inspire them to rise above themselves.

Once the battle of Agincourt is over, Henry himself relapses from his vision of a band of brothers. He sends for Gower, not to confer knighthood upon him (as Williams expects) but merely as part of the practical joke he is playing on Williams. The tone of this joke is highly subject to interpretation, depending on the spirit in which the King offers the gloveful of crowns and the spirit in which Williams accepts or does not accept it (see pp. 138–44). In any case the two are in no sense 'brothers' at this point. And when the King then reads a list of the dead, it is in a strictly hierarchical order and idiom reminiscent of his initial sense of community:

> Edward the Duke of York, the Earl of Suffolk,
> Sir Richard Keighley, Davy Gam Esquire;
> None else of name, and of all other men
> But five-and-twenty.   (4. 8. 103–6)

The next scene (5. 1) shows the previous coming together of British nationalities beginning to fall apart, with Pistol's slurs on the Welsh. The ennoblement of which the King spoke gives way to Pistol calling Fluellen a 'mountain-squire' and Fluellen calling him a 'squire of low degree'. Earlier the King had declared: 'We would not die in that man's company / That fears his fellowship to die with us' (4. 3. 38–9). Now fellowship in that sense no longer prevails; instead Fluellen disparagingly finds Pistol 'no petter than a fellow' (5. 1. 7).

Henry, however, has moved on to another kind of community, where again the expansion/elevation complex can be seen. His first words to the French court make the familial terms explicit:

> Peace to this meeting, wherefore we are met.
> Unto our brother France and to our sister,
> Health and fair time of day. Joy and good wishes
> To our most fair and princely cousin Catherine.   (5. 2. 1–4)

The King of France responds in kind to his 'Most worthy brother England'. The complex also has its mundane aspects. Henry loves France so much he will not part with a village of it and insists on every feature of his new title, both in French ('*notre très cher fils Henri, Roi d'Angleterre, Heritier de France*') and in Latin. Thus he fulfils his early promise in response to the Dauphin's insult: 'I will rise there with so full a glory / That I will dazzle all the eyes of France' (1. 2. 278–9).

Henry's marriage to Kate is more than a marriage of political convenience. They both make the effort to talk the other's language, and in the process create a unique form of communication that allows them to make something of a love-match as well. As before, this involves Henry's self-lowering in a sense, as when he very eloquently proclaims his own lack of verbal facility and puts down that of others. If she will follow his prompting, Kate, too, can stoop to conquer: 'take

me, take a soldier; take a soldier, take a king.' The peroration of his
suit to Catherine makes clear the new idea of community the King is
proposing:

> take me by the hand, and say, 'Harry of England, I am thine'—which word thou
> shalt no sooner bless mine ear withal, but I will tell thee aloud, 'England is
> thine, Ireland is thine, France is thine, and Henry Plantagenet is thine'—who,
> though I speak it before his face, if he be not fellow with the best king, thou
> shalt find the best king of good fellows. (5. 2. 234–40)

The central concern with enlargement and ennoblement in the
imagined world of *Henry V* throws light on the workings of the
performance-ensemble, as may be illustrated by considering in turn
the playgoers, the players, and the playwright.

Shakespeare challenges his spectators to a large-mindedness that
can rise to his occasion. In the rest of the Prologue, the Chorus is very
direct about the appeal he would make to our imaginary forces. First
he confers upon us some of the nobility he had wished for in his ideal
beholders: he dubs us 'gentles all'. Although in other places
Shakespeare regularly refers to his spectators as 'gentles', the Chorus's
earlier wish for 'monarchs to behold' the performance puts special
emphasis on our implied ennoblement. He then proceeds to specify
how (*noblesse oblige*) we can live up to our given title and grant his
concluding appeal 'gently to hear . . . our play'. Given the limitations
of the Elizabethan stage and actors, he calls on the audience to 'piece
out our imperfections with your thoughts'. This is not a vague 'appeal
to the imagination' nor is imagination to be exercised solely for its
own sake. The Chorus spells out precisely the faculties required for
this particular play and the particular purposes they are to serve. In
our minds we must expand what we see; make much of little,
multiply one warrior into many, 'into a thousand parts divide one
man', convert one crooked figure into a million. These exercises are
strenuous enough, but the Chorus then adds more arduous ones.[1] We
must with our thoughts 'make imaginary puissance', 'deck' kings,
convert what we hear into what we see ('Think, when we talk of
horses, that you see them, / Printing their proud hoofs i'th' receiving
earth'). Our assigned tasks climax in injunctions to defy space and
time: carrying the kings 'here and there, jumping o'er times'. No
wonder then that the Chorus—using military terms as if we were
soldiers—exhorts us: 'On your imaginary forces work'. Only thus
may we help his 'swelling scene' to be achieved.

---

[1] Cf. Michael Goldman's chapter on '*Henry V*: The Strain of Rule', in his
Shakespeare and the Energies of Drama (Princeton, 1972), 58–73.

The Chorus's methods are significantly similar to those of Henry. For the sake of his exalted dream-theatre, the Chorus humbles himself to pray our indulgence and co-operation. By so doing he builds a larger sense of community, one that appeals to us not as individual spectators but as an audience, and goes beyond that to make us collaborators with him and with the actors in accomplishing the challenging acts of imagination the play requires.

In particular, the audience must assist the playwright and performers by helping to imagine the victory at Agincourt. Olivier's film gloriously imagines it for its audience, with surging music and a climactic flight of arrows. But Shakespeare's challenge is more severe. To count ourselves among the happy few, we must ourselves do the hard work of assembling and piecing out the fragmentary battlefield incidents and enlarging and elevating them into the famous victory they only suggest.

The elevation is especially difficult. If the central action of the play is to be accomplished, we must make the heroic effort of crediting Henry and his men with the heroism necessary to winning at Agincourt a victory so extraordinary that even the victors wonder at it. Shakespeare, of course, does not make the victory depend altogether on the gallantry of the English. Henry is the first to acknowledge the hand of God in the battle and the French are shown to be weak and vain. Holinshed reported another factor: the innovative stratagem the English employed of using sharpened stakes to impale the French horses. Shakespeare significantly omits this factor and thus makes a more difficult claim on our credence. Whatever the shortcomings of the English, they must be seen to have a heroic potential. That is the very least that Shakespeare must make credible. For he does not present the French as being so weak nor divine influence so strong as to account for the famous victory otherwise.

Not that Shakespeare has addressed his play to a convocation of knights in shining armour. We too are allowed our frailties. While appealing to that part of our natures that roots for underdogs and prizes teamwork and self-sacrifice, he also makes due allowance for contrary impulses: to deride top dogs and to find sneaking amusement in shirkers and self-servers—and to discover an understandable humanity in them too. Like modern media, his play appeals to our need to make heroes of leaders and yet to relish the exposés that reveal their feet of clay. He requires us to allow both their due.

To his actors Shakespeare presents a similar challenge. They may not be the 'princes' the Chorus wishes for, but in their characterizations they must create believable human beings who, for all their imperfections, have the potential of princeliness. Shakespeare leaves it to the actors to interpret the degree of frailty and of genuine heroism to be shown by the English, the degree of grandiosity and weakness by the French. Recent performers (as well as interpreting critics) have often stressed the ways in which Henry falls short of perfection—the ferocity of his threats to Harfleur, the ruthlessness of his order to kill the hostages, the weakness of his arguments against Williams, and the insensitivity of his practical joke on him. There is no denying the reality of such frailties. Yet if Shakespeare's largest purposes are to be fulfilled, they must not be so emphasized as to undercut the essential heroism of the happy few who do, after all, achieve their impossible dream. The challenge to the actors, particularly to Henry, is believably to embody both the nobility that is achieved and the frailty it transcends.

It is to the good, it seems, if the performers are themselves responding to a comparable challenge in real life. Amid many practical wartime problems and risks, Olivier's film sought to celebrate the Battle of Britain, when the indomitable spirit of England again won out over seemingly overwhelming odds. In the 1975 Royal Shakespeare Company production, director Terry Hands and the company managed to triumph over reduced financial circumstances through the resourceful use of their imaginations. Unable to afford elaborate sets, they employed instead a single huge canvas, the underside of which—when raised—made a bright-coloured canopy for scenes at court and when lowered to the stage-floor became the muddy fields of France. In both cases the performers themselves had to rise above themselves and—perhaps in part because of this—they won famous victories of their own.

It is especially important, too, that the acting styles of the company be well tempered. The Britishness of the British side must come through, at the same time that the varied subgroups represented—the Welsh, Scots, Irish, taverners, nobility—are distinguished. Their fallings out and fallings short must not be so emphasized as to preclude an eventual, successful coming together. The Frenchness of the French must also come through. Almost always, these roles are played by English actors who tend to portray the French as the English perceive them. In a Stratford, Ontario, production in 1966 the roles were played by French Canadians, who took a French point of view—and to good effect. And yet the national differences should not be so emphasized as to undercut the harmony of the finale, however temporary.

Of course, there is more to *Henry V* than the achievement of community and nobility, or the failure to do so; and its actors and spectators are involved in experiences that have nothing directly to do with this pattern. I single out these factors because they are central to the imagined action of the play and because the Chorus gives them explicit prominence in his comments on his ideal players and playgoers. As such they illustrate the way in which central concerns of the imagined world can help to guide those who are engaged in re-imagining it, whether they are performing it or responding to it.

Such guidance can extend as well to our understanding of the playwright's role, at the time of creation and as an unseen presence at the time of performance. For Shakespeare's imagination itself participates in the shared experience of a given play. It not only provides the scenario for the other members of the dramatic ensemble but is caught up in the very processes it is creating. In *Henry V* this is clearest in the unique figure of the Chorus, whose high-flown rhetoric not only conjures up the 'swelling scene' to come but partakes of its swellingness. He is not to be simply equated with Shakespeare. When Ronald Watkins directed the play at Harrow in 1962, he made up the boy playing the Chorus to look like Shakespeare and kept him visible throughout, presiding over the play. This was plainly wrong. Shakespeare's presence is never so evident as that, even though the Chorus does carry out many of the playwright's functions. There are too many discrepancies between what the Chorus says and what the playwright actually shows us for the two to be equated. The Chorus is more precisely an embodiment of the play's expansiveness of spirit, its upward and outward reach.

Rather than as a direct spokesman for the playwright, the Chorus is best seen as a more mundane avatar of the same muse that inspired Shakespeare in writing *Henry V*. A royalist if there ever was one, the Chorus's dream-theatre, performed by and for aristocrats, is a literal-minded version of Shakespeare's ideal performance-ensemble for this play. Like a cheer-leader or adulatory sports writer, the Chorus at once expresses and unwittingly caricatures the very aspirations he would celebrate. His hyperboles clarify yet distort the heroism that in Shakespeare's overall rendering is complex and qualified; in his address to the audience he makes an exhortation of what in Shakespeare is an invitation to share in an ever larger sense of community.

At that, however, the Chorus's first prologue provides us with Shakespeare's most explicit invocation of the kind of performance-ensemble he would like for his play. Elsewhere he is less explicit, although in *A Midsummer Night's Dream*, he is in different ways almost as overtly helpful. In it, as in *Henry V*, the playwright, the players, and the playgoers are faced with an unusual feat of imagination. But in *A Midsummer Night's Dream* it is not the heroic moment of a famous victory that must be conjured up but the night-world of fairyland. It is an invitation to dream a little; or to put it more precisely, to open ourselves to the shaping fantasies that characterize the dreamer as well as the lunatic, the lover, and the poet. By doing so we can share in a dreamlike experience in which features of the ordinary world are recombined and transformed in ways that are undreamt of in our waking philosophies. Since dreaming is ordinarily a solitary activity, such sharing is a rare, possibly unique, opportunity. Hippolyta expresses this best toward the end when she observes that the minds of the young lovers were 'transfigured together'. Participation in this collective transfiguration makes extraordinary demands on all who are involved in it.

For the audience, such challenges, unlike those in *Henry V*, are not at first spelled out. Despite the play's title we may not at first realize what we have got ourselves into. It is not until the end of the forest sequence that we are made conscious of the special nature of the experience. That is as it should be since we do not recognize a dream for what it is until it is over. Nor is there a single spokesman for this awareness such as the Chorus; virtually every speaker in the post-forest section in one way or another helps the audience to come to terms with the 'dream' it has had—or is the dream what Bottom calls it, a 'vision'?

Our challenges as spectators are even more demanding than those for *Henry V*. We must imagine not only a single conversation around a camp-fire but a whole fairy-time, with appropriate lighting effects from the light of the moon and the stars to the onset of fog and total darkness to the coming of dawn. We must look at a normal-sized actor and see an Amazon or an elf. Very possibly Shakespeare's company aided his first audiences by casting the smaller boys as elves and the tallest one as the Amazon Hippolyta; yet even then an act of imaginative exaggeration was required. The muse of *A Midsummer Night's Dream* is wilder and freer than that of *Henry V*. We must see an actor and suppose him invisible, watch Robin Goodfellow (more commonly known as Puck) run off and suppose him capable of accelerating to the speed of a satellite. Like Hermia (3. 2) we must learn to trust our ears more than our eyes. We should have some fellow-feeling for Bottom in his synaesthesia: 'the eye of man hath not heard, the ear of man hath not seen . . . his tongue to conceive . . . what my dream was'. (4. 1. 208–11).

The Royal Shakespeare Company film of the play used camera-tricks to accomplish many of these feats. An animated cartoon might seem an even better medium for them. Yet this would be to mistake the way these challenges involve the audience in the very processes which animate the whole play. We too must transform what we see according to what we hear: magnifying it, miniaturizing it, erasing it, accelerating it. The best effect in the RSC film was the opening shot of an Elizabethan stately mansion, with the caption ATHENS super-imposed on it. That bold challenge to our powers of transformation was almost perfectly in tune with the play; it would have been still better if 'Athens' had been spoken, obliging us, as so often in the play, to see with our ears.

The players of *A Midsummer Night's Dream* must be no less than protean in their self-transforming powers. Those who play characters who are magically transformed must be able to portray multiple selves. Under the influence of love-in-idleness, the mortal young men must make changes of affection that are abrupt and complete; Titania must waken to express immediate and passionate devotion to a 'vile thing': 'What angel wakes me from my flow'ry bed?' With Bottom, on the other hand, much of the fun is in the gradualness of his inner metamorphosis. A bit of an ass in any case, he must grow more and more aware of his asshood ('methinks I am marvellous hairy about the face'), then—after the ass-head has been removed—this awareness must fade: 'Methought I was, and methought I had . . .' This kind of challenge was extended and heightened by director Peter Brook in the 1970 RSC stage-production when he doubled the roles of Theseus and Oberon, Hippolyta and Titania, Puck and Philostrate.

The mortal maidens are not influenced by external potions and remain constant in their affections toward their men, yet they too experience the pervading changeableness. Their performers must internalize the play's processes. Hermia is the only character who actually experiences a midsummer night's dream, a nightmare her performer must re-create so vividly as to make the audience live through it too. Helena wishes desperately that she might be 'translated' into Hermia and thus receive Demetrius's love; to Demetrius she declares: 'I am your spaniel.' The two must turn from bosom girlhood friends to arch love-rivals; Helena then seems to Hermia a 'canker blossom' (3. 2. 282) while Helena observes how emotion can change Hermia: 'When she is angry, she is keen and shrewd' (l. 324). Performers of the two roles thus must deal not only with the magical changes in fairyland but with the changeableness that pervades ordinary life.

The actor of Oberon must be able to declare with conviction 'I am invisible'. Other fairies have the power to make outer transformations of mortals. Puck is able to give Bottom an ass's head, Titania promises to purge his 'mortal grossness so / That thou shalt like an airy spirit go'. But only Oberon controls the power to change inner feelings—and that only by way of his special knowledge of transforming potions derived from the play's chief ruling deities, Cupid and Dian. He seems even to be able to invoke the power of Venus, whose love-light helps to accomplish the key transformation, the reawakening of Demetrius's affections for Helena:

> When his love he doth espy,
> Let her shine as gloriously
> As the Venus of the sky.   (3. 2. 105–7)

The lines should have the sound and power of an incantation.

Puck not only acts as Oberon's agent in wielding the magic potions but can change shapes at will. His actor must bring to these transformations the spirit of a mischief-maker and practical joker. He takes amusement in his own pranks but they also have a professional side; as court-jester he is concerned to make Oberon 'smile' and his retinue 'hold their hips and laugh'. Bottom has a similar proclivity for shape-changing, yet with a difference. Like Puck he has an eye to his audience but in an amateur spirit. His desire to play all the parts in 'Pyramus and Thisbe' is born of the sheer joy of histrionic impersonation, a joy so exuberant that Peter Quince (like Oberon with Puck) has trouble containing it.

With Quince, we come to the character most nearly comparable to the role Shakespeare assigns himself as playwright for this play. It seems that Quince is a carpenter of plays as well as houses, serving as the script-writer as well as director of the hempen-homespuns, who function very much like a theatre 'collective' of the 1960s. Almost certainly it was Quince who changed the script to adapt to the casting-decisions made at the first rehearsals; Bottom thinks of him as the one to write a ballad of his dream.

It is the transforming power of the poet that Shakespeare emphasizes. Even so sceptical and sober-sided an observer as Theseus can recognize this power. In famous lines he observes that the poet, like the lunatic and the lover, is 'of imagination all compact', and:

> Such tricks hath strong imagination
> That if it would but apprehend some joy
> It comprehends some bringer of that joy;
> Or in the night, imagining some fear,
> How easy is a bush supposed a bear!   (5. 1. 18–22)

Not only do Quince and company exercise the transforming powers of theatre-magic but they are aware of these powers and its dangers. Shakespeare takes time to enjoy their literal-minded worrying of its mysteries (3. 2) and gives full force to their fears of giving offence.

This last concern seems to reflect Shakespeare's own fear that his imagination may have got out of hand and gone too far. In the Epilogue, the performer of Puck worries 'If we shadows have offended' and Quince as Prologue to 'Pyramus and Thisbe' begins:

> If we offend, it is with our good will.
> That you should think: we come not to offend
> But with good will.   (5. 1. 108–10)

The repetition of 'good will' may be significant. Is there a suggestion of 'good Will Shakespeare' in it? Did he perhaps play the role of Quince?

How has the playwright offended? His vision is of a cosmic *mélange*, a world that resembles the mispunctuated prologue to 'Pyramus and Thisbe': 'like a tangled chain, nothing impaired, but all disordered.' It works in ways that are disturbingly different from those we ordinarily suppose. It transports us into 'Love's mind', a place where the mating-impulse has gone wild. Beerbohm Tree was right to include live *rabbits* in his stage-forest! Even Egeus is caught up in the match-making, his problem is that he insists on a mismatch. This is a place where reciprocated romantic love is not to be enjoyed until one has either doted (loved more than one is loved) or been doted upon. There are suggestions of sado-masochism. Theseus believes that he has won Hippolyta's love by doing her injuries; Helena believes that she can win Demetrius' love by suffering them ('beat me as your spaniel'). Oberon takes satisfaction in mating his wife with some 'vile thing'. Yet it is through these nightmarish experiences that the king and queen of fairies are restored to amity and that the young mortal couples can enjoy their blessed slumbers.

Not that Shakespeare proclaims his unsettling world-view. On the contrary, he is sly about bringing it out. Puck's Epilogue is dismissive—at least ostensibly:

> If we shadows have offended,
> Think but this, and all is mended:
> That you have but slumbered here,
> While these visions did appear;
> And this weak and idle theme,
> No more yielding but a dream,
> Gentles, do not reprehend.

We remember a similar ploy, practised on the mortal young lovers; Oberon instructs Puck that

> When they next wake, all this derision
> Shall seem a dream and fruitless vision.   (3. 2. 371–2)

And we know that the lovers did not dream. On the other hand, Bottom feels that he has 'had a most rare vision'. Perhaps rightly, he also feels that 'Man is but an ass if he go about t'expound this dream'. None the less, the claims that the vision is 'fruitless' and 'weak and idle' protest so much as to invite us to do just that.

When we do, we can scarcely avoid the realization that the mad ways of the wood (the pun on 'wod' meaning 'mad' is to the point) are not so different from the ways of the world. In real life are our own inexplicable changes of heart the secret work of Oberon—or Puck? Indeed, the play lets us see that not only may this be so (since Demetrius remains under the influence of love-in-idleness) but also that it is for the good; before the young lovers leave the wood the foursome is blessed by Oberon 'with league whose date till death shall never end'. Thus Hermia's defiant decision 'to seek new friends and stranger companies' (1. 1. 219) is rewarded.

Shakespeare would seem to bespeak poetic licence for his wayward muse, no matter how foolish, childish, freakish, lunatic, or painful its carryings-on. He rewards a similar impulse in his spectators, repeatedly inviting us to take 'delight in disorder'. The worse the actors of 'Pyramus and Thisbe' are, the more we enjoy their performance; and the same is true for its on-stage audience—the rude mechanicals' play succeeds as a wedding entertainment precisely because it fails as a tragedy.

No production of the play has embraced its anarchic impulses more enthusiastically than did Peter Brook's. Its Puck, John Kane, describes an early rehearsal in which 'Spirits' (who doubled as Titania's fairies and stage-hands) were given complete licence:

They were free to wander where they pleased and assist or screw-up whatever they liked whenever they liked. It soon became obvious that the Spirits that morning were certainly mischievous if not downright malevolent. The forest and its inhabitants exuded a primitive savagery that infected everyone who came in contact with them. As the group feeling grew, a wild gaiety seized the company. With books in one hand and a hoop or a cushion in the other, we whipped the play along like some frantic bobbing top until it eventually exploded during the Titania/Bottom confrontation in a welter of torn newspaper, cardboard phalluses and Felix Mendelssohn. As the noise and the laughter died away, we looked around the room and as though awakening from

2. Puck (John Kane) on stilts terrifies Demetrius (Ben Kingsley).

a dream ourselves we realized that we had been possessed by some wild anarchic force . . .[2]

Through his characters Shakespeare defines a spectrum of options as to the degree of delight to be taken in the play's disorders. At the very least he seems to expect from us the kind of indulgence Theseus

[2] John Kane, *The Sunday Times* (13 June, 1971), 27.

extends toward himself and others. In his youth he may have consorted with Titania but now the realm of imagination has a carefully limited place in his world of reason and law. Philostrate is given his due; his entertainments serve to beguile the time. Yet there is something philistine about Theseus's attitudes. He worries that these night-time beguilements may encroach on his daytime functions: 'I fear we shall outsleep the coming morn / As much as we this night have overwatched.'

Puck, at the other extreme, exuberantly takes positive pleasure in mix-ups. He is notably unrepentant about his miscue in recombining the lovers; indeed, there is reason to wonder, along with Oberon (3. 2. 346–7), if the error was accidental; for Puck takes open delight in the consequences: 'those things do best please me / That befall prepost'rously.' Yet there is something inhuman as well as non-human about Puck. His shape-changing can go beyond mischief to malice, as when he misleads 'night-wanderers, laughing at their harm'. There is something unfeeling and detached, too, about his famous couplet:

> Shall we their fond pageant see?
> Lord, what fools these mortals be! (3. 2. 114–15)

The play's muse seems warmer than that. It invites us not only to see the fondness of the 'fond pageant' but also to see it *fondly*.

No single character represents a fully approved attitude. For me, it is Bottom who comes closest to embodying the spirit of the play. It is he who chiefly experiences the play's characteristic processes of re-combination and transformation. His match-up with Titania involves the most extreme joining of contraries—the animal-headed mortal with a fairy, the commoner with a queen. He undergoes the most radical transformation, combining asshood and humanity not only in his head but in his inner life: he retains, for example, a 'reasonable good ear in music' (at least so he thinks) while acknowledging 'a great desire to a bottle of hay'. And he undergoes these experiences with remarkable aplomb. It is true that he is at first frightened, especially by the horror with which his friends regard him. But he soon regains his composure and is to be seen comfortably settling into his new status. On his release from his spell, he has a compelling sense of wonder at what has befallen him yet soon finds ways to come to terms with his experience and fit it into his ongoing life. Bottom thus sets an example for the audience. If we are often inclined to exclaim with Horatio 'O day and night, but this is wondrous strange!' Shakespeare seems to reply with Hamlet: 'And therefore as a stranger give it welcome' (*Hamlet*, 1. 5. 167).

For by accepting that there are more things in heaven and earth than were hitherto dreamt of in our philosophies, we can join the play in its huge embrace of life. Here again Bottom is exemplary. He is able to make himself at home in fairyland as in Athens. He shows the same capacity to move comfortably between two worlds during 'Pyramus and Thisbe', when he acts as intermediary between the spectators and the play; he steps out of his character Pyramus to explain that Thisbe 'is to enter now, and I am to spy her through the wall. You shall see, it will fall pat as I told you. Yonder she comes' (5. 1. 183–6). Bottom the weaver is in the right occupation.

So are Snug the joiner and Starveling the tailor. There is a strong sense of community and accommodation among this group. The first concern of their first scenes together is 'Is all our company here?' (1. 2. 1) and 'Are we all met?' (3. 1. 1). It is as a team that they confront the problems of their production. As such they parody, as they exemplify, the play's imperative that we be 'transfigured together'. Yet the togetherness they embody is not an easy one. It is impaired when Bottom is translated, and his fellows abandon him in fright. Like every other love relationship in the play, their fellowship must show itself able to survive violation. Flute the bellows-*mender* is well named. It is he who is most concerned about the absence of 'sweet bully Bottom' (4. 2) just before Bottom's triumphant return to their midst.

In the same way, by the end of the fourth act, the members of Theseus's court who had separated have all come together again, as have the Fairy King and Queen. For the wedding festivities all three of these groups are assembled. It is true that their togetherness is less than complete and immediate. Theseus is not able to sustain his ideal of a tolerant ruler who can graciously take satisfaction in a heartfelt expression of duty however mistakenly rendered; nor does Hippolyta sustain her concern for the feelings of the rude mechanics. Both join in the patronizing ridicule of 'Pyramus and Thisbe' that is led by the young bridegrooms, whose recent transfigurations seem not at all to have enhanced their imaginative faculties. The young brides say nothing at all. Still, a final harmony is found: by the deaths of the two fictitious lovers, 'the wall is down that parted their two fathers'; Theseus brings himself to declare the interlude a fine tragedy and very notably discharged; and the Fairy King and Queen 'hand in hand' bless the marriage beds.

Even Puck in his Epilogue wants to make things right with the audience. Fearful of having given offence, Puck first tries to explain it away. Think it but a dream, he suggests. He does not leave it at that, however, but proceeds to his next appeal: the promise of future amendment in return for present pardon. As if fearing that that is too much to ask, he then hurries on to offer to make 'amends ere long' if only we won't hiss. Since we know him to be an arch-deceiver, his repeated protestations, 'as I am an honest puck' and 'Else the puck a liar call' are not as reassuring as he might wish them to seem. Presumably, however, there are no hisses to be heard; so he wishes 'good night unto you all' and may start to leave the stage, or seem to. At any rate, his final couplet seems a postscript, albeit one of those ostensible afterthoughts that in fact reveals the ulterior motive behind the preceding letter. Puck ventures a final appeal, again promising future amendment in return for immediate award:

> Give me your hands, if we be friends,
> And Robin shall restore amends.

The couplet is always glossed simply as a bid for applause, as in part it obviously is. But it is of the essence that the bid is expressed in the form of a gesture of friendship. Is it significant that Puck at this point refers to himself as Robin (Goodfellow)? In the Peter Brook production, Puck was at this point full of goodfellowship; 'give me your hands' was the cue for him to shake the hands of the other members of the cast and audience and embrace them. Brook thus underlined Shakespeare's invitation to all concerned not only to be 'transfigured' but to be 'transfigured together'.

So much then for these preludes for performance-ensembles. They were possible because in *Henry V* and *A Midsummer Night's Dream* Shakespeare was unusually helpful. To proceed to other plays which do not provide these helps will require further groundwork. Before beginning my main line of argument, I need to clear the ground and deal with an immediate and obvious objection. Does not this view of a playwright who is very much present, playing an active part in the performance-ensemble, run counter to the long-held perception of Shakespeare as the writer of all writers who simply holds the mirror up to nature? Is he not the prime exponent of the dramatic point of view, entailed by the very nature of the genre, in which an impartial objective creator enters with universal sympathy inside all his creations?

3

Point of View and Viewpoint:
Henry IV, Part One and *Macbeth*

An author in his book must be like God in the universe, present
everywhere and visible nowhere.

FLAUBERT

THE illusion that the life of a play is, like real life, taking place before
our eyes, at that very moment, is one of the most powerful of dramatic
appeals. It has often been cheapened by the modern literalist theatre,
which has sought to create this effect through mere slice-of-life
fidelity to surfaces. But at best it has kept its powers intact. For this
first-hand point of view is an appeal unique to the dramatic form.
Other forms can only aspire to it. Flaubert and Henry James, and their
followers, have sought to adopt a dramatic point of view in the novel;
yet in the nature of the form we can never actually see or hear their
characters: we can only read their words. Film and television come
closer; yet the camera's eye, however privileged, never seems as free
and trustworthy as our own eyes. For full effect, we must feel that we
are seeing for ourselves, without intermediary, as in life.

Of all dramatists it is Shakespeare who has rightly been recognized
as the master of this effect. By common consent, it is he who appears
best to carry out Hamlet's injunction to 'hold the mirror up to nature'
without apparent distortion or partiality. With him above all, the
writer seems not to 'tell' his story at all but simply to 'show' it.

Eastern drama, by contrast, often includes an on-stage narrator or in
other ways enhances a narrative quality in its dramaturgy. It was
instructive to see what happened when *Macbeth* was adapted to the
style of Yakshagana, a narrative folk-drama of southern India, in
Barnam Vana (Birnam Wood), presented in New Delhi in 1979.
Although the translation was faithful to Shakespeare's lines, the
presence of an on-stage orchestra of drums, bells, and gongs, the
strong infusion of dance-movement, and the extensive use of
processional entries and exits completely altered the impact of the
original. Everyone there, it seemed, was on a fore-ordained journey.
Moonstruck (it was done in the open air), the audience was invited to

contemplate the ritual enactment of a twice-told tale. Lost completely was the excitement one feels at *Macbeth* of being caught up in an event unfolding before one's eyes, and with that loss went something very close to what makes drama 'dramatic'—at least as drama is felt in the west.[1]

Of course, the contrast is a matter of degree. The narrative frame of Eastern theatre does allow some amount of direct character-to-character interaction to occur. The point of view shifts from telling to showing and back again. In Western drama the closest thing to this effect is in *Our Town* (1938), itself deeply influenced by Thornton Wilder's exposure to oriental theatre in his formative years. The Stage Manager provides a narrative frame and speaks both to the actors and to the audience; yet within this frame, key vignettes allow the characters to work out their own destinies.

In the West, such overt shifting back and forth between telling and showing is more common in fiction than in plays. At an extreme, think of the interleaved essays in *Tom Jones* and *War and Peace*. Even in fiction that pretends to a strictly dramatic point of view, there is a great deal of more or less overt authorial telling and commenting. As Wayne Booth demonstrated in *The Rhetoric of Fiction* (Chicago, 1983), pure showing is very rare. The same (I want now to propose) is true of drama, even though the dramatist is characteristically neither visible nor audible. Booth's critique of 'dramatic point-of-view' in fiction needs to be extended to drama itself.

In that direction, Oscar Wilde has gone so far as to say that 'A play is as personal and individual a form of self-expression as a poem or a picture'. And Eric Bentley writes in *The Playwright as Thinker*: 'the playwright has always been a thinker, a teacher, or, in modern jargon, a propagandist. Born out of Greek religion, reborn out of medieval catholicism, Occidental drama has almost never rid itself of its admonitory tone and its salvationist spirit' (p. 256). One need not go so far as they in order to recognize that, far from presenting an impartial mirroring of life, playwrights through the ages have found all sorts of ways of conveying a very definite view of things, whether of advocacy (Ibsen, Shaw, Brecht, Miller) or satire (Jonson, Molière) or even of virtual autobiography (O'Neill's *Long Day's Journey into Night*, Williams's *Glass Menagerie*). 'Extra-dramatic' devices are not uncommon, whether of actual choruses (as in Greek tragedy) or 'choric' commentators. And in less overt ways—through structuring

---

[1] For more details see my review, '*Macbeth* Distilled: A Yakshagan Production in Delhi', *Shakespeare Quarterly*, 31 (1980), 439–40.

of plot and skilful directing of audience sympathies—playwrights regularly stack the deck and load the dice.

It is not too much to say that Shakespeare is one of the very few dramatists to whom the theory of dramatic point of view seems to apply at all well. The fullest study of this matter is *Shakespeare the Dramatist* (London, 1961), in which Una Ellis-Fermor maintains that 'Of the greatest dramatists of the world's literature, one alone, so far, has used the dramatic mode, and only the dramatic, for the revelation of his underlying thought' (p. 11). She recognizes that a 'reading of life' is implied through Shakespeare's artful interrelation of the basic elements of drama with one another (p. 12), the imagery and verbal music of his dialogue (p. 14), and other 'secret influences' (chapter 2). All the same, she holds to the traditional view of Shakespeare's 'universal sympathy which has at once the balance of impersonal detachment and the radiance of affection' (p. 19): 'He enters into the minds of his characters and speaks, as it were, from within them, giving thus a kind of impartiality to his picture of life.' This, in her view, is the essence of the dramatic, and she finds 'in Shakespeare not only a dramatist but *the* dramatist, the only one in the great company of dramatic poets who is wholly and continuously dramatic'.

In putting it thus strongly, she is doing no more than pushing to its logical conclusion a generally held way of thinking about Shakespeare and the drama. Yet, on further reflection, what a strange way of thinking it is—to hold to the definition of a genre for which there is only one true example! Shakespeare's genius is so great that it is understandable that it should skew our thinking in his favour; yet isn't it more likely that it is he who is the exception to the rule? or that the rule needs to be differently defined?

Moreover, Ellis-Fermor's claim that Shakespeare extends an impartial and universal sympathy towards his characters needs to be modified. After all, he obviously gives some of his characters more attention than others. It is true that he can, in a line or two, give his minor characters more life than most authors do; yet he also creates first, second, and third gentlemen with little or no personality, and his minor characters are understood in less depth than are his major ones. Of the major characters all are understood from within, but some to greater depths than others. The profound explorations are primarily conducted in his tragic protagonists and a few of the most memorable characters from the histories and comedies. Of these, some are regarded with admiration, some with amusement, some with pity, others with horror.

It thus appears that Shakespeare in his characterization seeks the *effect* of dramatic point of view more than its reality. The same is true of his plots. At their best, they seem to unfold of themselves. But on further reflection we can see that their apparent inevitability is in fact the result of the author's sensitive response to the stories and their implications and a very subtle direction of our expectations so that we want to see exactly what he has chosen to show us. To speak of this direction of our expectations as Shakespeare's 'manipulation of the audience' is too heavy-handed a way of putting it, as if our attention were a camera lens to be mechanically adjusted to his liking. Shakespeare is infinitely responsive and tactful in his rapport with his viewers, sometimes challenging, sometimes luring, bold here, subtle there—all depending upon the nature of the ground to be covered. But his influence is none the less present and active.

I conclude therefore that Shakespeare—the one supposed adherent to a pure dramatic point of view—does not truly adhere to it but only seems to. From this it follows that he is not so different after all from other dramatists. The true difference is that he is the dramatist most concerned with sustaining the *illusion* of dramatic point of view and the one who is most adroit at doing so. The effect he creates of rendering unmediated life is something of a vanishing act: in truth, Shakespeare is anything but absent from the scene, he is ever-present in it, selecting, emphasizing, relating, reiterating, contrasting, dilating, framing, and so on. He is so much and so skilfully involved that he seems not to be involved at all.

If one then asks what, apart from appearances, is the actual practice of Shakespeare and other dramatists in matters of point of view, one finds virtually no critical help. As Robert Scholes has observed in *Structuralism in Literature* (New Haven, 1974), 'the concept of point-of-view' in the sophisticated sense of current fiction theory is 'seldom encountered in the criticism of drama'.

Fiction theory can provide more help, given some adjustment for the differing forms. In Shakespeare's tragedies and the most popular of the histories and comedies the prevailing point of view is that of a third person who chiefly follows the fortunes of a leading character or pair of characters. It is omniscient in that the playwright shows whatever events he deems pertinent and can—through soliloquies and asides and confidences—disclose the inner thoughts and feelings of whatever characters he likes. It is rare for a character to know something that the audience does not. In other respects, however, Shakespeare is highly selective in exercising his omniscience. When his attention ranges from the immediate concerns of the characters in the main plot, it is most commonly to turn to the working out of a subplot. He rarely rambles or dawdles or asks us to attend to incidents whose importance is not evident. He looks into the inner lives of relatively few of his characters, and surprisingly often these are not sympathetic characters, with whom he might be expected to invite a deeper understanding, but villains, whose deceptions need clarifying or whose perverse motives need explaining.

In general, Shakespeare's plays show us in the audience how our own lives would look if we were enlightened enough to detach ourselves slightly from them and look at ourselves from the outside as well as the inside—with a fuller understanding of the influences that are exerted upon us, a more detached perspective on our own formulations of experience, and a greater awareness than usual that others see things differently from ourselves and have inner lives, too.

At times the dominance of a leading character can be so strong as to approach an autobiographical point of view. The beginning of *Richard III* is an exceptional case in point. Each of the first two scenes is framed by soliloquies in which Richard first tells us what he is going to do and at the end crows over his success in having done so. In the process the audience is brought not only to see how Richard sees the world but also— to an alarming extent—to share his gleefully wicked way of seeing it. At the outset the play becomes his story, and he tells it. In the rest of the play this dominance is lessened. After the first and until the last act, Richard has asides but no soliloquies; he confides his plans and attitudes to Buckingham. His last soliloquy is an extraordinary revelation of his character but does nothing to re-establish the dominance of his point of view.

In general, it is hazardous to trust a Shakespearian character to tell us what to think. At times a character may speak with special authority, as when the Fool insists on King Lear's folly or Flavius on Timon's profligacy or Emilia on Othello's jealousy. At those moments they do speak for the playwright, driving home to the most obtuse or inattentive some key dramatic point. The hazard comes when interpreters generalize this local choric function. As discussed in Chapter 2, those who think they hear Shakespeare's voice in the choruses of *Henry V* are mistaking the part for the whole. Or to take another example, Philo's disapproval of Antony has been taken as the keynote of a whole Roman view of the tragedy that is attributed to Shakespeare. To do so, however, is to neglect his counterbalancing presentation of an Egyptian view of it. It is the essence of drama that its characters express with conviction and eloquence views that may be diametrically opposed.

Yet there is a way in which point of view in Shakespeare extends beyond what he chooses to show us as a story-teller. He does provide a certain kind of guidance as to the 'viewpoint' from which we should respond to the story. He seems, however, much less interested in telling his audience *what* to think about a given play than in suggesting *how* best to go about understanding it.

Each play defines its own epistemology. One of Shakespeare's methods of definition is to present a character who practises the exact opposite of the preferred way-of-knowing. Egeus in *A Midsummer Night's Dream* is an example of an anti-viewpoint character. He is the most rigidly authoritarian of fathers in a play which was shown in Chapter 2 to bespeak a degree of poetic licence, both in its working out of a happy ending for its characters and for the enjoyment of this process by the audience. Egeus's folly in choosing his daughter's mate is underlined when her own choice tells his rival:

> You have her father's love, Demetrius;
> Let me have Hermia's. Do you marry him.   (1. 1. 93–4)

Even when the young lovers have in unorthodox fashion arrived at a 'gentle concord', Egeus persists in holding to the law until Theseus intervenes: 'Egeus, I will overbear your will' (4. 1. 178). Clearly, a rigid insistence on orthodoxy is not the way for an audience to enter into the world of this play.[2]

For a more extended example, consider *1 Henry IV*. It is in large part about 'making history', and the play challenges its audience to a sophisticated understanding of just how this is done. It shows its leading characters engaged not only in doing the deeds that make history but in trying to control the way these deeds are understood by others. The deeds themselves are swift and brief. The bulk of the play is devoted to the conflicting versions of reality to which the characters try to give currency and thus 'make history' in a second sense. Shakespeare sharpens the challenge for his audience by making the alternative versions highly plausible and by choosing a style of dramaturgy that at first seems heavily realistic, even naturalistic. Only gradually do we learn not to take it at its face value.

The implicit lesson begins in the first scene. To all but the most acute it must come as a surprise when, at the end of the scene, the King speaks of Hotspur and his withholding of prisoners:

> But I have sent for him to answer this;
> And for this cause awhile we must neglect
> Our holy purpose to Jerusalem.

---

[2] For an interesting modification of Egeus's intransigence in the Folio edition, see Barbara Hodgdon, 'Gaining a Father: The Role of Egeus in the Quarto and the Folio', *Review of English Studies*, NS 37 (1986), 534–42.

How can one reconcile this speech with the King's opening speech in which he had reaffirmed his determination to proceed with his long-planned expedition to the Holy Land? Note that the King now says, 'I *have sent* for him' not 'I *will send* for him'. His use of the past tense here makes it clear that at the time of his opening speech he had already decided not to make the crusade he there *says* he is going to make. Is he hopelessly befuddled? or Shakespeare careless? Or, as I believe, has the King been acting out a 'pseudo-event'?—one in which the virtuous King may be publicly seen to be regretfully deflected from his holy crusade by the need to deal with insurgents at home?

It may be that only the most alert spectators will catch the clues that give away the King's manipulation of appearances; few commentators have. The second scene is more overt. For the first part of the scene, we think we are seeing a slice of life in the behaviour of the wastrel Prince and his dissolute companions. We may already have seen that Sir John Oldcastle (later renamed Falstaff) was busy trying to put his own self-serving construction on events, one that would place himself in the role of royal crony. He said to the Prince: 'Do not thou when thou art king hang a thief' (1. 2. 60–1). 'No, thou shalt', was the Prince's reply, which Sir John was quick to interpret to his own advantage: 'Shall I? O rare! By the Lord, I'll be a brave judge!' The Prince was not to be so easily manipulated: 'Thou judgest false already. I mean thou shalt have the hanging of the thieves, and so become a rare hangman.' Only at the end of the scene does Shakespeare have the Prince reveal the master-plan of his own manipulativeness: 'I know you all . . .' (1. 2. 192–214). By re-enacting the story of the prodigal son, the Prince can play along with Sir John's scheme for self-advancement and in the end turn it to his own benefit.

The third scene shows Hotspur in the process of interpreting the past. His long and entertaining attempt to excuse his battlefield refusal of prisoners due the King is promptly undercut by the King's observation that Hotspur still withholds the prisoners.

For those in the audience who are still not sufficiently alerted against taking appearances at face value, Shakespeare introduces poor Francis who, in his unthinking credulity, serves as an anti-viewpoint character. At the beginning of this episode Prince Hal tells Poins, 'Step aside, and I'll show thee a precedent'. The practical joke they then play on Francis may serve to teach Shakespeare's precedent as well. If we—like Francis—take things at face value, we will be duped as he is.

If this caveat is challenging to the audience, Shakespeare as usual accompanies his challenge with rewards, in this case the sheer delight that can come from the free play with appearances. In the Gadshill robbery episode, we are allowed to see the real events as they occur and then to enjoy Sir John's attempt to revise them to his liking. Part of the fun is that it is so knowing. All of the principals know that the fat rogue is prevaricating, and to a degree they all know that the others know it. His increase of the number of men in buckram from two to four to nine to eleven cannot have truly been meant to deceive. He did it in part for the joy of seeing how far he could go before the Prince and Poins would protest. And they in turn egg him on; when the Prince at first remonstrates that Jack increased the number of men from two to four, Poins backs Sir John: 'Ay, ay, he said four.' An alert spectator may also see that old Jack's mock-prevarication here is not all exuberant play. For it suits the ultimate purposes of this would-be court-jester to inflate his bubble of heroism so that the heir-apparent may have the pleasure of puncturing it.

Properly alerted, we in the audience thus may discern layers and sub-layers of appearances and realities within the horseplay. We can also see at once beneath the role-playing when the Prince and plump Jack rehearse his coming interview with his father. The two are in fact acting out a psychodrama in which they address their own relationship, a subtext that rises to the surface for all to see in the course of the playlet.

In the actual interview between father and son, we may marvel at the astuteness of the King's manipulation of public 'opinion' in his usurpation of the throne but even more at the precocious sophistication of the Prince, who we can see to be tacitly reversing his father's techniques. Instead of making himself scarce and thus to be wondered at, he makes himself seem common—the better to highlight his eventual reform. Furthermore, he succeeds in winning his father's support in this scene without ever confiding his master-plan. And that is very much to his purpose, for the grief of the father over the prodigality of his son is a key part of the plan.

With the rebels, the alertly sceptical members of the audience will have little doubt about the duplicity of Northumberland's 'illness' on the eve of battle; it will be confirmed as 'crafty-sickness' in Part Two. We may remark the irony that Hotspur, who was so impoliticly open in his scepticism about Glendower's magical powers, is so easily duped by Worcester, when he suppresses the King's offer of amnesty.

By the time of the battle, the alerted members of the audience should be ready for its riot of counterfeiting—from the King's multiple selves to Sir John's falsities, the playfulness of his pretence to heroism at Gadshill now turned sour with his desecration of Hotspur's corpse and cynical claim to reward for having killed him.

We may also have gained a special insight into the heroism of Prince Hal, shown not only in his ability to do the deeds that make history but in his ability to control the way he and his actions are understood by others. He has mastered both reality and appearances. The Prince's response to Sir John's claims about Hotspur is, however, a disturbing foretaste of Part Two: 'if a lie may do thee grace, / I'll gild it with the happiest terms I have' (5. 4. 154–5). For in the sequel the manipulations of appearance and reality will be crude and overt. Shakespeare will initiate his audience into this viewpoint, not by the gradual process I have traced in Part One but by bringing on as his prologue 'Rumour [*in a robe*] painted full of tongues'.

Let us now consider matters of point of view and viewpoint in *Macbeth*. The illusion of dramatic point of view is particularly important to its effect. Its master paradox depends upon it. Macbeth must seem free to work out his own destiny—only to find at his final undoing that he has done no more than fulfil the prophecies he had sought to outdo. For the paradox to hold, the process must not seem rigged: the outcome—though predetermined—must seem to have resulted from a free play of character and circumstance.

Shakespeare succeeds brilliantly in creating just this effect. Obviously he does not pretend to show the whole story. His style is too economical and his pace too swift for that. He does not, for example, choose to present the scene of public inquiry into the assassination that Banquo and Macduff urge and that all concerned, including Macbeth, feel to be in order. Yet its absence does not seem an omission. He has already shown Macbeth under questioning, squirming and playing the hypocrite. The scene of inquiry could only be more of the same. Besides, the flight of Malcolm and Donalbain seems at the time to obviate further investigation. Not everything is shown, it seems; only the essentials. It is the key actions that the playwright appears to lay bare, whether they lie deep inside the secret counsels of Macbeth and Lady Macbeth or in far-away England, when the forces against them are gaining adherents.

On analysis, however, this effect may be seen to be indeed illusory. As elsewhere, the mirror that *Macbeth* seems to hold up to nature proves in fact to be an artfully created image, the product of uncountable acts of selection and emphasis by the playwright, some of which daringly defy a literal mirroring of events.

Technically speaking, from what point of view does Shakespeare present his play? *Macbeth* represents a unique variant of 'omniscience', if by an omniscient point of view we mean that the playwright knows and reveals all to the audience that is important to be told as the story unfolds. What is unique is that in *Macbeth* Shakespeare does more than that, and less.

In certain respects, his general point of view is *prescient*, since we are given foreknowledge of what is to occur, much of which proves true. This exceeds the kind of advance information that we enjoy when we eavesdrop on characters who are laying plots against one another and then see the plots carried out. It is more than the foreshadowing with which Shakespeare habitually hints at tragic events. The foreknowledge he discloses in *Macbeth*, as rendered by the Weird Sisters, glimpses a whole order of things beyond the human. It resembles the predictions in Queen Margaret's curse in *Richard III* yet with some crucial differences. Margaret seems to be in touch with a divinely ordained retribution for sins: with Providence. Her prophecies are clear-cut, openly delivered, and in due course straightforwardly fulfilled. The Weird Sisters, on the other hand, disclose forbidden knowledge, ordinarily denied to playgoers as well as the characters. Their prophecies are unclear and subject to surprising fulfilment. They tantalize, by offering knowledge that is privileged yet partial.

The association of the Sisters with forbidden knowledge is established in the first scene. Heralded by thunder and lightning, three bearded women enter. The First Witch asks 'When shall we three meet again? / In thunder, lightning, or in rain?' At first it seems that she is freely proposing a possible time for their next meeting. Yet it soon becomes clear that she is asking the others' help in a piece of future-telling, seeking to divine the preordained time they are to meet again. The Second Witch has more definite foreknowledge: 'When the hurly-burly's done, / When the battle's lost and won.' It is the Third Witch who is the most precise: 'That will be ere the set of sun.'

Are they sharing a common vision, each adding to the others' account? Or are there degrees in their prescience? The next round of prophecies indicates the latter, for it shows the same pattern of graduated knowledge as does the first. The First Witch again asks a question: 'Where the place?' The Second Witch knows that 'the place' is to be 'Upon the heath.' But it is the Third Witch who knows that it is not only 'we three' who will be meeting but that a fourth will join them: 'There to meet with Macbeth.'

The sense of powers beyond powers is most strong in their final sequence, in which they respond to their supernatural familiars. The First Witch submissively cries, 'I come, Grimalkin'. The Second Witch seems less subservient, simply acknowledging that 'Paddock calls.' The Third Witch seems to be telling whoever is calling her: 'Anon.' Again, she seems the most powerful of the three, responsive to her familiar yet with a degree of free will and independent authority.

Like the first, the second scene begins with loud sounds (*'Alarum within'*) and a horrific sight: *'a bleeding Captain.'* Duncan continues the idiom of a question ('What bloody man is that?') followed by a confident prediction ('He can report, / As seemeth by his plight, of the revolt / The newest state.'). His prediction is accurate. Lennox, too, can foretell by appearances what to expect. When Ross enters, he exclaims:

> What haste looks through his eyes! So should he look
> That seems to speak things strange.

Sure enough, Ross then tells of the remarkable victory of Macbeth over Macdonald and 'that most disloyal traitor / The Thane of Cawdor'.

The connection of the scene with the Macbeth story is then settled at the end by the King's decision to award Cawdor's former title to Macbeth. Again, Shakespeare gives inside information about something that is about to happen to Macbeth. And the parallels with the first scene are completed by the concluding lines:

ROSS I'll see it done.
KING DUNCAN
What he hath lost, noble Macbeth hath won.

Duncan's unwitting echo of the Sisters' 'When the battle's lost and won' and the rhyme of 'won' with 'done' give the audience its first instance of an order of things that is working through human affairs in its own mysterious ways, outside the ken of its human participants.

It is with a certain familiarity that we greet the second appearance of the three Witches (we may note that the First Witch was right the first time: they do meet in thunder). Their words, however, are cause for new alarm. For this time it is their destructive powers that are revealed. Again it is the First Witch whose limits are emphasized. She can torment the 'master o'th' Tiger' in reprisal for his wife's affront, make him 'dwindle, peak and pine' among other torments; yet she is not all-powerful: 'Though his barque cannot be lost, / Yet it shall be tempest-tossed.' To accomplish her purposes, she seems to need the help of the winds commanded by the other two, although she has 'all the other'. The odd chiming of the Sisters with their circumstances is emphasized when their 'thumb / come' rhyme precedes the sounds of a drum within. The Third Witch spells out the effect: 'A drum, a drum—/ Macbeth doth come.' Even the beating of Macbeth's drum fits into their rhyme-scheme.

Their responses to Macbeth's 'Speak, if you can' follow the pattern I have been tracing. The First Witch's salutation—'All hail, Macbeth! Hail to thee, Thane of Glamis!'—tells us something we had not known for sure: this hitherto unidentified character *is* the Macbeth we have been hearing so much about. Yet clearly the Second Witch has greater knowledge: 'All hail, Macbeth! Hail to thee, Thane of Cawdor!' Thanks to the second scene, we are in a position, before Macbeth is, to give credence to her words. Yet just as we are feeling that our foreknowledge is complete, Shakespeare gives us a jolt. The most momentous of the pronouncements, delivered by the most authoritative of the three, comes as a complete surprise: 'All hail, Macbeth,' says the Third Witch, 'that shalt be king hereafter!' Our knowledge, too, we are made to realize, is partial though privileged.

This is by no means the only such surprise that Shakespeare gives us in the course of his play. At the end we do not learn until Macbeth does that 'Macduff was from his mother's womb / Untimely ripped'. By that time, though, we (unlike Macbeth) may well have begun to expect an unexpected meaning in the prophecy. The most disturbing of Shakespeare's surprises comes in 1. 4 when we, with Macbeth, have been expecting Duncan to name him as the next in line to the throne. Instead, the King names his son Malcolm, the Prince of Cumberland. We in the audience had again been led to feel that we had been granted a special vantage. With our privileged knowledge of the new Cawdor's murderous broodings, Shakespeare had invited us to take sardonic amusement in Duncan's blind trust in him. At the very moment Duncan was acknowledging his error with respect to the previous Cawdor ('He was a gentleman on whom I built / An absolute trust'), in walked Macbeth. Furthermore, the playwright had clearly raised our anticipation of some further honour due Macbeth. Ross had called his promotion to Cawdor 'an earnest of a greater honour' and Duncan himself had said that 'More is thy due than more than all can pay'. When Duncan then begins 'We will establish our estate upon . . .' we—as much as does Macbeth—expect that he will be the one who is named. And as much as he, we feel tricked when he is not. Shakespeare's muse in *Macbeth* is sly.

It is also secretive. It offers us the inside story of crime in high places yet we are not allowed to see the key moment, the actual killing of Duncan. In his film version, Polanski made the serious mistake of actually showing the crime. For one thing, it further diminished his already weakened Macbeth, making the killing altogether an act of fear, carried through because the King woke up enough to recognize Macbeth as he was about to strike and thus forced Macbeth to complete the act lest he be punished for the attempt and not the deed. More fundamentally, the off-stage crime is one of those challenges to the imagination—like those of the magnified armies in *Henry V* and the miniaturized elves in *A Midsummer Night's Dream*—by which Shakespeare draws his audience actively into the ways of his imagined world. In what is perhaps the boldest stroke of point of view in all of Shakespeare, we are obliged to join Lady Macbeth in imagining it, in straining to hear what we are not allowed to see, as Macbeth is 'about it'. Macbeth, too, is intent on hearing. He, of course, wants his crime to be unheard as well as unseen. He had earlier felt the need for a 'stealthy pace' lest 'the very stones prate of my whereabouts'. After the crime he listens hard for any sounds that might threaten discovery. Every noise appals him. All concerned are intent on listening.

Shakespeare's other great secret has to do with Macbeth's inner-most motives for killing the King. Although we are made privy to Macbeth's most closely concealed interviews and most private self-examinations, we can never be quite sure why he did the deed. From the raptnesses with which he meets the fateful developments at his first appearance, we are repeatedly left wondering what exactly is going on inside his mind. It is not too much to say that for the first half of the play, the workings of Macbeth's psyche are as tantalizing a secret as is the working out of his destiny.

This is partly because of his continual involvement with confidants in reaching his decisions. Although most of Shakespeare's leading characters have confidants, Macbeth is unique in the number of 'partners' he takes and the degree to which he relies upon them. First it is Banquo, then his wife. Later, the two Murderers will serve that function, followed by a brief reprise with Lady Macbeth at the appearance of Banquo's ghost. Finally, he goes to the Weird Sisters. His scenes with his partners give unusual insight into his inner life, yet only up to a point. For his attitudes are defined and importantly influenced by the very interactions that reveal them, thus leaving us finally unsure about what his private feelings and purposes actually are.

In his soliloquy at the end of 2. 1, we see most deeply inside Macbeth's mind just before his crime, and what do we find? Still another partner. This time it is his dagger that is influencing him, marshalling him 'the way that I was going'. It is worth noting that

Macbeth's imagination here blanks out the actual doing of the deed, just as we have seen the play's dramaturgy to do. He sees the dagger before the deed and then after it: 'And on thy blade and dudgeon gouts of blood, / Which was not so before.' He declares, 'I go, and it is done.' The bell he hears invites him to do the deed; he also hears in it the knell that follows it. In all three instances, the awful moment of the crime is left out. If the deed were to be done, 'then 'twere well / It were done quickly', he had said earlier; now his imagination is doing it so quickly that it leaps immediately from past to future. In this respect, too, we are left staring at a blank.

So inscrutable is the heart of Macbeth's mystery that even he cannot pluck it out. In one of the most revelatory of his soliloquies, he asks himself:

> why do I yield to that suggestion
> Whose horrid image doth unfix my hair
> And make my seated heart knock at my ribs
> Against the use of nature?   (I. 3. 133–6)

He cannot fathom his own attraction toward the murder.

The mystery is compounded by the succession of traumas he undergoes. Again traumatic changes are anything but rare in Shakespeare, that close student of Ovid's *Metamorphoses*. Hamlet is much altered from the student-prince Ophelia cherished; like Othello, Lear finds his occupation's gone. But no Shakespearian character experiences so many traumas as does Macbeth. He suffers the visitation of the Weird Sisters, the abrupt alterations in his social status, the radical change in his wife's personality after she unsexes herself, the killing of Duncan (that unleashes his wild killing of the chamberlains), the vision of Banquo's ghost, the ghastly 'shows' by the witches, his wife's mental illness and death—each with its strong impact on his personality. Not only is his inner self only partially revealed, even to himself, but that self is repeatedly altered radically.

Our understanding of Macbeth's character is thus very much like our understanding of the prophecies and the murder-plot. We have been given unusual advantages, yet these are accompanied by unusual limitations and difficulties. Although the point of view of *Macbeth* verges on omniscience, the knowledge it affords is of a peculiarly insecure variety. A radical dubiousness prevails. We cannot be sure what can reliably be known and what cannot. We inhabit a world of graduated knowledge, where—as with the First and Second Witches— our information is much less than complete. The Third Witch knows more than they, yet her knowledge is less than that of Hecate, and so on. We cannot even be sure how to gain reliable knowledge. The playwright himself can seem unreliable. Whether by choice or because he does not know, he does not reveal all, either about the killing of Duncan or Macbeth's motives for doing it. He even misleads us, where Duncan's naming of a successor is concerned.

From what viewpoint *are* we to know the truth in *Macbeth?* Certainly we must be careful not to trust in appearances. Duncan in the Cawdor scene is the anti-viewpoint character who illustrates what not to do. The folly of his straightforward trust in Macbeth is underlined by the fact that he makes this mistake even while realizing that appearances—as with the previous Cawdor—can be deceiving. Duncan's own promises can be misleading—as Macbeth (and we) learn in this same scene. The Witches' prophecies are particularly insidious. Even Macbeth is at first sceptical of them. Often in performance he and Banquo break the tension with laughter after the first round of prophecies. Macbeth's 'Went it not so?' and Banquo's 'To the self-same tune and words' invite a sceptical tone. Certainly their tone here is much lighter than after Macbeth is named Cawdor, thus confirming the second prophecy. Macbeth's scepticism has then begun to give way. He puts forth a transparent feeler: 'Do you not hope your children shall be kings?' Banquo catches his drift immediately and repudiates its implication: 'That, trusted home, / Might yet enkindle you unto the crown.' Then comes his warning to Macbeth about the theological hazards he sees: 'oftentimes to win us to our harm / The instruments of darkness tell us truths, / Win us with honest trifles to betray's / In deepest consequence.' Yet so insidious is the power of the prophecies' appeal that even Banquo eventually weakens:

> If there come truth from them—
> As upon thee, Macbeth, their speeches shine—
> Why by the verities on thee made good
> May they not be my oracles as well,
> And set me up in hope?   (3. 1. 6–10)

His question is soon answered, but not quite as he had hoped.

In *Macbeth,* as elsewhere, the best way to know is to await the event. When that is not possible, Malcolm's approach with Macduff in 4. 3 seems best, cumbersome as it is. His intuitions are as dubious as his father's: where Duncan could not tell a traitor when he saw one, Malcolm fails to recognize Macduff's loyalty at first sight. However, Malcolm has good reason to be suspicious of Macduff since he has left his family behind. To test Macduff, Malcolm is obliged to resort to duplicity, and Shakespeare does not overlook the irony that results from this. Macduff is at first as bewildered by Malcolm's duplicitous innocence as was Macbeth by duplicitous evil: 'Such welcome and unwelcome things at once / 'Tis hard to reconcile' (4. 3. 139–40). None the less, Malcolm's device does serve its purpose: it confirms Macduff's loyalty without losing his support.

His success depends ultimately on Macduff's moral courage, his readiness—no matter how difficult and confusing the circumstances— to trust his own convictions and pronounce the monster that Malcolm pretends to be not fit to govern: 'No, not to live.' The same may be said of the test that Shakespeare gives his audience. However difficult he may make it for us to be sure of things, the effect of his play will depend finally on our ability to know evil for what it is and repudiate it.

Although the prescience of *Macbeth* is unique in Shakespeare (and in dramatic literature), it may serve to illustrate how actively involved Shakespeare can be in matters of point of view and viewpoint. As much as it may serve his purposes to appear to be detached, Shakespeare's approach is in fact far from that of Stephen Dedalus's dramatic artist, 'indifferent, paring his fingernails'. In this respect, as in many, Shakespeare's is an art that hides art. Dedalus was closer to the mark when, in the same passage, he finds that the dramatist, 'like the God of the creation, remains within . . . his handiwork'.[3]

Since Shakespeare has thus been shown to be an active participant in the performance-ensemble, just what is his role within it? Chapter 2 sampled his work within the implied ensembles of *Henry V* and *A Midsummer Night's Dream*. Historically, what have been the actual roles played by Shakespeare and other playwrights in the production of their plays? This will be the subject of Chapter 4.

---

[3] James Joyce, *A Portrait of the Artist as a Young Man* (London, 1985), 194–5.

4

The Roles of the Playwright

THE roles that a playwright may play within the performance-ensemble have received surprisingly little attention. Where modern Western theatre is concerned, what has been written on the subject reads like propaganda issued from entrenched positions or communiqués from an on-going battle. The combat has concentrated mostly on questions of primacy. Some one of the participants in the performance-ensemble may be felt to be dominant throughout, in which case there is talk of a dramatist's theatre or a director's theatre or an actor's theatre. Bayreuth, for example, was originally a dramatist's theatre but has become a director's theatre. Gordon Craig dreamed of a designer's theatre. One doesn't hear of a playgoer's theatre, but no one doubts the power of the box-office and of the season-subscription to give the audience the last word. Or the periods of dominance may be regarded as sequential. It is sometimes said backstage that a play belongs at first to the playwright. During rehearsals, it belongs to the director. After opening night, it belongs to the actors. And after it has run for a few weeks, it belongs to the audience, to whose responses the actors cater. Peter Shaffer's term for this process of appropriation is 'The Cannibal Theatre'.

Shaffer is relatively reconciled to the process, painful as it may be. He sees it as a kind of sacrificial death for the playwright that ultimately frees him for his next effort:

Of course, the playwright doesn't merely accept this role; he needs and demands it. He also seeks rebirth, and the only way for him to achieve it is to be liberated from his old play, to have the obsessional demon who first beat it from the cover of his unrest haled out of his body in the fullness of performance. The actor is the playwright's exorcist.

But the actor, too, needs freeing. He also lives in isolation and needs to be released, through the harness of a text from the intensity of feeling unyoked to purpose. Thus each of these incomplete beings is living in the other and released by the other . . .[1]

Other modern playwrights have been more insistent than Shaffer in

[1] Peter Shaffer, 'The Cannibal Theatre', in *The Making of Theatre: From Drama to Performance*, ed. R. Corrigan (Glenview, Ill., 1981), 178.

their claims to primacy, even though they have often been defeated. In *See-Saw Log* (New York, 1959), William Gibson has given a blow-by-blow account of his losing power-struggles with the director and leading actor of his *Two for the See-Saw*. Arthur Miller has excoriated the stupidity and ignorance of the policies of the Lincoln Center Theatre, for which he was to have been house-playwright.[2] John Arden fought his battle with the Royal Shakespeare Company management in public and on-stage.[3] Some playwrights have taken executive authority into their own hands. Samuel Beckett, Edward Albee, and Tom Stoppard have directed their own work; Richard Foreman and Kobo Abe have formed their own theatre companies. Like Charles Chaplin and Orson Welles, Woody Allen often directs his own filmscripts as well as acting in them.

Scholars have characteristically sided with the playwright. Eric Bentley, for example, inveighs against 'theatricalists' like Gordon Craig and Max Reinhardt, who 'try to make drama without the help of a dramatist'. He maintains that 'the dramatist not only charts out a plan of procedure'; 'he conceives and realizes a work of art which is already complete—except for technical reproduction—in his head and which expresses by verbal image and concept a certain attitude to life.' The director's function is properly 'to be utterly faithful and subordinate' to his author's words.[4] This view is widely held. Most Shakespeare scholars would subscribe to it.

Such dominance by the playwright has been challenged by performers, most radically by Antonin Artaud.[5] Himself a frustrated actor and director, Artaud is concerned to displace the prevailing theatre of 'storytelling psychology' (of which he saw Shakespeare as a prime exponent) with one of ecstasy. To that end he wants to overthrow the authority of the playwright. Instead of 'our purely verbal theatre', in which theatre is no more than 'a performed text', he advocates a kind of theatre which overthrows 'the supremacy of speech' in favour of production values, one which indeed 'eliminates words' and speaks instead 'the language of everything that can be said and signified upon a stage independently of speech'—that is to say, dance, song, pantomime, spectacle. In a latter essay, he puts it less strongly: 'It is not a matter of suppressing speech in the theatre' but of giving it a reduced position in which it is one element among many, where 'gesture, word, sound, music' are on a par. But he still

---

[2] Arthur Miller, *Theater Essays*, ed. R. Martin (New York, 1978).
[3] John Arden, *To Present the Pretence* (London, 1977), 159–72.
[4] Eric Bentley, *The Playwright as Thinker*, 239.
[5] Antonin Artaud, *The Theatre and its Double* (New York, 1958).

maintains that in 'pure theatre' there is no place for 'the author who uses written words only'. His battle-cry against the tyranny of the dramatist is famous: 'No More Masterpieces!'

In Artaud's wake, many modern directors have asserted their own primacy, to which they see the playwright and his words as properly subordinate. In *Environmental Theater* (New York, 1973), Richard Schechner insists that the playwright's skills are 'literary, poetic, the mastery of language as distinct from the mastery of action'. In his view the director is the master of action. For Peter Brook's *Orghast*, poet Ted Hughes provided dialogue in a new language he had invented to meet Brook's requirements. To John Arden, however, someone who simply 'puts pen to paper and sets down dramatic dialogue' is no more than a scriptwriter, 'a semi-skilled sub-contractor to the theatre', not the fully-fledged playwright Arden aspires to be: 'in control of his or her work right through to the final exit of the audience from their seats in the theatre.'[6]

And so the dispute has gone on, with a ferocity that makes one wonder how, in a collaborative effort, productions ever reach the boards. Surely John Whiting, the dramatist, is wise in his observation:

There is an old argument as to whether the direction and performance of a play is interpretive or creative. The question can be answered: the writing, directing, designing and acting of a play are each creative in their own part to the whole. More important, surely, is that they are interdependent.[7]

It is worth remembering also that various playwrights have produced masterpieces within performance-ensembles of various sorts. Few have had the kind of total control to which Arden aspires. Molière led his own company. Strindberg had his Intimate Theatre. After years of struggle with opera managements, Wagner at Bayreuth had his own theatre and company. Brecht led the Berliner Ensemble. Sometimes a major playwright has been especially associated with a certain company, as was Chekhov at the Moscow Art Theatre, O'Neill with the Provincetown Players and Theatre Guild, Odets with the Group Theatre. But it has been much more common for the playwright to be a freelance, dependent for the performance of his work on its selection by an actor-manager, producer, or in the case of the ancient Greeks by a festival official and a financial sponsor.

The subject is a fascinating and neglected one. The roles that

[6] Arden, 209.
[7] John Whiting, 'Writing for Actors', in *The Making of Theatre: From Drama to Performance*, 173.

playwrights have played in the production of their own work deserves its own book. It is time now, however, to look at Shakespeare and the role that as theatre-poet he assigned himself as playwright. Chapter 2 sampled the ideal performance-ensembles he implied in *Henry V* and *A Midsummer Night's Dream*. What is known about the actual production circumstances within which he worked?

The general theatre conditions of Elizabethan England differed from ours today in a number of basic ways that influenced the workings of the performance-ensemble during Shakespeare's time. All professional productions in London were done by all-male repertory acting companies. Although all-boy companies were important, Shakespeare apparently had no connection with them; so I shall focus on the companies of men, in which boys acted only the roles of women and children. The adult companies were made up of between ten and twelve permanent sharers—leading actors who shared in the expenses and profits—plus numerous 'hired men' engaged as needed. The sharers were the centre of artistic and economic power. They were often indebted, however, to the housekeeper, the owner of the theatre in which they performed. Since this impresario also shared in the proceeds and was often the source of immediate funds for costumes, wages, and the purchase of plays, he was another major economic factor.

Politically, the acting companies had to cope with divided authority. They were favoured by the court (each company had its noble patron, certain ones were invited periodically to entertain the queen or king) but opposed by the City of London and its Lord Mayor, who for many years kept theatre buildings outside the City proper. They were subject to regulation by both court and City, including censorship of their scripts by the Revels Office.

Usually, the companies bought scripts outright, for cash plus a benefit performance, and retained ownership of the scripts. Most playwrights freelanced; a few (probably fewer than a dozen in all) had more lasting relationships with a single company. Today, we would call the latter 'house playwrights'. In *The Profession of Dramatist in Shakespeare's Time* (Princeton, 1984), G. E. Bentley calls them 'attached' dramatists. They wrote exclusively for a given company (which apparently had only one attached playwright at a time), refrained from publishing their scripts (unlike the freelancers), and often did various odd jobs, such as updating old scripts, collaborating with freelancers on company plays, composing prologues and epilogues. In general, it is not too much to say, as does Andrew Gurr in *The Shakespearean Stage 1574–1642* (Cambridge, 1980), that

'Playwrights were the servants of the players, in economic servitude to them' (p. 19).

For all these and other differences, the Elizabethan theatre scene was in numerous ways very like our own. It was commercially competitive, based in the chief population centre of its area, financially precarious for most yet richly rewarding for the most successful few. Especially familiar was the atmosphere of conflict among participants in the theatrical enterprise. Every relationship within it was the subject of dispute. In 1591 a group of players warned James Burbage, the owner of The Theatre, that if he continued to withhold money due them, 'they wold compleyne to ther lorde & Mr. the lord Admyrall, and then he in a rage, litle reverencing his honour & estate, sayd by a great othe, that he cared not for iii of the best lordes of them all' (Gurr, p. 38). In 1597 Francis Langley, owner of the new Swan playhouse, sued players who were in his debt (Gurr, p. 42). In 1615 Lady Elizabeth's Men drew up 'Articles of Grievance and of Oppression against Phillip Henslowe', the theatre-owner (Gurr, p. 56). In 1623 Mrs Baskerville, the widow of a sharer, took members of the Red Bull company to court for money due her. In 1624 Anne Elsden, a member of the playgoing public, alleged that she was defamed in a play called *Keep the Widow Waking* (Gurr, p. 54). Around 1639 the owners of the playhouse in Salisbury Court and the members of Queen Henrietta's company took their attached playwright Richard Brome to court for failing to meet his agreed quota of plays and doing work on the side for another company (Gurr, p. 21; Bentley, p. 112).

In their turn, playwrights had harsh words for one another (as in the War of the Theatres). They attacked poor acting; Thomas Dekker in his address to the readers of *The Whore of Babylon* compares players to musicians and laments: 'that in such consorts many of the instruments are for the most part out of tune. And no marvel; for let the poet set the note of his numbers even to Apollo's own lyre, the player will have his own crotchets, and sing false notes . . .' The satirists sometimes engaged in personal attacks. They kept up a running battle with their Puritan critics. Almost to a man the playwrights disparaged the poor judgement of their audiences, especially that of gallants and the garlick-mouthed, greasy-apron nutcrackers who stood in the yard.[8] Audiences might 'mew' (hiss) a play. At Shrovetide in 1617 some rioting apprentices seriously damaged the Cockpit (Gurr, p. 208). According to one account 'the

[8] David Klein, *The Elizabethan Dramatists as Critics* (New York, 1963), 178–84.

benches, the tiles, the laths, the stones, oranges, apples, nuts, flew about most liberally'.

These instances are only a sampling of the suits and disputes on record. Of course, the records very likely give a distorted version of the whole picture, exaggerating the times of dissonance and taking the harmony for granted. At the core there must have been a good working relationship within the Elizabethan performance-ensemble, for—amid the acrimony during this era—a remarkable kind of imaginative collaboration was achieved. The sort of performance-ensemble studied in this book was indeed one of the major accomplishments of Elizabethan drama. In *The Rise of the Common Player* (London, 1962), Muriel Bradbrook has sketched the process by which it evolved from Chaucer declaiming his narratives at court to the fully-fledged drama of Kyd, Marlowe, and the early Shakespeare. She sees the process as a 'search for literary form, which should capture and display the social relations between player and audience as they shared together the imaginative acts which the poet had conceived for them'. Completion of the process required a certain loss or immersion of self by all concerned. For the members of the audience to be able freely to lose themselves in the play, the actors had to transform themselves into their roles and the playwright to make the 'imaginative feat of detachment' which would result in 'the establishment of *direct* relationship with the audience to the actors'. Marlowe and the great actor of his leading roles, Edward Alleyn, 'imposed themselves by grand, obliterating majesty'. It was left to Shakespeare and the great actor of his leading roles, Richard Burbage, to take the final steps of self-submergence that would invite, rather than demand, the audience's involvement.

Burbage was famous for his total immersion in his roles, 'so wholly transforming himself into his part and putting off himself with his clothes, as he never (not so much as in the tiring house) assum'd himself till the play was done'. It was just at this time that 'personation' came into the language to describe just this kind of acting (Gurr, p. 98). The audience involvement that complete personation could inspire is celebrated by Thomas Heywood:

What English blood, seeing the person of any bold Englishman presented, and doth not hugge his fame, and hunnye at his valor, pursuing him in his enterprise with his best wishes, and as beeing wrapt in contemplation, offers to him in his hart all prosperous performance, as if the Personator were the man personated? So bewitching a thing is lively and well spirited action, that it hath power to new mold the harts of the spectators.[9]

[9] Thomas Heywood, *An Apology for Actors (1612)* (New York, 1972), Book 1.

So the personator leaves his ordinary self to seem the man personated, and the resulting lively action, by theatre-witchery, in turn transforms its witnesses. The contribution of the playwright to this act of mutual imagination is brought out by Thomas Dekker; he writes in the prologue to *If It Be Not Good* (1610):

> That man give me, whose breast, fill'd by the Muses
> With raptures, into a second them infuses:
> Can give an actor sorrow, rage, joy, passion,
> Whilst he again, by self-same agitation,
> Commands the hearers; sometimes drawing out tears,
> Then smiles, and fills them both with hopes and fears.
> That man give me. And to be such a one
> Our poet this day strives, or to be none.

Such is the chain of emotion to which Dekker aspires. The poet must be such a one as to transmit the raptures he receives from the Muses to a receptive actor and thereby to responsive hearers.

Shakespeare was just 'such a one'. His theatrical circumstances were remarkably conducive to this achievement. Structurally, they were much the same as those that generally prevailed but whether through good fortune or his own good management, his working conditions were singularly advantageous. His acting company was by far the most stable and long-lived of his time. Politically, it was in such good standing with the court that under Elizabeth I it survived unscathed its involvement with the Essex Rebellion (some of the rebels had commissioned the company to perform *Richard II* on the eve of the uprising), and under James I it received royal patronage as the King's Men. The company was in such good standing with the City of London that when in 1608 the Blackfriars precinct for the first time came under City jurisdiction, its performances at the Blackfriars Theatre were allowed to continue without hindrance (Gurr, p. 53).

Economically, too, Shakespeare was in an extraordinarily strong position. Although Bentley does not make the point, it would seem from surviving evidence that he was the first of the 'attached' playwrights. As an actor, he was a sharer in the company, and one of the very few 'attached' playwrights who was also a sharer. He may well have been the first of these. Certainly, he was the first such playwright/sharer who was also a housekeeper (he was one of the sharers brought in to help to finance the building of the Globe Theatre).

Actor, sharer, housekeeper, attached playwright, Shakespeare was, more than any other Elizabethan playwright, a complete 'man of the theatre'—and amid particularly harmonious circumstances. Compared with playwrights of his time, his popular reputation was second to none. And the era's most discerning drama critic, Ben Jonson, could see his stature in the dramatic literature of all time. Within his acting company, the sharers clearly had more than a business relationship. To read through their biographies in E. K. Chambers' dictionary of Elizabethan actors is to marvel at their collegial feelings.[10] With the exception of Thomas Pope, who was the first to die, the wills of all of the original and continuing sharers in the King's Men involve mention of other sharers, as witnesses or legatees or trustees or recipients of memorial rings. Perhaps it was Augustine Phillips, who died a year after Pope, who encouraged this custom. He was especially generous to his theatre-associates, as Chambers has summarized:

There are legacies of £5 to 'the hyred men of the company which I am of', of 30s pieces to his 'fellowes' William Shakespeare and Henry Condell, and his 'servant' Christopher Beeston, of 20s pieces to his 'fellows' Laurence Fletcher, Robert Armin, Richard Cowley, Alexander Cook and Nicholas Tooley, of silver bowls to John Heminges, Richard Burbadge, and William Sly and of £20 to Timothy Whithorne.

In his will Shakespeare himself gave rings to all of the surviving original sharers, Richard Burbage, Henry Condell, and John Heminges. Clearly, Heminges was the hub of the company. A man of unusually upright character, he managed the company's business affairs successfully and fairly. Again and again his fellows name him in their wills as executor, overseer, trustee. In his own will, he left ten shillings for a ring 'unto every of my fellows and sharers, his majesties servants' (Chambers, p. 322). With his colleague and neighbour Henry Condell, his posthumous gift to Shakespeare was to see to the publication of the collected plays of his 'Friend & Fellow'.

From most indications, Shakespeare entered intimately and harmoniously into his theatrical circumstances. He is unique among his contemporaries in the courtesy with which he addresses his spectators as 'gentles all'. In *As You Like It* he honours the memory of that 'dead shepherd' and fellow playwright, Christopher Marlowe. In the First Player in *Hamlet* he recognizes the personating powers an actor can command. It was customary for an Elizabethan playwright to read his play through for the company, and there are Restoration traditions that Shakespeare instructed the players in particular roles. Hamlet is

---

[10] E. K. Chambers, *The Elizabethan Stage*, 4 vols. (Oxford, Clarendon Press, 1923), ii. 295–350.

very much the Elizabethan playwright, in 'pronouncing' the speech as he wishes the player to perform it.

In general, Hamlet has a strong theatrical streak in him; he successively takes the role of critical spectator, author, and quasi-performer—Ophelia thinks him as good as a Chorus and he himself thinks he might qualify for a fellowship in a 'cry of players' (Horatio thinks perhaps half a share). But he cannot be taken simply as a spokesman for Shakespeare. Hamlet's advice to the Players is very much in his own character. He is a born exhorter. The Player is by no means the only one he charges to change his ways completely and 'reform it altogether'. He is also much given to expatiation. It is very like him, having written a speech of a dozen or sixteen lines, to expound a whole philosophy of drama in the course of explaining how he wishes it delivered.

Every inch an author, Hamlet takes an aggressive stance. His first concern is for the speeches of a play, then for its structure—the necessary questions of the play and the 'digestion' of the scenes. He assumes that to render the speech properly the Player need only repeat it 'as I pronounced it to you'. Although he makes individual exceptions, he is highly critical of players and playgoers in general. He welcomes the Players as 'good friends' and marvels at the First Player's ability to feel his role; but most of his comments on acting are harshly critical. He disparages the 'million' in the audience, especially the groundlings. He reserves his praise for the few who are 'judicious', among which number he counts himself (although he does acknowledge that there are 'others, whose judgments in such matters cried in the top of mine'). Of course, his authority as author and critic is re-enforced by the fact that he is the Crown Prince of the realm and special patron for the performance to come.

Hamlet's comments, none the less, are best understood as the brilliant *aperçus* of an aristocratic amateur of the stage. Shakespeare's approach as a working professional is of quite another order.

Not that Shakespeare was simply a purveyor of successful scripts for his company. The remarkable length of many of them, far beyond the 2,500 lines ordinarily performed on the Elizabethan stage,[11] suggests a writer who was following his muse where it led him regardless of the practicalities of performance. And he seems to have been a leader rather than a follower of theatrical trends—as in his early concern with the history play, his revival in *Hamlet* of the

[11] Alfred Hart, 'Stage Abridgement', in his *Shakespeare and the Homilies* (Melbourne, 1934).

revenge play, and, very possibly, his focus on tragicomic romances at the end of his career.

Nor was he altogether content with his theatrical lot. Two of his Sonnets express his feeling that, by pursuing his career in the theatre, he has betrayed his better self. Thus he feels 'my nature is subdu'd / To what it works in, like the dyer's hand' (Sonnet 111), and again:

> Alas, tis true, I have gone here and there
> And made myself a motley to the view,
> Gored mine own thoughts, sold cheap what is most dear . . .
>
> (Sonnet 110)

As shown in the Pageant of the Nine Worthies in *Love's Labour's Lost* and 'Pyramus and Thisbe' in *A Midsummer Night's Dream*, he was alive to the follies of amateur actors and their patronizing patrons. The first Prologue in *Henry V* may express a private frustration with the limitations of his 'wooden O'. Actors are disparaged in some of his later plays, as they are not elsewhere in the canon. Ulysses tells Agamemnon about how Achilles mimics him:

> Like a strutting player, whose conceit
> Lies in his hamstring and doth think it rich
> To hear the wooden dialogue and sound
> 'Twixt his stretched footing and the scaffoldage . . .
>
> (*Troilus and Cressida*, 1. 3. 153–6)

Macbeth compares life to a 'poor player / That struts and frets his hour upon the stage' (*Macbeth*, 5. 5. 23–4). Cleopatra foresees how the 'quick comedians' will degrade her tragic relationship with Antony into 'Alexandrian revels':

> Antony
> Shall be brought drunken forth, and I shall see
> Some squeaking Cleopatra boy my greatness
> I'th' posture of a whore.
>
> (*Antony and Cleopatra*, 5. 2. 214–17)

In *Shakespeare and the Idea of the Play* (London, 1977), Ann Righter Barton finds in such instances signs of 'Shakespeare's disillusionment with the stage' at this phase of his career (p. 171). These passages are, however, too deeply coloured by the personalities and purposes of their speakers to shed reliable light on Shakespeare's own attitudes.

Whatever Shakespeare's private feelings, what can be concluded about his role as playwright in his actual performance-ensemble? Although the evidence is far from complete, everything points to a relationship based on mutual regard among all the participants, something very close to the ideal ensembles implied in *Henry V* and *A Midsummer Night's Dream*—gracious and harmonious, challenging yet ultimately loving. Unlike many playwrights, then and now, Shakespeare was present in person at the Globe, very much a participant at rehearsals and—as an actor—at performances of his plays. He seems not, however, to have been an all-dominating figure but rather a key member of the inner circle of his acting company. Indeed, no one member of the performance-ensemble at the Globe appears to have been dominant.

In trying to picture this relationship, one should put aside the power struggles of the modern theatre and recall that a successful theatre-event is after all a collaborative act, one in which playwright, players, and playgoers are linked in a kind of love-relationship as they mutually imagine the events of the play. In *Blessings in Disguise* (London, 1986) Alec Guinness catches this collaborative spirit between player and playwright in describing Ernest Milton as Hamlet: 'He neither did Shakespeare a favour, as some of our actors manage to imply they do, nor kow-towed to him; he met him, in Hamlet, on mutual and loving ground' (p. 172). In a highly instructive anecdote, Laurence Olivier adds the audience to the loving collaboration:

I daresay that artistry in acting lies somewhere in the relationship with the audience. Between an actor and a spectator wanting to be entertained, there can be a kind of invisible ray. It's like a string of a bow or a harp or a violin, upon which you can play if you're clever enough. That is the moment of artistry to an actor. I used to sit closer and closer to watch Sid Field, one of England's greatest comedians, and I used to see this marvelous energy bursting out of the pores of his skin and shooting out of his eyes. This all has something to do with love, I think.

I finally discovered this for myself when playing what was considered the secondary and extremely difficult and rather lousy part of Sergius [in Shaw's *Arms and the Man*]. I knew I wasn't good in it. I was in my habitual relationship with the critics. I'd always hated them. And for the most part I'd felt antagonistic toward audiences. Shortly after the play opened, Tyrone Guthrie and I walked back to the hotel after the performance. He looked down at me from his great height and said, 'Liked your performance very much.' And I said, 'Oh, thanks.' And he said, 'Do you enjoy it?' and I said, 'Are you out of your mind? How can anybody enjoy that idiotic, pantomimic, absurd character?' He looked down at me, as I say, from his great height, and he said, 'Well, of course, if you don't *love* Sergius, you'll never be any good in the role, will you?'

Well, stretch that around a bit, and you get a young man who had never thought of loving an audience—whereas Sid Field had never thought of anything else. This may sound sentimental. All right. Everybody can sneer if they want, but it actually made the entire difference to my whole life. I'm very sorry but it is absolutely true. The key word is 'love'.

Only a couple of weeks later [playing Richard III], I finally felt the proper rapport between myself, the work, the critics, and the audience—all as a single entity . . .[12]

Within that 'single entity', I would add, the participants keep a certain identity and autonomy. The collaboration that Shakespeare the theatre-poet invites might be compared to that of a musical group in which each voice follows its own line yet together they make an ensemble—freer than the voices in a string quartet, less free than those in a jazz combo.

There is something similar in Noh, which relies even more on the imagination than does Shakespeare. In Noh, the movements of the actors do little more than suggest the action of the work. There is no possibility of a complete rendering of it on stage, as there is in literalist theatre. At most a symbolic property may be used, plus occasional mimetic gestures in the dances. Often a priest will take three slow steps, then talk of having made a long trip quickly. The playwright's text, chanted and sung by the chorus and actors to drums and flute, is also allusive. Both player and playwright thus openly depend upon the imagination of the playgoer, which in turn is prompted by the words, music, and movements. Their mutual dependence is thus evident and accepted, even as the distinctness of their contributions is kept clear.

In Shakespeare, where much more of the imagined action is simulated on stage than in Noh, the division of labour is much less clear. In Noh, since the style of the dialogue is not much concerned with characterization, there is no mistaking the playwright's voice. In Shakespeare, the style of the dialogue does a great deal to characterize the speakers, making it much more difficult to hear the playwright's voice. To make it out, one needs to look analytically at Shakespeare's text, determining the relative reliability of its various indicators of his purposes and weighting them accordingly. That will be the aim of the next two chapters.

[12] Richard Meryman, 'The Great Sir Laurence', *Life*, 56 (1 May 1964), 97–8.

5

The Playwright in the Play:
Macbeth, Romeo and Juliet, The Tempest

> It is the task of the dramatist so to coordinate his play, through
> the selection of episodes and speeches, that though he is himself
> not visible, his point of view and his governing intention will
> impose themselves on the spectator's attention, not as dogmatic
> assertion or motto, but as self-evident truth and inevitable
> deduction.
>
> THORNTON WILDER

I F one asks in a general sort of way what is identifiably 'Shakespearian'
about a play by Shakespeare, one is in familiar territory. One may
think of an extraordinary breadth in his scope and depth in his insight,
a wonderful vitality and variety in his characters and a supercharged
energy in their actions, an eloquence and memorableness in his
dialogue at its best, an amazing ability to match character and
language that is celebrated in T. S. Eliot's paradox: 'Each character
speaks for himself, but no other poet could have found these words for
him to speak.'[1] All of these are included in a view of human nature
that makes a unique blend of truth and compassion—at once hard-
headed and soft-hearted.

When one tries to identify in detail Shakespeare's presence in individual works and parts of works, one is on much less familiar ground.
For in one place the author's hand may seem bold and clear while in
another place he seems to allow his players options for interpretation
or his playgoers options for response, and in yet other places his
surviving text gives no reliable direction at all.

There is little help to be had from the comments of other
playwrights. What they have said about the collaborative process, as
discussed in the preceding chapter, has mostly been in the form of
protests when something has gone wrong. When the collaboration has
succeeded, they have kept quiet (this, too, is an art best hidden); and
thus they have not revealed much about how this fact of their artistic
lives has entered into their writing. As a consequence, there is not

---

[1] T. S. Eliot, *On Poetry and Poets* (New York, 1957), 248.

much comment as to where various playwrights have drawn the lines of their authority: where they have wished to claim their due, where they have been willing to allow the performers and spectators to play their parts in their own ways.

The great exception to this reticence is a remarkable essay by Thornton Wilder, 'Some Thoughts on Playwrighting'.[2] It deserves to be better known for its own sake and should be read entire, but I will extract from it those parts that provide the most guidance to an understanding of Shakespeare's practice. Although Wilder is the best available guide for this purpose (to my knowledge, he is the only such guide), he is nevertheless not ideal. He is obviously a very different kind of playwright from Shakespeare. While welcoming his help in general, therefore, I will also need to take into account those places where it may be misleading.

Wilder begins by emphasizing the fact that 'The theater is an art which reposes upon the work of many collaborators'. He accepts this, a bit reluctantly, as a fact of a dramatist's life. He is well aware that his intentions are constantly endangered by 'the distortions effected by the physical appearance of actors, by the fancies of scene painters and the misunderstandings of directors'. And he is plainly one of the 'many dramatists' who regret 'the absence of the narrator from the stage, with his point of view, his powers of analyzing the behavior of the characters, his ability to interfere and supply further facts about the past, about simultaneous actions not visible on the stage, and above all his function of pointing the moral and emphasizing the significance of the action'. His Stage Manager in *Our Town* (a role Wilder himself played on occasion) in fact performs all these functions.

By nature, then, Wilder is more a novelist than a dramatist. This is in a way a drawback, yet it also has its advantages. For just because of the effort it takes for him to assume a playwright's role, he has been the better able to see it clearly. And having done so, he has been especially conscious of compensating vitalities in the dramatic form and of ways by which the dramatist can capitalize upon the collaborative situation: 'The dramatist through working in the theater gradually learns not merely to take account of the presence of the collaborators, but to derive advantage from them.'

The other general reservation that needs to be kept in mind is that, like most theorists who are also creative writers, Wilder's views are at times distorted by his own predilections as a playwright. For instance,

[2] Thornton Wilder, 'Some Thoughts on Playwrighting', in *The Intent of the Artist*, ed. A. Centeno (Princeton, 1941).

he deplores the way in which modern staging reduces Juliet to 'this one girl, in one place, at one moment in time' whereas: 'When the play is staged as Shakespeare intended it, the bareness of the stage releases the events from the particular and the experience of Juliet partakes of that of all girls in love, in every time, place and language.' There is truth to this, but it is not the whole truth. Wilder's formulation comes very close to being the whole truth about his own heroine Emily in *Our Town*. But Shakespeare never '*releases* the events from the particular': his Juliet is both a unique girl and a representative one.

These provisos entered, we can proceed to appreciate in general the keenness of Wilder's observation about the participants in the performance-ensemble and their distinctive contributions to the theatre-event. Although he does not use these terms, he has a keen awareness of the resources available to a theatre-poet. He points out how the largeness of a theatre audience creates a 'group-mind' with its own special proclivities towards forward-moving action and broad appeals, how theatre conventions need not deaden but in fact can stimulate an audience's imagination. He analyses the specific skill of a good actor and how a good script provides the 'highly characteristic utterances' and 'concrete actions' through which an actor may define his or her character. But his chief concern is with the playwright and his role in the performance-ensemble and with how he—while making the most of what his collaborators can bring to their joint effort—can control what is essential to his own function.

I want now to consider Wilder's analysis in detail and see how it may be applied to Shakespeare. I shall take up the dramatic elements in turn, surveying their salient features and their relative reliability as indicators of Shakespeare's purposes. The reader should be advised that the results may seem surprising. For character and theme—those favourite subjects for scholarly attention—come out as the least reliable of the indicators, whereas actions and large features of the dialogue are the most. Since action is the most important of these (Aristotle called it 'the soul of drama') and yet it has received the least attention from Shakespearian commentators, I will have the most to say about it.

ACTION

Wilder repeatedly stresses that it is the dramatist's control of the action of the play that is the key to his control of its essentials: 'The theatre is unfolding action and in the disposition of events the author may exercise a governance so complete' as to reduce any misinterpretations by his collaborators to 'relative insignificance': 'the shock and countershock of circumstances; the flow of action; the interruption of action; the moments of allusion to earlier events; the preparation of surprise, dread, or delight—all that is the author's and his alone.'

Wilder's observation is as profoundly true of Shakespeare as it is of most other dramatists. Even though Shakespeare did not often invent his plots but usually drew them from other works, still his unvarying practice was to rework them in such a way as to make them his own. And in performance his plots remain his 'and his alone'. Of the dramatic elements, the succession of events is the least subject to interpretation—unless performers make large cuts or transpositions, in which case they have strictly speaking not 'interpreted' Shakespeare's text but 'adapted' it.

Scholarly practice has been all too willing to recognize the reliability of what we can know about the action. It has been regarded as so definite as to be 'obvious', and commentators have been inclined to avoid and deplore 'plot summary'. Yet no less than with other dramatic elements, the effort to say exactly what happens in a play can benefit from analysis, dispute, and re-analysis and can yield consequent rewards. Usually, Shakespeare's indications will prove definite enough, if only we attend to them precisely and refrain from filling in what he has chosen to leave blank, or from drawing bold outlines where he provides shadings.

As a case in point, let us try to determine how Macbeth reacts when he first encounters the Weird Sisters. Here are Bradley's comments (I choose Bradley precisely because he is in general such a sensitive and fair-minded witness):

That the influence of the first prophecies upon him came as much from himself as from them, is made abundantly clear by the obviously intentional contrast between him and Banquo. Banquo, ambitious but perfectly honest, is scarcely even startled by them, and he remains throughout the scene indifferent to them. But when Macbeth heard them he was not an innocent man. Precisely how far his mind was guilty may be a question; but no innocent man would have started, as he did, with a start of *fear* at the mere prophecy of a crown, or have conceived thereupon *immediately* the thought of murder. Either this thought was not new to him, or he had cherished at least some vague dishonorable dream, the instantaneous recurrence of which, at the moment of his hearing the prophecy, revealed to him an inward and terrifying guilt. In either case not only was he free to accept or resist the temptation, but the temptation was already within him.[3]

[3] A. C. Bradley, *Shakespearean Tragedy* (New York, 1951), 343–4.

Bradley's key imprecision is that he assumes that Macbeth 'fears' the first prophecies whereas the text tells us no more than that Banquo asks him: 'Good sir, why do you start and seem to fear / Things that do sound so fair?' We can't be sure, at the time or in retrospect, whether Banquo's surmise 'seem to fear' is reliable or not. Certainly, Macbeth 'starts' and is rapt. Both are outwardly observable. But even Banquo does not claim as Bradley does that Macbeth 'fears', only that he *seems to* fear. Macbeth himself in his letter to his wife does not mention a feeling of fear but only of being 'rapt in the *wonder* of it'. Could Macbeth's 'wonder' have been mistaken by Banquo for fear?

But surely Banquo is a reliable observer and interpreter? Bradley certainly likes to think so. Of Banquo's response to the Sisters, Bradley observes that he 'is scarcely even startled by them, and he remains throughout the scene indifferent to them'. Indifferent? Certainly he claims to be:

> Speak then to me, who neither beg nor fear
> Your favours nor your hate.

But if he is truly indifferent, why does he charge them to speak to himself at all? Later it is he who questions 'have we eaten on the insane root / That takes the reason prisoner?' and who observes:

> oftentimes to win us to our harm
> The instruments of darkness tell us truths,
> Win us with honest trifles to betray's
> In deepest consequence.

This is far from indifference. It is fearful. It seems almost as likely that Banquo is projecting his own fears on Macbeth as that Macbeth is himself fearful. My point, however, is that we cannot be sure whether Macbeth's start was truly fearful or merely seemed so to Banquo.

Of course, what Bradley is most concerned with is the degree of Macbeth's moral guilt—the extent to which he is of his own free will to blame. With his usual fairness of mind, Bradley observes of Macbeth: 'Precisely how far his mind was guilty may be a question'; yet he then adds, 'but no innocent man would have started, as he did, with a start of *fear* at the mere prophecy of a crown, or have conceived thereupon *immediately* the thought of murder' (Bradley's italics). With 'immediately', Bradley again exaggerates. Macbeth's thought of murder is not expressed until some ninety lines later—an intervening period of great emotional intensity, during which in addition to hearing the prophecies Macbeth has had partial confirmation of them.

A great deal of emotional ground has been covered. His thought of murder certainly comes *soon*, along with 'present fears'. The potential for ill in the prophecies certainly works faster on Macbeth than on Banquo. None the less, Bradley is putting it more strongly than the text warrants when he says that Macbeth's murderous thought comes immediately.

What underlies these distortions by even so careful a reader as Bradley is his strong desire to know what is in Macbeth's mind at this point, and that it be 'abundantly clear' what it is. This is, I believe, the wish that Shakespeare wants his audience to have. He may well wish us to sense, as Bradley elsewhere speculates, that Macbeth had previously 'harbored a vaguely guilty ambition, though he had not faced the idea of murder'.[4] But students of Shakespeare's artistry need to recognize that he does not confirm this surmise or otherwise satisfy the audience's wish for Macbeth's inner attitudes here to be 'abundantly clear'. Having recognized this, one can then see how much Shakespeare gains by doing so. For we in the audience are thus left as curious about Macbeth's secret life as we are about the prophecies. And it is thus, in part, that we are led into complicities that we will later regret.

In sum, what happens when Macbeth hears the first prophecies? One can be quite definite. He starts and grows rapt. Of his inner life at this point, however, the audience like Banquo (and perhaps Shakespeare himself) can only surmise.

The larger organizations of the plot allow more room for interpretation. Even so, Shakespeare's hand is relatively clear and rewards close attention. Indeed, it is hard to think of studies that have added more that is durable to our understanding of Shakespeare in this century than Bradley's chapter on 'Construction in Shakespeare's Tragedies', Empson's pages on double plots in *Some Versions of Pastoral*, Frye's essay on 'The Argument of Comedy', with its paragraphs on the visit to the 'green world' sequence in certain Shakespearian comedies, and Mack's essay on 'The Jacobean Shakespeare'.[5]

The most important recent contribution is in Emrys Jones's *Scenic Form in Shakespeare* (Oxford, 1971). In it he calls attention to Shakespeare's tendency to group scenes into sequences, among which

---

[4] Bradley, *Shakespearean Trageay.*
[5] William Empson, *Some Versions of Pastoral* (Norfolk, Conn., n.d.); Northrop Frye, 'The Argument of Comedy', in *English Institute Essays, 1948* (New York, 1949), 58–73; Maynard Mack, 'The Jacobean Shakespeare', in *Jacobean Theatre*, Stratford-upon-Avon Studies (New York, 1960).

characterization, style, and other features may be quite distinct. He himself puts his case more strongly, proposing that for the tragedies, histories, and such tragicomedies as *All's Well that Ends Well*, *Measure for Measure*, and *The Winter's Tale*, 'a play will usually be found to divide into two movements (corresponding roughly to the first three acts and the last two acts)'. He argues for a single interval or intermission between the two movements. This formulation fits certain of the plays readily (such as *Julius Caesar* and *Richard III*) but other plays less clearly, as he is the first to admit. Since there is no exterior evidence that any interval was normal, there is no need here to pursue that practical problem. What Jones's analysis does establish incontrovertibly is a habit of mind on Shakespeare's part, a tendency to divide his plays into distinctive sub-sequences.[6]

Jones's analysis of *Macbeth* is particularly helpful. He finds in it 'a three-part division, in which Part One ("Duncan") occupies Acts One and Two, Part Two ("Banquo") Act Three, and Part Three ("Macduff"), Acts Four and Five'. With Jones's sequences marked out, one can then go on independently to see that each of them is concerned with circumstances leading up to a murder, its execution, and its consequences. There are more detailed parallels as well. Shortly before each murder we are taken deeply 'inside' Macbeth. Towards each, Macbeth follows a pattern of attraction, revulsion, and recovery. The murders are progressively more repulsive, and the reactions against them by others grow stronger and stronger. To the murder of Duncan, there is some initial moral resistance expressed by Banquo and Macduff but the flight of Malcolm and Donalbain effectively overcomes that. The murder of Banquo rebounds with the appearance of his Ghost. The killing of Macduff's family is followed by the invasion of Scotland by Malcolm and Macduff.

Furthermore, one can see large progressions in Macbeth's inner life that conform to these sequences. His prime motive in Part One is ambition for the glory of the crown; in Part Two he is most concerned

---

[6] From this vantage one can go beyond Jones to recognize that, besides continuity of time, tone and rhetorical structure may be decisive bases for such divisions—as in the break in *Romeo and Juliet* between the 'comic' sequence ending with the lovers' marriage and the 'tragic' sequence ending with their deaths. In *As You Like It* the break comes when the action moves to Arden. One can also observe in Shakespeare a comparable tendency to group whole plays into sequences. For example, G. K. Hunter has shown that the two parts of *Henry IV* conform to the pattern of the 'Elizabethan Two-Part Play', with some of the same features of 'rhyming' between parts that Jones observes between sub-groups (*Review of English Studies*, NS 5, 1954, 236–48). This habit of mind also seems to extend to still larger groupings among the history plays, as in the loosely linked 'tetralogies'.

with keeping safe the continuity of his line; while in Part Three he adds to that a concern for his own survival. As he wades further and further into blood, the degree of his resistance to violence against others grows progressively less. In Part One the audience wonders 'Will he or won't he?'; In Part Two, 'What will he do next?'; in Part Three, 'What won't he do next?'

I would go one step further than Jones. He himself grants that Part Three 'divides into two phases'. I would propose that the last act be regarded as Part Four, 'Macbeth', since it is concerned with the immediate circumstances leading up to *his* death and its consequences. True, we would not then in Part Three see the consequences of Macbeth's murder of the Macduff family coming home to him as we do in each of the earlier parts. But otherwise this further division seems to me an improvement. We can then, for example, recognize final phases in the progressions already observed. At the end it is the respect of his fellows that—in its absence—he realizes he most values. He is no longer concerned for his own life but in fact needs to dissuade himself from suicide; and his resistance to violence toward others is almost entirely gone—except for his feeling that he already has shed too much of Macduff's blood. We can also see that in each of the four parts Macbeth appears only after the audience has been given indications of the developments with which he must immediately deal. Before his first entry we learn of the Weird Sisters and of the King's decision to name him Thane of Cawdor. In Part Two, he does not enter until we have heard Banquo confess his hopes about the prophecies. Part Three (which seems to me to start at 3. 5) begins with Hecate and the Sisters and news of Macduff's defection. In Part Four, we are shown his wife's mental derangement in the sleep-walking scene and the hostile troops on their way to Scotland.

Recognition of these sequences also throws light on the typically interwoven plot-strands of the play. At the beginning of Act 3 of *Macbeth* Banquo summarizes the upshot of the action to that point:

> Thou hast it now: King, Cawdor, Glamis, all
> As the weird women promised; and I fear
> Thou played'st most foully for't.

Each of his lines cites one of three main story-lines that Shakespeare develops:

1. the rise and fall of Macbeth in rank and power;
2. his attempt to learn and control his destiny;
3. his moral degeneration (and his parallel loss of social status).

Each line runs through the play and is inseparably interwoven with the others; yet each follows a different rhythm and pattern of climax. Their relative importance is thus subject to interpretative emphasis. Yet Shakespeare provides clear guidance for determining their importance.

The story of Macbeth's rise and fall in rank and power reaches its climax early, with his successful assassination of the reigning king and accession to the throne himself. Of his various crimes, it is the killing of Duncan that requires the greatest risk for Macbeth and brings the greatest political benefits. The later killings that he orders are essentially defensive actions on his part, involving victims who are of less and less political consequence to his regime and who pose less and less immediate danger to the continuity of his line and the preservation of his own life. Macbeth's rise thus holds much more interest than does his fall; yet Shakespeare devotes two acts to the former and three to the latter (contrast *Richard III* in which the usurper does not attain the throne until the fourth act). Clearly Shakespeare is relying on additional sources of interest.

Of the three strands, the Witches' prophecies are the most consistently important throughout the play, but they come into particular importance in Macbeth's killing of Banquo. They are of course important in Duncan's death; but in that case they are one instigating factor among many, whereas with Banquo they are a prime consideration: the prophecies are the principal reason given for Banquo's hopes and Macbeth's fears. The prophecies in Part Three provide a second set of influences that affect the rest of the play. They are important in the killing of the Macduff family. For Macbeth is warned to beware not only Macduff but all future holders of his title ('the thane of Fife'). This logic is so lightly indicated, though, that few commentators have noticed it. Nor is Macduff made to seem a serious threat to Macbeth's political power. Shakespeare's chief emphasis in this part of the play is on the third story-line: Macbeth's desperate unscrupulousness, his drive to satisfy his own needs whatever the cost to others: 'From this moment / The very firstlings of my heart shall be / The firstlings of my hand.'

The gradual emergence of this plot-strand as an important one brings out another distinctive feature of Shakespeare's story-telling. For like certain oriental scrolls, as his story unrolls its whole frame of reference is progressively altered. It is not simply that a later part has a different or larger frame of reference from what has gone before but that everything that has taken place is redefined as subsequent events occur. Part One, for instance, at the time it occurs, seems primarily a success story of a sort; it tells of a war-hero who aspires to the power and (especially) the glory of the crown and whose better nature is unable to resist the strong external influences which reinforce this aspiration and together lead him to kill the reigning king. He suffers terribly from the deed, both in prospect and retrospect, yet he recovers sufficiently to overcome the suspicions of some of the nobles and take the throne himself.

It's true that Shakespeare, by omitting the coronation, takes care to avoid too strong a sense of closure and to mute the satisfactions of Macbeth's success: his overall emphasis is on the miseries of the crown. Yet the feeling of a completed unit is even so quite clear.

With Part Two, Macbeth is no longer thane but ruler; he enters 'as King' (according to the stage direction). He is now suffering kingly fears about the safety of his line and rightly identifies Banquo as a threat. But it is chiefly his rivalry with Fate that is uppermost. Part One is now subsumed as an early phase of this struggle. There, he had merely hurried his destiny; realizing that chance might crown him king he nevertheless went ahead to force the issue. Now he is seeking to alter his fate, to keep the Sisters' prophecies from being fulfilled. Even after suffering the repercussions of his deed in the horrors of the apparition of Banquo's ghost, he recovers his aggressiveness to defy the ghost and to resolve to go himself to the Weird Sisters.

With Part Three, all that has gone before is again redefined. Macbeth's killing of Duncan and Banquo are now seen as progressive steps in his moral degeneration. Macbeth's killing of Duncan plainly went against his better nature, a whole set of circumstances had to conspire to bring him to the act. The killing of Banquo came easier to him, yet it still seemed that he was as much bringing himself to do the deed as inciting his underlings to it. They themselves require no such incitement (note their immediate agreement without urging; this is after all their second such meeting). When in Part Three Macbeth goes to the Weird Sisters, however, he has become, as they discern, a 'wicked thing'. Although he feels sorry for his 'unfortunate' victims, his decision to kill them is almost immediate. Looking over the three killings, one can see that it has taken less and less time and less and less anguish for him to reach his murderous decisions and that his victims have been less and less able to defend themselves.

In Part Four all three plot-strands reach their culmination. Macbeth's power and rank decline to the point that his men desert him and the forces opposing him at last deprive him of both. His destiny is revealed in its entirety. And his inner life has so declined as to be virtually dead. Beyond this, there is a sense in which Macbeth himself joins those seeking his death. Looking back one can now see that in killing Duncan and Banquo and the Macduff family Macbeth was in fact destroying a part of himself all along, his own dearest aspirations. Before he kills them he praises in turn Duncan's kingly virtues and Banquo's 'royalty of nature':

> 'Tis much he dares,
> And to that dauntless temper of his mind
> . He hath a wisdom that doth guide his valour
> To act in safety. (3. 1. 52–5)

These are the very traits which he most values for himself. He has been killing himself slowly throughout the play, and from the inside out.

The plot of *Macbeth* is especially important because so much happens in the play relative to its very short length and because these happenings are so richly patterned in relation to one another. The 'governance' that Wilder sees the playwright as exercising through the disposition of events is consequently especially clear and strong. *Macbeth* is an extreme case, although still representative of Shakespeare's general practice. Even here, however, his governance leaves considerable room for interpretative choice. Certain of the four parts may come in for particular emphasis; so may certain of the three plot-strands. While allowing for such emphasis, the overall organization of the play's action remains 'the author's and his alone'.

That Shakespeare's plots may be analysed into parts and strands has of course long been a staple of commentary, although not so often considered lately as in the past. A more recently observed characteristic is the choreography of gestures, movements, stage pictures, and verbal kinetic imagery that Shakespeare outlines. It takes various forms. In *Julius Caesar* certain key gestures (such as kneeling, stabbing, shaking hands) are perverted by Caesar's assassins, only to be turned upon themselves by Antony.[7] In *Measure for Measure*, more general kinetic factors are stressed. In the course of the play, those who have been too free are confined (the street people end up in prison, including Lucio), while those who have been too confined or self-confined are freed (Claudio, Mariana, Isabella, Angelo, the Duke all end up in the streets). At the same time, those who have been separated are at the end reunited, and what has been secret becomes open, made visible by the dramatic unhooding of the Duke and Claudio. Such choreography is closely related to plot and is almost as clear an indicator of the playwright's purposes.

[7] See my article, 'Speak Hands for Me: Gesture as Language in *Julius Caesar*', *Drama Survey* (1966), 162–70.

In *Romeo and Juliet*, it is the pace and rhythm of the choreography that is most important, as I should like to examine in detail. In Verona, as has often been observed, haste is a way of life. Brents Stirling has shown that this is true, even of Friar Laurence. When Romeo tells him 'I stand on sudden haste', the Friar replies: 'Wisely and slow: they stumble that run fast.'[8] Yet this saying proves all too literally true when the Friar hurries, too late, to Juliet's tomb, exclaiming, 'Saint Francis be my speed! how oft tonight / Have my old feet stumbled at graves!'

Romeo is a significant exception, however. Although he is usually equated with Juliet as a recklessly passionate lover, a close inspection of his stage movements helps to bring out that he is for much of the play much more a delayer of action than a hurrier of it. It's true that he is impetuous about initiating courses of action, especially in his love at first sight for Juliet, which soon has him leaping orchard walls. Yet he lacks follow-through. His response to Rosaline's disfavour was to pen himself private in his chamber, feeling 'bound more than madman is'; it is Benvolio who must prevail on him to attend Capulet's feast. Some of his reluctance to do so comes from a misgiving that 'Some consequence yet hanging in the stars / Shall bitterly begin his fearful date / With this night's revels' (1. 4. 108–10). Yet it also seems part of his general state of mind; he refuses, for example, to be one of the dancers: 'I am not for this ambling; / Being but heavy, I will bear the light' (ll. 11–12).

In the balcony scene, his initial impulse is overtaken by Juliet's controlling ardour. He still is not finished declaring his love before she is planning their marriage. Reinforced by his love for Juliet, Romeo's inclination to hold back from action comes close to seeing him through Tybalt's challenge, but it is not proof against Mercutio's onrushing intervention. Circumstances then make it possible for him to act immediately on his impulse to retaliate for his friend's death by killing Tybalt. But this act leaves him dazed and immobile. Benvolio must hurry him off: 'away, be gone. . . . Hence, be gone, away.' Later, Friar Laurence must make plans for his wedding night and departure, Romeo's response having been to 'fall upon the ground . . . taking the measure of an unmade grave'.

The crucial change comes in 5. 1; when Balthasar reports Juliet's supposed death, Romeo declares: 'Is it e'en so? Then I defy you, stars.' Previously, in keeping with his general passiveness, Romeo had seen himself as fortune's fool, the subject of destiny: 'he that hath the

---

[8] Brents Stirling, *Unity in Shakespearian Tragedy* (New York, 1957), 10–25.

steerage of my course / Direct my sail!' Now he defies such forces.

If his passion were not so imperious and his plight generally so touching, there would be something ludicrous about the elaborately systematic folly with which Romeo goes about preparing to enact his love-death. It is his first plan—the one impulse we have seen him follow through on his own—and it is worthy of Tom Sawyer. In Shakespeare's source, Romeo simply writes to his father and takes to horse. In Shakespeare he also *plans* to do so. The effect of over-elaborateness is further emphasized in the apothecary incident. Although he carries a dagger, Romeo could not simply stab himself, he must have poison, and on a holiday (Shakespeare's touch) must hunt up a special source of it. He arrives at the tomb fully equipped with 'a torch, a mattock, and a crow of iron' and remembers to dispatch Balthasar with the letter to his father before resolutely carrying through his ill-fated plan. If only he had developed sooner an ability to form and carry out an independent plan!—say to take Juliet with him to Mantua. Or if only he had remained dependent on the Friar and others just a little longer, at least to the extent of asking Friar Laurence about Juliet's death! Romeo's choreography thus points up still another way in which *Romeo and Juliet* is a tragedy of mistiming.

Romeo and Juliet's choreography of haste and delay is unusually clear and full. At that, it is anything but complete. Shakespeare's stage directions are characteristically sparse. Much is left to the discretion of the performers. At most his scripts sketch in the main outlines of choreography, with certain moments highlighted in detail. All the same, general patterns of stage movement are there to be found, and as outward and visible signs of things otherwise unseen, interpreters should give them their full authority.

CHARACTERS

It is about the extreme variability in interpretation to which their characters are subject (or are subjected) that dramatists have had most say. Jean Giraudoux has ruefully commented on 'the sad and slightly ridiculous position of the playwright toward those of his characters he has created and given to the theatre'.[9] Before being played by an actor, a character is 'docile toward the author, familiar, and part of him'; but 'once he appears before the audience he becomes a stranger and indifferent'. The same is true, he adds, of the whole play: 'From the first performance on, it belongs to the actors' and 'after the hundredth performance, particularly if it is a good play, it belongs to the public'.

[9] Jean Giraudoux, 'Two Laws', in *Playwrights on Playwriting*, ed. T. Cole (New York, 1960), 62.

As he wittily remarks: 'In reality the only thing the playwright can call his own is bad plays.' But it is especially about his characters that he broods: 'while the hero of your novels follows you everywhere, calling you "father" or "papa", those of your stage characters you chance to meet—as I have—in Carcassonne or Los Angeles, have become total strangers to you.'

Christopher Fry is at once more accepting of this variability and less passive about it. In his foreword to *The Lady's Not for Burning*, he first acknowledges: 'As for the people of the comedy, there may be more ways than I know of playing them.' But he then goes on to hold out for certain essentials: 'The *musts* are few: the Mayor is fretfully embrangled in his chains of office; Tappercoom is fat . . . ' and so on. He concludes. 'I like to think it is all there in the text.' T. S. Eliot seems positively to welcome the interpretative variables that actors can bring to his text. As he wrote in a letter to E. Martin Browne about *Murder in the Cathedral*:

I am by no means now sure that it is not better to have the knights played by different actors from the tempters. I like to leave questions for the audience to resolve for themselves, and one question which is left for them if the knights and tempters are different actors, is whether the fourth tempter is an evil angel or possibly a good angel. After all, the fourth tempter is gradually leading Becket on to his sudden resolution and simplification of his difficulties.[10]

Where Shakespeare is concerned, Eliot has remarked: 'If you seek for Shakespeare, you will find him only in the characters he created.'[11] His remark is doubly misleading. As already discussed, Shakespeare is to be found not only in his characters but elsewhere as well. Nor has Eliot allowed sufficiently for their varying inter-pretability by actors. For it appears to be true of Shakespeare, as Wilder says it is of himself, that the playwright makes 'a conscious preparation of the text whereby the actor may build upon the suggestions in the role according to his own abilities'.

Superabundant evidence of this variability in Shakespeare is to be found in theatre history and literary criticism. Although individual interpreters have felt that they have at last found the one true nature of a given character, the cumulative effect of generations of such finds had undermined the definitiveness of any one of them. Stage historians of a play sometimes marvel at the range of interpretations that actors have given its characters, as if it were an exceptional

[10] E. Martin Browne, *The Making of T. S. Eliot's Plays* (Cambridge, 1969), 58.

[11] T. S. Eliot, *On Poetry and Poets*, 248.

feature of their chosen play.[12] As these histories increase, the apparent exceptions are proving to be the rule. Of course, some of Shakespeare's characters are more subject to interpretation than others. No matter how different one Hamlet may be from another, most Horatios are very much alike. It is the major roles that have proved to be the most variable.

Several features of Shakespearian characterization especially contribute to their variability. Since they usually depict complex personalities, they invite various weightings among the complicating features. What these features are is fairly well agreed; the question always is how much of each? Even for secondary roles Shakespeare shows a taste for richly mixed and blended attitudes. To what extent is the Nurse teasing Juliet when she is so slow to reveal the result of her visit to Romeo? Or is she genuinely hot and tired and cross? To what extent is Celia teasing Rosalind when she is disparaging Orlando? Is it purely to give her friend the joy of defending her lover? Or is she, like the Nurse, beginning to feel a bit 'left out' by her confidante's new attachment to a man? We can be sure from the playful tone of the exchanges that there is some element of teasing in both; and the fact that it takes the form of complaint or criticism confirms some underlying resentment. But what degree of each should enter into their mixed emotions is left to the discretion of the interpreter.

The fact that the leading characters undergo significant change in the course of the play also invites varied emphases on the successive parts. Some actors of Macbeth have favoured the sensitive soul of the beginning, others the insensitive butcher of the end. Some Cleopatras have stressed the witty siren of the beginning, others the transfigured queen of the finale. The fact that Shakespeare's scripts give only the barest indications concerning the appearance and manner of his character further enlarges their variability.

Wilder goes so far as to say that 'Characterization in a play is like a blank check which the dramatist accords to the actor for him to fill in—not entirely blank, for a number of indications of individuality are already there, but to a far less definite and absolute degree than in the novel.' His image of a largely 'blank check' fits Wilder's own practice as a playwright better than it does most other dramatists, including Shakespeare. In support of his view, however, Wilder uses Shakespeare as an example. He contrasts Irving's Shylock, 'a noble,

---

[12] Examples are: Toby Lelyveld, *Shylock on the Stage* (Cleveland, 1960); Joseph G. Price, *The Unfortunate Comedy* (Toronto, 1968).

3. Henry Irving as Shylock (1879).

wronged, and indignant being, of such stature that the Merchants of Venice dwindled before him into irresponsible schoolboys' with Gémier's Shylock, 'a vengeful and hysterical buffoon': 'at the close of the trial scene Shylock was driven screaming about the auditorium, behind the spectators' back and onto the stage again, in a wild Elizabethan revel.' Wilder concludes: 'For all their divergences both were admirable productions of the play.'

My own reaction would be: 'Good theatre, perhaps; but not Shakespeare.' To me it seems evident that both Irving and Gémier pushed the liberties that Shakespeare grants his interpreters to the point of license. They have each put asunder what Shakespeare had joined. In successive scenes we see Shylock nobly indignant ('Hath not a Jew eyes?'), then hysterical ('my daughter . . . my ducats'). For Irving or Gémier to play only a part of the role and treat it as the whole, is to distort it and perform an unacknowledged act of adaptation. Shakespeare's Shylock is both wronged and vengeful. That is what is special about him. Overplaying the former tips Shakespeare's tragic–comic balance toward sentimentality; overplaying the latter tends toward melodrama or, in Gémier's case, toward farce.

Given its due, Shakespeare's plot resists such imbalances. In the trial scene, Shylock must be vengeful enough to sharpen his knives to be ready to carry out his legalized murder, yet he must not be so wildly vengeful that when Portia has taken away his legal protection he attacks Antonio anyway. Shakespeare's dialogue also resists over-simplification. Consider Shylock's 'Hath not a Jew eyes' speech. Although it has been played as simply a plea for human understanding or simply a justification for revenge, in any valid rendering it must be something of both. Its rhetorical frame, especially its order of climax, emphasizes his desire for vengeance. Yet his appeal to the common humanity of all men exceeds in length and scope the demands of his argument, for which he needed only to develop the resemblances of Jews to Christians. Seen thus, the speech still allows its speaker options of emphasis, yet Shakespeare's guidelines for Shylock's character here and in general are much tighter than Wilder supposes. The 'check' that Shakespeare writes allows the actor to fill in his own name, but he himself in round numbers fills in the amount.

Although Wilder exaggerates the latitudes that Shakespeare allows his interpreters, still he and the other dramatists I have quoted seem to be fundamentally right in their recognition that characters in a play are validly subject to varied interpretations. Broadly considered, Shakespeare makes clear enough the personalities of his leading characters. He vividly delineates the features that make them what

4. Firmin Gémier as Shylock (1917).

they are; and what they do is even clearer, since it involves action, the clearest of his indicators. But when one tries to determine exactly how these personality features are balanced and patterned, the degree of this and the emphasis on that—then one is among the least positive indicators of Shakespeare's purposes. Indeed, he seems deliberately to have left such matters open to interpretation.

DIALOGUE

The great omission in Wilder's survey is the power of the dramatist's words to guide the interpretation of his play. This is the more surprising because Wilder in his own plays does suit his words to his actions and elsewhere has commented on their importance: he calls attention to the significance of the recurring numbers in the text of *Our Town*, for example.[13] It seems, then, an oversight on his part rather than a deliberate omission. To those who chiefly read the plays, indeed, the authority of the dialogue may seem more important than that of the action. It should be remembered, however, that in performance we see the action before our eyes, with full visual and kinetic impact, whereas the aural appeals of the dialogue are less powerful. Furthermore, it is particular words and lines which carry the most force in a theatre; yet these are the parts of the dialogue that are most subject to interpretation—to the tone, emphasis, pace of their speaker.

Well aware of the powers of oral interpretation, actors and directors have tended to underrate the independent authority of Shakespeare's dialogue, treating their lines simply as a facet of characterization. Accustomed as we are to the dialogue of realistic drama, it is hard to imagine a kind of performance in which the playwright's share in the dialogue has a degree of autonomy. An example of such autonomy is to be found in Bunraku, the Japanese classical puppet-theatre, where the chanter always begins his performance with a ritual salute to his text. All of the playwright's words are spoken by a chanter on the side of the main stage, who never looks at the movements of the puppets, although speech and movement are perfectly synchronized. Most of the words are interpreted by the chanter's impersonation of the characters, with as much colouring as by live actors, if not more. Yet the separation of speaker and puppet gives the words a special independence, an effect that is strengthened by the meditative and narrative passages that the chanter delivers in his own voice.

[13] Thornton Wilder, *Three Plays* (New York, 1957), p. xii.

Shakespeare's verbal art is not autonomous to the same degree, nor is it as distinct as is the score of an opera. Yet it is certainly more so than is the dialogue of modern realistic drama; and it is especially in the verbal implications that go beyond realistic conversation that his presence in the dialogue is most directly to be felt. To take an extreme instance, for me one of the pleasures of the Russian film of *King Lear* is that the Shakespearian subtitles glowing on the screen lead a semi-independent existence. They are enhanced by the tones of voice on the sound-track yet not confined by them.

An acting exercise devised by Peter Brook is to the point.[14] In it he has taken the farewell scene between Romeo and Juliet and cut from it everything that is not necessary to a rendering of it as modern realistic dialogue, substituting pauses of the same length as the lines that have been cut. The original passage reads as follows:

JULIET

Wilt thou be gone? It is not yet near day.
It was the nightingale, and not the lark,
That pierced the fear-full hollow of thine ear.
Nightly she sings on yon pom'granate tree.
Believe me, love, it was the nightingale.

ROMEO

It was the lark, the herald of the morn,
No nightingale. Look, love, what envious streaks
Do lace the severing clouds in yonder east.
Night's candles are burnt out, and jocund day
Stands tiptoe on the misty mountain tops.
I must be gone and live, or stay and die.

JULIET

Yon light is not daylight; I know it, I.
It is some meteor that the sun exhaled
To be to thee this night a torchbearer
And light thee on thy way to Mantua.
Therefore stay yet. Thou need'st not to be gone.

ROMEO

Let me be ta'en, let me be put to death.
I am content, so thou wilt have it so.
I'll say yon grey is not the morning's eye;
'Tis but the pale reflex of Cynthia's brow;
Nor that is not the lark whose notes do beat
The vaulty heaven so high above our heads.
I have more care to stay than will to go.
Come, death, and welcome; Juliet wills it so.
How is't, my soul? Let's talk. It is not day.   (3. 5. 1–25)

---

[14] Peter Brook, *The Empty Space* (London, 1968), 109–11.

The cut version reads:

JULIET
Wilt thou be gone? It is not yet near day. It was the nightingale [pause] not the lark. [pause]

ROMEO
It was the lark [pause] no nightingale. Look, love [pause] I must be gone and live, or stay and die.

JULIET
Yon light is not daylight; [pause] therefore stay yet. Thou need'st not to be gone.

ROMEO
Let me be ta'en, let me be put to death. I am content, so thou wilt have it so. [pause] Come, death, and welcome; Juliet wills it so. How is't, my soul? Let's talk. It is not day.

The cut version pays full respect to Shakespeare as a maker of actions. His stipulation, that the lovers must part not in 'sweet sorrow' as in the balcony scene but in 'dry sorrow', has been met. This version has also respected the 'twist' that Shakespeare has made in the inner action at this point. Instead of Romeo at first wanting to stay longer and Juliet urging him to go, the reverse is true. In the balcony scene it had been Romeo who was fearlessly risking death and romantically denying reality, whereas Juliet had been fearful for his life and insistent on the real dangers to it. How is Romeo now to be realistic about his need to leave before the setting of the watch without seeming ungallant and husbandly? How is Juliet to indulge her wishful thinking without seeming unfeeling for Romeo's safety?

As Brook points out, but without giving specifics, the cut lines reveal 'unspoken thoughts and feelings'. The element of self-delusion on Juliet's part is brought out in the original by the fact that she protests too much. Brook's version cuts her protestations: 'Believe me, love'; 'I know it'. In addition, the cutting of her endearment 'love' loses a softening effect. She never directly tells Romeo: 'Are you afraid?—when you were wooing me, you seemed fearless!' She does, though, in one of the omitted lines speak of the 'fear-full hollow of thine ear'.

Romeo might have explained that at first he had had no fear because he had nothing really to lose (not having her love) and everything to gain; now he has their mutual love to protect. But Romeo doesn't say this or anything like it. Instead, he comes very close to accusing Juliet of wishing him dead: 'let me be put to death. I am content, so thou wilt have it so.' Or is he trying to shock her into awareness?—as if slapping someone in a daze. In the cut version there is then a pause, while in the original Romeo speaks five lines before again saying: 'Come, death, and welcome; Juliet wills it so.'

Sometime between the first of Romeo's charges and her response, Juliet must awaken to reality and the need for Romeo to leave. This is an example of Shakespeare leaving options as to when exactly a character-change takes place. It is possible that she may still not fully have 'come to' even at Romeo's second charge. He seems to be calling attention to her silence with 'how is't, my soul? Let's talk. It is not day.' The implied 'pause' that Shakespeare gives Juliet here is more telling than any that Brook gives her. Only after it does Juliet realize: 'It is, it is. Hie hence, be gone, away.'

The cut passages suggest further unspoken thoughts and feelings. This has been the lover's wedding night. There is a clear secondary sexual suggestion in Juliet's saying it was the nightingale 'that pierced the fear-full hollow of thine ear'. Is Juliet, after her sexual initiation, more ardent than Romeo, who remarks that 'Night's candles are burnt out'? Is that a factor in the 'switch'?

Why does Romeo speak of 'jocund day', when it is daylight that is tearing him away? Always before it has been night that he has welcomed. Is it just his conventional poetic diction? Or is he after all hurrying for dear life? 'I must be gone and live, or stay and die.' He also comments on the lark, presumably in flight, 'whose notes do beat / The vaulty heaven so high above our heads'. Is one part of him wishing to 'take flight'? It is Juliet, after all, who must stay behind. If he is looking up from their 'loft', she at the end of the passage is looking down from it, as into a tomb. The suggestion of Romeo's apostasy to their love may echo the scene in which Mercutio and Tybalt were killed, where he allowed friendship and personal honour finally to take precedence over his love for Juliet. Note that even after he has declared his intention to remain, he uses the double-edged word 'care': 'I have more care to stay than will to go.' It is only after Juliet has begun to urge him to go that he returns to his former enmity to day: 'More light and light, more dark and dark our woes.'

What Brook cut altogether from the passage is its imagery. As Spurgeon has shown, images of bright, brief light against darkness recur a number of times. Here we see that image in eclipse. The lover's parting is a time of 'grey', or dim dawn, when they themselves are no longer shining, even in one another's eyes, but 'pale'. Only at the end of the play will their association with brilliant light return.

Although these implications seem to me certainly there in the text, Shakespeare is discreet about them. They are hints for subtle shadings that interpreters may play up if they choose. In every performance I have seen to date, the actors have chosen to ignore them and to play down the 'switch' in attitude between the two lovers. They prefer to perform a conventional scene of 'sad farewell'. As it happens I have seen the Peter Brook exercise performed by Helen Mirren, in a film about his experimental studio in Paris. I found her performance in the cut version much more moving than in the original version, partly because of the camera's intimate revelation of her very expressive face during the pauses, partly because she was less at home with the more imaginative language. In this she was like almost all modern Shakespearian actors. Brook's cutting only makes graphic what goes on most of the time in ordinary productions; the actors in fact play the part of the text that might, as in the exercise, be lifted out in prose paraphrase. The rest largely goes by the way. As a consequence, Shakespeare's voice in the dialogue, subtilizing, ramifying, extending the bare gist of his words, is often lost.

 The most durable and distinguishable contribution of the playwright to the dialogue is to be found in overall features that transcend the language of single speeches or characters. Concerning a new play, for example, reviewers will often comment on the playwright's 'ear' for contemporary idiom or on a prevailing kind of eloquence or style that is peculiarly that of Tennessee Williams or Harold Pinter or David Mamet. In Shakespeare this sense of a prevailing idiom extends to individual plays, to the fancifulness of the language in *Romeo and Juliet* or the rhetorical flatness of the speeches in *Julius Caesar* or the luridness of the imagery in *Macbeth*.

 The images that recur in a given play (such as brilliant light in *Romeo and Juliet* or hidden disease in *Hamlet*) have received special attention from scholars. Caroline Spurgeon thought that the 'iterative images' she discovered revealed Shakespeare's way of visualizing a whole play or situation. G. Wilson Knight used such images and words as the basis for his visionary readings of the plays. Certainly at the time the images occur in the dialogue, they can serve to crystallize what is happening into a vivid picture, and when they recur they gain added impact. Yet in the course of a play there are many such crystallizations, not only in the dialogue but in the choreography. And in the theatre, interplay of character and circumstance is so compelling that one is rarely conscious of the image patterns that may be analysed in the study. Their impact in performances is at most subliminal. Bradley was closest to the mark in finding that the verbal imagery helps to create a prevailing 'atmosphere'.

 More recently, students of Shakespeare's dialogue have begun to notice in it what I call 'modes of speech'. These are ways of speaking that are so common in a given play as to constitute a prevailing idiom—a 'universe of discourse' for the particular 'world' of that play, a manner of speech that reflects its typical way of life.[15] The inhabitants of *Julius Caesar*, for example, live in the imperative voice, while those of *Macbeth* live in the future tense. As an extended example, I should like to look further at the dialogue of *Romeo and Juliet*, especially that of Romeo.

The dominant mode of speech in the first two acts is that of counselling. Romeo and Juliet are subjected to unremitting advice from those around them. At Lord Montague's urging, Benvolio counsels Romeo to 'forget to think' of Rosaline. Lady Capulet counsels Juliet to 'think of marriage now' to Paris, and the Nurse chimes in: 'he's a man of wax'. Friar Laurence counsels Romeo not to stand on such 'sudden haste'. Mercutio advises him 'if love be rough with you, be rough with love'.

Immediately after the secret marriage, the 'hot days' begin and the prevailing mode changes to that of quarrelling. Mercutio first quarrels in fun with Benvolio, then in earnest with Tybalt. To the Nurse Juliet 'chides' Romeo for killing Tybalt, then turns on her when she joins in: 'Blistered be thy tongue.' In general, the docility with which the two lovers accepted counsel earlier is replaced by resistance. When Friar Laurence tries to 'dispute' with Romeo about his banishment, Romeo tells him to 'talk no more': 'thou canst not speak of that thou dost not feel.' Lord and Lady Capulet explode when Juliet resists their plans for her marriage to Paris.

Of course, the modes in the two parts of the play are not altogether distinct. The play begins with a quarrel; Capulet's ball is marred by Tybalt's outburst. Through most of the latter part Romeo and Juliet continue to be counselled by the Friar. After Romeo's final dispute with Paris, and Juliet's break with the Friar, the play ends in modes of confession, counsel, and reconciliation. Still, the modal emphasis in the two parts of the play is clear.

To a considerable extent the lovers participate directly in these prevailing modes. The movement from being counselled to disagreement marks a process of maturation for each of them, as they increasingly come to direct their own destinies. After her initial compliance Juliet comes immediately to a mature ability to counsel herself and Romeo. As we saw when considering his choreography, Romeo is much slower to come of age.

At first, it is true, Romeo is pictured as 'his own affections'

[15] See my article, 'Shakespeare's Thematic Modes of Speech: *Richard II* to *Henry V*', *Shakespeare Survey*, 20 (1967), 41–9.

counsellor', but as such he is ineffectual. With the failure of his initial
approaches to Rosaline, his unrequited love is frustrated, secluded,
paralysed. Only the good counsel of Benvolio shakes him out of it.
With Juliet it is she who plans their marriage; Romeo does little more
than set the time for her to send to him. He is not altogether passive in
this part of the play, especially with servants. He directs the Nurse in
details of the marriage (2. 4. 187 ff.) and arranges for delivery of the
rope-ladder. However, his attempt to question Capulet's servant Peter
is more characteristic:

ROMEO . . . Whither should they come?
[PETER] Up.
ROMEO Whither?
[PETER] To supper to our house.
ROMEO Whose house?
[PETER] My master's.   (1. 2. 73–8)

As advisee, Romeo has often been subjected to just this kind of
questioning. But his attempt to turn the tables here gets him nowhere
until the servant volunteers: 'Now I'll tell you without asking.'

As with his choreography, the crucial change in Romeo's speech
comes when he learns of Juliet's supposed death. His words are now
those of preparation and command; he tells Balthasar: 'Thou knowest
my lodging. Get me ink and paper, / And hire posthorses. I will hence
tonight' (5. 1. 25–6). So complete is his change that by the end of the
scene it is he who is offering sage moral counsel. He admonishes the
apothecary about the poisonousness of money, concluding: 'buy food,
and get thyself in flesh.'

The new note of command continues through Romeo's speech in
the last scene. He gives Balthazar final instructions and the blessing:
'Live and be prosperous'. He expresses the same wish to Paris to
'live' and urges him to 'be gone'. His self-command is most explicit in
his last speech, as he bids his eyes to 'look your last', his arms to 'take
your last embrace', and his lips 'to seal with a righteous kiss / A
dateless bargain to engrossing death'. Finally, he commands his 'bitter
conduct' to 'run on / The dashing rocks thy sea-sick weary barque!'

With each other the two lovers speak their own mutual language.
The prevailing modes of speech are made to serve the expression of
their love. So the asking and answering of counselling become the
praying and granting of the sonnet they share at first meeting. So in
the quarrelling second part, the *aubade* I have been considering takes
the form of loving disagreement. Without second thought, they take
bold liberties with language. In their sonnet they play with the

vocabulary and rites of religious worship. They would change Romeo's name from Montague to Love. Juliet, if necessary, would speak with the false language of coyness. Later she will play out a false 'confession' to Paris. Although both lovers try to tell others of their love—Romeo to Tybalt and Paris; Juliet to her parents—both are misunderstood. In the service of their love, they both end up telling lies.

Their independence of society goes much further than this. As the language indicates, their love is profoundly extra-social. Their use of nature imagery is more than conventional. As they see it their love is a natural force, with a power even beyond such natural forces as the inconstant moon. It is beyond the kind of institutionalized love that the older generation has in mind. It is even anti-social. In an innocent way, the society-of-two that Romeo and Juliet create anticipates that of Antony and Cleopatra, the Duchess of Malfi and her secret husband, the incestuous lovers of *'Tis Pity She's a Whore*. They are two against the world. Indeed, their love involves a dislocation from reality as it is generally understood. To them life together is heaven; separation is death.

In contrast to the very explicit modes of counselling and disagreement which surround them, communication in their society-of-two goes on intuitively, outside the ordinary modes of language—often through violating these modes. For example, they no sooner fall in love than Romeo starts talking to himself and Juliet to herself. Yet in the balcony scene Juliet's talking to herself proves to be the way in which she expresses her love to the eavesdropping Romeo. Romeo is much more inclined toward following the set patterns of 'exchanging vows' while Juliet sets the pace in breaking these patterns. She does all the talking for Romeo (2. 1. 127 ff.) and interrupts his attempts to express himself. She talks on one plane; he on another: She is insistently practical ('How cam'st thou hither, tell me, and wherefore?') while he persists in playing the poet ('With love's light wings did I o'erperch these walls'). Much of the gentle humour of the balcony scene comes from such dislocations of language. Yet in the process their love gets communicated. In contrast to the formal, calculated communication around them, theirs is spontaneous, direct, free. The two seem most in rapport when Juliet returns to say that she can't remember what she has to say (l. 170).

As responsive as they are to one another, however, their love-rapport is far from complete. One of the most touching things about their 'bud of love', as Juliet calls it (2. 1. 163), is that it dies just as it is coming to flower. This is pointed in the tomb. Juliet understands much more from Romeo's silent body than he from hers. For all his fanciful words, he is all too literal-minded, wondering at length at her beauty without ever thinking that she might be alive. Spontaneously and intuitively she sees it all and acts accordingly with a minimum of words. She is in a position to understand Romeo's mistake, and his 'true-love' sacrifice:

> What's here A cup closed in my true love's hand?
> Poison, I see, hath been his timeless end.   (5. 3. 161–2)

She has a sense of the accident of time: 'Thy lips are warm!' She tries his lips, not to 'die with a kiss' but in the hope that the practical means of sacrifice will be there. Even if the Watch were not coming, a soliloquy such as Juliet delivers in the source-story would be unthinkable. Her meaning is in the act itself, as she seizes Romeo's 'happy' dagger and stabs herself.

As usual in Shakespeare, action finally takes precedence over words. Eloquent as he was, Shakespeare knew the limits as well as the resources of language. Yet before reaching their limits, his words serve to provide an enormously rich context for his actions and characters. His dialogue cannot be cut without loss. When the lines and speeches he gives his characters are taken individually, however, they are so subject to varied interpretation that it is difficult to hear the playwright's voice within them. In their delivery we hear instead an actor's interpretation of their speaker. It is in large features of the dialogue that Shakespeare makes himself heard most clearly, features that involve several characters and numerous passages (such as the prevailing 'modes of speech' in *Romeo and Juliet*). These large features seem to me, next to the plot and choreography, the most reliable indicators of Shakespeare's purposes.

THEMES

In defining the nature of the dramatic 'transaction', Wilder finds at its heart 'a succession of events illustrating a general idea'. The dramatist must be a born story-teller and the combination of idea and illustration is the hallmark of successful story-telling, as it is in its parent forms of myth, parable, and fable. In Wilder's view, Melville, Meredith, and George Eliot, 'for all their intellectuality', (indeed because of it) fail to achieve such a combination. An idea alone is not enough. Yet to Wilder a single, central, unifying idea is indispensable, and he does not shrink from emphasizing 'the didactic, moralizing employment of a story' in its service. Jane Austen is his example of a 'pure story-teller'.

Wilder's views will seem congenial to most scholarly interpreters of Shakespeare's plays, and to many directors of them. Yet to me it seems the aspect of his essay most biased by his own approach to writing a play. Certainly he is right to stress the need for a fusion of idea and illustration. And his focus on a single, central, unifying idea fits playwrights with a philosophic message (like Pirandello and Wilder himself), those with a social message (like Ibsen in *A Doll's House* or Miller in *All My Sons*), and certain satirists (like Aristophanes and Molière). In each of these categories, however, one may value as well (or more) the less doctrinaire aspects of the playwright's work. One reason that Shaw's plays have worn better than his prefaces is that the plays dramatize the process of his thought, whereas his prefaces expound his conclusions. But about the much larger realms of tragedy and comedy, tragicomedy and farce, Wilder's views are at best a half-truth.

Certainly ideas are an important element in Shakespeare's plays, in some of them more than in others. But if each play is meant to illustrate a single meaning in the manner of *Pride and Prejudice*, he has failed in the effort. For when it comes to saying what that idea is for a given work, generations of dedicated interpreters have not been able to agree. True, individual scholars have thought they had discerned such an idea. Alfred Harbage declares roundly: '*Macbeth* is the shortest of Shakespeare's tragedies and the simplest in its statement: *Thou shalt not kill.*' Such obvious oversimplification condemns itself, yet it only reduces to absurdity a common inclination to tie up a play's manifold implications into one neat package.[16] The truth is that each play develops a distinctive set of ideas or themes which function to engage our minds in various ways—to see more deeply into a situation, sharpen a dilemma, complicate an apparent simplicity, highlight a humorous aspect or an ironic twist. Together, this set of ideas functions, not to point a single moral, but to provide a rich frame of reference, within which the action may fully resonate.

This is true even of a play whose title may seem to point toward a single meaning. *Measure for Measure* is centrally concerned with ideas of justice and mercy. But these make up only one theme in a symphony of further concerns. Matters of life and death are at stake,

---

[16] Richard Levin documents in detail the excesses of thematic interpretation in *New Readings vs. Old Plays: Recent Trends in the Reinterpretation of English Renaissance Drama* (Chicago, 1979).

as is life after death, and the return to life after presumed death. Honour and shame tie in closely, for several of the characters must face a choice between honourable death and a 'life of shame'. Honour and shame connect with praise and slander and they in turn with questions of truth/honesty and seeming/lying. The latter questions, since the Duke's plot involves what he regards as beneficent deception, lead into complex questions of virtue and vice, which in their turn intertwine with questions of law and nature. In this Vienna, leniency can lead to licence, restraint can harden to stricture and then to cruelty. The range of meanings that may be drawn from these and other interconnections is thus very wide. This is not to say, however, that some ideas are not more important than others. Frequency of reference, relevance to plot and character, connection with other ideas—all of these criteria may serve to distinguish a major idea from a minor one. Nor is it to say that *Measure for Measure* can mean anything one may wish. It does not praise either unbridled licence or a fugitive and cloistered virtue. The play rewards the characters who seek to fulfil yet govern the 'promptures' of their blood, and such understanding as they achieve comes about from experience, from knowing life in all its seaminess (and seeming-ness). Yet within these limits it leaves wide latitudes for interpretation concerning the nature of responsible governance and wise understanding.

For a more extended example, consider *The Tempest*, the play by Shakespeare most often regarded as allegorical. With its air of fantasy, semi-human beings, and arbitrarily controlled sequences, it does seem to invite such a reading. Yet none of the allegories that interpreters have advanced has persuaded many for long. Like Shakespeare's other plays, it instead presents a constellation of ideas. One major preoccupation is with art of various kinds: magic (black and white), books and education, music, dance. Another has to do with conduct: pity and anger, the noble and the vile or monstrous, chastity and lust, reason and madness or drunkenness, the ways of the court and of the isle. Shakespeare's perennial concern with illusion and reality is here uniquely focused on the strange and wonderful—on shows, dreams, charms, liquor, and on symbolic clothing (whether it is Prospero's robe, the courtiers' garments that are made like new by the sea-water, or the 'glistering apparel' that enchants Stefano and Trinculo).

Taken together, these concerns are unique to *The Tempest*. They grow out of the action of the play and provide a meaningful frame of reference for it; but they do not add up to a single allegorical meaning.

Lately, interpreters of *The Tempest* have been particularly concerned with its ideas about politics, finding in it a 'political testament': one interpreter sees a warning about the iniquity of rebellion;[17] another sees 'a statement about *homo civilis*—about the "fair and reasonable blending together" of men into a society, about the renovation of a political structure, and about the self-education of its fallen ruler in the skills and magnanimity of an ideal governor'.[18] More sophisticated studies have seen the play as an ambivalent defence of colonialism.[19] These messages can be plausibly extracted from the set of ideas the play provides, but to the neglect of complicating or contradictory factors.

It is true that Shakespeare is very much interested in the political implications of the action in *The Tempest*. Like *Richard II* its characters espouse a spectrum of attitudes toward the political science of its situations, thus ventilating such issues as tyranny, rebellion, usurpation, and the like. In *Richard II*, however, these attitudes are conventional and traditional whereas in *The Tempest* Shakespeare is much more exploratory in his approach.

Shakespeare sets this exploration under way in the very first scene, by making much of the reversals of authority that occur when 'the King's ship' is in a storm at sea as compared with the ordinary lines of authority on land. It begins with the shipmaster giving orders to the Boatswain, who gives orders to the mariners. The chain of command is clear and functioning; the Boatswain repeatedly uses the word 'master' towards his superior. In this emergency, however, his subservience to his superiors on land is altered. When the King of Naples tries to intervene, the Boatswain courteously urges, 'I pray now, keep below.' To the more aggressive Duke of Milan, he responds in kind: 'You mar our labour. Keep your cabins; you do assist the storm.' To Gonzalo, the Boatswain makes the point explicit: 'You are a councillor; if you can command these elements to silence and work peace of the present, we will not hand a rope more. Use your

[17] Dean Ebner, '*The Tempest*: Rebellion and the Ideal State', *Shakespeare Quarterly*, 16 (1965), 161–73.

[18] Gary Schmidgall, *Shakespeare and the Courtly Aesthetic* (Berkeley, 1981), 154.

[19] Lorie Jarrell Leininger, 'Cracking the Code of *The Tempest*', in *Shakespeare: Contemporary Critical Approaches*, ed. H. Garvin (Lewisburg, 1980), 121–31, concludes that the play 'has forced the audience into a position of partiality toward Prospero'; Francis Barker and Peter Hulme, 'Nymphs and Reapers Heavily Vanish: The Discursive Con-texts of *The Tempest*', in *Alternative Shakespeares*, ed. J. Drakakis (London, 1985), 191–205, see the play as an instance of uneasily colonialist discourse. Malcolm Evans, in his *Signifying Nothing* (Athens, Ga., 1986), gives an anti-Prospero reading of the play, inspired by the journal of a disillusioned colonizer who taught Shakespeare appreciation in British Honduras (Belize).

authority.' Later, instead of the 'peace of the present' we hear a shouting match, in which Sebastian and Antonio find the Boatswain an 'insolent noise-maker' and he declares their howling 'louder than the weather, or our office'. In the event, no human authority can shout down Prospero's 'tempest'. At the end of the scene Gonzalo humorously extends to the gods the scope of these issues of rule and obedience: 'The wills above be done, but I would fain die a dry death.'

In the next scene Prospero not only gives Miranda an account of Antonio's palace revolution but freshens the subject of subverted authority by acknowledging his own unintended complicity in the wrongdoing; he explains how, by his preoccupation with 'liberal arts', negligence of his duties as ruler, and excessive trust, he brought out the worst in his brother. The scene then goes on to show the patterns of authority that now prevail between the magician and his strange underlings, a spirit (Ariel) and a monster (Caliban). Shakespeare develops the two relationships by playing them off against each other. In both Prospero is a harsh taskmaster, although with Ariel his severity is in the form of a threat ('If thou more murmur'st, I will rend an oak, / And peg thee in his knotty entrails till / Thou hast howled away twelve winters') whereas he actually inflicts cramps on Caliban. Bizarre as they may be, these relationships follow familiar lines of dominance. Ariel's subservience is a kind of indenture while Caliban's is slavery. Within these patterns, Ariel and Prospero share a mutual regard whereas Caliban and Prospero have come to hate one another. The scene ends by turning to another facet of Prospero's authoritarianism, as he *pretends* to play the tyrant. He accuses Ferdinand of being a traitor who 'hast put thyself / Upon this island as a spy, to win it / From me the lord on't', and spurns his daughter's attempt to intercede: 'What! I say, / My foot my tutor?' In a single scene these shifting perspectives on Prospero as an authority figure thus afford an impressive array of subtle and complex insights into his personality.

In the next scene, Gonzalo expatiates on still another, and more radical, political option, dreaming of a commonwealth without any servitude or authority, with 'no name of magistrate', 'no sovereignty'. From this extreme, the scene then turns to another, as Antonio brings Sebastian to the verge of a *double* usurpation, planning not only to kill his brother the king but then to appropriate the crown from his elder sister Claribel, to whom it should rightly descend.

Further changes on the theme of dominance and servitude are rung in 3. 1 by developing the idea of voluntary, loving service. At the beginning Ferdinand persuades himself that he rejoices in his labour of stacking logs because of the presence of his 'mistress which I serve'. Miranda knows better. She wants to help him and says she would do so 'With much more ease, for my good will is to it, / And yours it is against'. Later they declare their love as a form of freely accepted bondage. Ferdinand tells her:

> The very instant that I saw you did
> My heart fly to your service; there resides
> To make me slave to it.

Miranda puts it still more strongly:

> I am your wife, if you will marry me.
> If not, I'll die your maid. To be your fellow
> You may deny me, but I'll be your servant
> Whether you will or no.

In a neat twist, Ferdinand might thus become an involuntary master! Shakespeare seems intent on playing every possible variation on the theme of mastery and service, not to convey a single 'message' but to further a free play of ideas on the subject, enlarge the range of the play's political reference, and sharpen its immediate relevance to his characters and the situations they are in. Thus Gonzalo's dream of a utopian community not only contributes to the political theme but also highlights his characteristic combination of good nature and foolishness. By this distraction, the old counsellor is attempting to ease the mind of his sorrowing king; yet the commonwealth of which Gonzalo imagines himself 'king' is one with 'no sovereignty'. Sebastian and Antonio lose no time in exposing the absurdity of this; but in so doing they reveal their own ill nature, which is then underlined by the double usurpation they plot. At the other extreme, the voluntary service that Ferdinand and Miranda offer one another provides a metaphor for the devotedness of their love.

Of course, to show that the political theme makes various local contributions to other features of the play is not necessarily to prove that the theme itself does not bear a single message. It does, however, illustrate that bearing such a message may not be the only reason for the theme to recur. It should further be observed that the play does not take a single, consistent view of political authority. How, for a prime example, are we to regard Prospero's assumption of rule on the isle? As Prospero sees it? Or as Caliban does? The play does not say for sure. As a contributor to this play of political ideas, Caliban is no less important than Prospero. As Caliban sees it, Prospero is a usurper: 'This island's mine, by Sycorax my mother, / Which thou tak'st from me'; 'for I am all the subjects that you have, / Which first was mine own king.' He does Prospero's bidding, none the less, capitulating to powers of sorcery that could subjugate a god:

> I must obey. His art is of such power,
> It would control my dam's god Setebos,
> And make a vassal of him.   (I. 2. 375–7)

Thus Prospero's usurpation is given a religious dimension.

Under the influence of drink, Caliban then voluntarily takes a new master, Stefano, the thrice-double folly of his choice being underlined by his extremes of exaltation ('be my god') and self-abasement ('I will kiss thy foot'). In his drunken celebration of his escape from Prospero's tyranny ('Farewell, master'), he ironically overlooks his new bondage: ' 'Ban, 'ban, Cacaliban / Has a new master.—Get a new man! . . . Freedom, high-day, freedom!'

At first, Stefano might well seem to Caliban an improvement on Prospero. His first command in 3. 2 is 'Servant monster, drink to me', an order with which Caliban is only too willing to comply. Stefano promotes Caliban to 'be my lieutenant, monster, or my standard' and stands up for him against Trinculo: 'The poor monster's my subject, and he shall not suffer indignity.' When Caliban offers Stefano the rule of the isle, his own service, and Miranda in return for killing Prospero, Stefano responds handsomely: 'Monster, I will kill this man. His daughter and I will be king and queen—save our graces!— and Trinculo and thyself shall be viceroys.' Their give-and-take unwittingly parodies a traditional exchange of service and reward between subject and sovereign. Only later is Caliban undeceived.

What has been primarily a secular issue (with only suggestions of a theological aspect) is transposed into a predominantly religious key in the next two scenes. In 3. 3, amid talk of devils and fiends, Ariel 'like a harpy' denounces in the name of destiny and fate the 'three men of sin' who 'From Milan did supplant good Prospero'. In 4. 1, amid talk of Heaven and Paradise, Prospero's wedding-show depicts Iris, the ever-obedient subject and messenger of Juno, queen o' th' sky, summoning Ceres to join her sister in blessing the young couple and their 'contract of true love'. A further royal 'summons' is extended to the naiads ('Juno does command'). As befits the gravity of the two scenes, Shakespeare thus invokes a context of classical myth and, to a lesser degree, Christianity.

The celestial harmonies of the occasion are, however, soon interrupted by reminders that Prospero's control is not yet complete, either of events or of himself. He is strangely agitated (Miranda has never seen him 'so distempered') when he realizes that he 'had forgot that foul conspiracy / Of the beast Caliban and his confederates'. Although he realizes that the 'minute' of Caliban's plot 'is almost come' and forthwith dismisses the spirits in his wedding masque, he none the less takes time to look at the 'gorgeous palaces' of his vision from a new, philosophical perspective, drawing a parallel between the melting of the spirits into thin air and the dissolving evanescence of 'the great globe itself'. Only then does he return to his immediate political problem and summon Ariel to deal with Caliban's intended coup. In due course he will appear in person to set his spirit-dogs on the trio: 'Fury, Fury! There, Tyrant, there!' Not until he has ordered his goblins to 'grind their joints / With dry convulsions' does he conclude that 'At this hour / Lies at my mercy all mine enemies'.

Lest his finale seem too pat, Shakespeare does not allow Prospero to handle this total supremacy with a spontaneous magnanimity. The master must be taught a key lesson in human fellow-feeling by the servant. When Ariel intercedes for the King and his followers, Prospero responds:

> Hast thou, which art but air, a touch, a feeling
> Of their afflictions, and shall not myself,
> One of their kind, that relish all as sharply
> Passion as they, be kindlier moved than thou art?

There is reason, indeed, for wondering whether Prospero has fully learned Ariel's lesson. For, as this passage indicates, his change seems inspired as much by emulation of his servant as by charity towards his enemies. There is reason, too, for wondering whether Prospero does not go on to make the very mistakes in governance that he made in the first place. Is he not again trusting his brother too far? As many have observed, he forgives Antonio's faults—'all of them'—even though Antonio is notably silent, never acknowledging his faults as such or asking that they be pardoned. Can we hear Prospero declare his intention to 'retire me to my Milan, where / Every third thought shall be my grave' without thinking, 'Here we go again'?

Shakespeare plays his final variation on the theme of rule and subservience when, in the Epilogue, he makes his bid for applause. The actor playing Prospero prays to the audience as gods whose clapping and cheers can set him free.

Obviously Shakespeare seeks to engage the minds of his audience, and never more so than in *Measure for Measure* and *The Tempest*. His characters never stop trying to make sense of their experiences and neither do we. To differ with Wilder about the function of ideas in his plays is not to diminish their intellectual appeal. On the contrary, it is to broaden it. For instead of approaching the plays as if they were essays in dramatic form, 'a succession of events illustrating a general idea', one can follow the fluid and wide-ranging interplay of ideas through their kaleidoscopic permutations and observe the varying perspectives they provide on other aspects of the play. Because this process is so free-wheeling, performers and readers have great interpretative freedom as to what ideas are of special interest and what are not. It should be remembered, though, that in Shakespeare the play of ideas is a process of exploration rather than of demonstration.

This long yet selective survey is intended to present a general rule-of-thumb estimate of the relative authority of the various elements of Shakespeare's composition. His plots are our best guides to Shakespeare's intentions. They are the most clear-cut of the dramatic elements and in performance are carried out through choreographies of compelling visual and kinetic impact. The large features of the dialogue are the next most reliable element, yet they are aural and more subtle, even subliminal. Characters are delineated in their broadest features, but in detail they are highly and properly subject to interpretation, as are details of line-readings. Themes are best understood in terms of areas of interest rather than of single 'messages'.

A composite picture of the playwright's share in a given text should thus reflect these various degrees of authority, starting from the more reliable elements of plot and dialogue and from them gaining guidance concerning characters and themes. We have already followed this sequence concerning the characterization of Romeo. Having sampled various features in various plays, let us now apply this approach to all the features in a single play, *Hamlet*.

6

The Playwright's Share in *Hamlet*

PRACTISING what was preached in the previous chapter, this chapter will first approach *Hamlet* through its most reliable sources of guidance as to the playwright's presence: it will analyse in order the play's plot, its choreography, and its large patterns of speech. In the light of these findings, it will then consider some of the more debatable aspects of its dramaturgy: its characters and themes. Its conclusion will explore the implications of this analysis for an understanding of the play's theatre-poetry.[1]

ACTION

The Tragedy of Hamlet, Prince of Denmark is well named. At its core, the action of the play is the story of Prince Hamlet, particularly of his struggle against his mighty opposite, King Claudius. It may be divided into four phases:

Phase One (1. 1–1. 5. 114): Prince Hamlet learns of Claudius's murder of his father and resolves to revenge it.

Phase Two (1. 5. 115–3. 3): The Prince and the King plot to find out one another's secrets; as a result of the play-within-a-play, they identify one another as mortal enemies.

Phase Three (3. 4–4. 7): Mistaking Polonius for the King, the Prince stabs him, an act with manifold consequences, including his own deportation, the death of Ophelia, and Laertes' determination to revenge *his* father's death.

Phase Four (5. 1–5. 2): The Prince returns and at long last kills Claudius but only after being fatally wounded himself by Laertes.

So bald a summary may leave the reader thinking first of what has been left out, the numerous characters and events that are left

---

[1] *Hamlet* exists in three versions, of which the Second Quarto and the Folio appear to have Shakespeare's authority. Textual experts differ about which of the two should be preferred. Since the differences between them are not crucial to my argument, I have not seen a need to make a choice and have felt free to use occasional examples that are to be found in Q2 and not in F and vice versa. My generalizations, however, seem to me true of both.

unmentioned. Obviously much more goes on in each of the phases than I have outlined. I have tried to specify the key events that define the phases.

They are worth distinguishing because within the general world of Elsinore each of the four phases has its own atmosphere and dominant modes of action and speech. As the play unfolds, it seems at first to be simply a revenge story; in Phase Two it becomes more of a detective story; in Phase Three, as the parallels ramify between the Hamlet family and the Polonius family, it opens up to become an encompassing Tale of Two Families; in Phase Four, the story, which has embraced so much of human life in all its diversity, at last reveals itself as a dance of death, in which not only the two mighty opposites but all those who came between their 'fell incensed points' have—one by one—met their deaths. Only Horatio, unwillingly, survives.

Although these phases may be thus marked off, their differences should not be exaggerated. The phases are not as distinct as conventional act divisions. As in *Macbeth* they flow from one to the next like an unrolling oriental scroll, each new phase subsuming and redefining what has gone before. The differentiating features of the phases, furthermore, are part of a coherent way of life for the denizens of Elsinore. It is a very different place at the end of the play than it was at the beginning. Yet the differences are not arbitrary; they have come about because of changing circumstances, reflecting and refracting the unfolding core of action.

The Elsinore of Phase One is a place where, despite difficulties, people are sure of their ability to use their acts and words to achieve their purposes. The Ghost comes reliably at its expected hour, Horatio rightly believes that the Ghost will speak to Hamlet, Marcellus correctly asserts that he knows where Hamlet is to be found. Claudius conducts the affairs of state in an unhurried but decisive fashion, including the awkward business of his rapid marriage to his brother's wife. Hamlet after careful questioning of Horatio and the guards proceeds to his rendezvous with the Ghost and pursues their encounter with determination, breaking free from those who would restrain him from it.

All of the citizens of Elsinore seem sure about how life should be lived and do not hesitate to tell one another how to do so. So Claudius and Gertrude admonish Hamlet on the commonness of death and the proprieties of mourning. So Laertes advises Ophelia, Polonius advises Laertes, and even Ophelia ventures to advise her brother to follow his own advice.

This idiom is established in the first scene of the play. It is true that it begins with a question, as Barnardo calls: 'Who's there?' Shakespeare likes to strike an immediate keynote, and the play's interrogative mood is its most distinctive feature. Yet its modes of certainty are no less important, and in the first part of the play they are dominant. The next lines are in that mode. Barnardo's question is misplaced (it is the guard on duty not his relief who should do the challenging) and Francisco corrects him: 'Nay, answer me.' And then he gives the proper command: 'Stand and unfold yourself.' Barnardo obeys, with a vow of allegiance: 'Long live the King!' Francisco then correctly guesses who it is: 'Barnardo?' And after Barnardo's confirmation ('He'), Francisco remarks on his punctuality, 'You come most carefully upon your hour', to which Barnardo agrees. Thus their lines establish the universe of discourse that will prevail in Phase One. In it commands are given and obeyed, immediately, and with declarations of loyalty. Duties are performed reliably and punctually.

Such certainties provide a supporting context for the key event in Phase One: the Ghost's command to revenge his death and Hamlet's vow to remember his command and carry it out. It is paralleled by Polonius's command to Ophelia to break off with Hamlet and by her response: 'I shall obey, my lord.' The lines of authority in the Polonius family are clear: Laertes 'with laboursome petition' has obtained his father's permission to return to Paris; Polonius in turn joins him in seeking their King's permission that he should do so; and the King—having confirmed the father's approval—graciously sends him on his way with good wishes.

Claudius's assertion of authority in denying Hamlet's request to return to Wittenberg is more complicated. Hamlet clearly refuses his invitation to think of him 'as of a father'. Hamlet's words of obedience are towards his mother—'I obey you, madam'—which the King blandly proclaims as his 'unforced accord'. In general, although Claudius often gives commands, he rarely does so when he can serve the same purpose by request or persuasion. Perhaps privately insecure in his usurped authority, he is publicly careful not to presume upon it. His directions are regularly accompanied by some explanation of his purposes. His speech is full of such expressions as 'I pray you' and 'I entreat you'. To Hamlet the King is particularly unctuous:

> we beseech you bend you to remain
> Here in the cheer and comfort of our eye,
> Our chiefest courtier, cousin, and our son.

Is 'bend' accompanied by a gesture of bowing? Of course, beneath

Claudius's velvet glove is the image of 'bending' Hamlet to his will—as he in fact does here since Hamlet does not contest the King's veto of his return to Wittenberg.

In contrast to Claudius, there is no doubt whatsoever about the authority of the Ghost, who is at the centre of the play's imperatives. The only major character who never asks a question, he always speaks with ponderous certainty. He gives the key command ('Revenge') and the key prohibition ('Taint not thy mind, nor let thy soul contrive / Against thy mother aught'). And his son's devotion is so complete as to suggest monomania:

> thy commandment all alone shall live
> Within the book and volume of my brain
> Unmixed with baser matter. (1. 5. 102–4)

No sooner does he conclude his vow of remembrance, 'I have sworn't' (l. 112) than Horatio and Marcellus appear, the mood changes abruptly, and Phase Two begins.

In Phase Two many of the modes of certainty continue. Rosencrantz and Guildenstern for example, positively abase themselves before their King's authority:

> we both obey,
> And here give up ourselves in the full bent
> To lay our service freely at your feet
> To be commanded. (2. 2. 29–32)

But in Phase Two it is mistrust that dominates. All of the authority figures of Elsinore are called into question. The King has just been accused of being a murderer; before the phase is over, the accusation will have been confirmed by Claudius himself. In only a few lines the Prince will refer to the Ghost of his revered father as 'true penny' and 'old mole'; soon he will suspect that the Ghost is the devil. Only after the play-within-a-play does Hamlet 'take the ghost's word for a thousand pound'. To Ophelia, the Prince confesses himself an 'arrant knave'. In the scene with Reynaldo (2. 1), the King's highly esteemed councillor of Phase One is aptly dubbed 'old Polonius' in the stage direction and made to seem a laughably absent-minded busybody.

By repeatedly swearing Horatio and Marcellus to secrecy—over their protests—Hamlet introduces the prevailing note of mistrust. And in determining to 'put an antic disposition on', he introduces another feature of Phase Two, the practice of deceptions. The scene that follows, between Polonius and Reynaldo, is very much in the new idiom. Just as Polonius in a lighter vein reflected the principal plot-element of Phase One (the command of a father to his obedient child), so in Phase Two he pushes mistrustfulness to ridiculous extremes. Not only is he deceptive and indirect in his methods, but he introduces the concern with spying that is another of the hallmarks of this phase.

The theme of parental checking-up on a son is then immediately developed further with the interview between the King and Queen and Rosencrantz and Guildenstern. At first it is the Prince's secret that is at stake. Why is he behaving so strangely? Then he in turn goes to work to test out Claudius's secret.

Phase Two is pre-eminently a time of questioning. It includes literature's most famous question, 'To be, or not to be; that is the question.' Yet the philosophical cast of Hamlet's question is not representative; only he and the First Clown are much given to posing such questions. Most of the questions in *Hamlet* are concerned with immediate, practical matters, the natural reaction of strong-minded people to a court full of secrets. The 'interrogative mood' of the play is not primarily musing but investigative.

Since the King and the Prince are working at cross purposes, it is not surprising that they and their adherents are often frustrated. The play is unique, however, in the extent to which these frustrations are pushed to a point of utter impasse or paralysis. Hamlet, of course, feels acutely his own inaction. In his 'rogue and peasant slave' soliloquy, he berates himself for it at length before arriving at a new resolve: 'the play's the thing / Wherein I'll catch the conscience of the King.' Yet the next time we see him, fifty-five lines later, he is lost in the thoughts of his 'to be, or not to be' soliloquy, at the end of which he comments on the very process we have just seen illustrated:

> And thus the native hue of resolution
> Is sicklied o'er with the pale cast of thought,
> And enterprises of great pith and moment
> With this regard their currents turn awry,
> And lose the name of action.   (3. 1. 86–90)

To a lesser degree Claudius experiences a similar paralysis. In *Scourge and Minister* (Durham, NC, 1951), G. R. Elliott puts it too strongly when he says, 'It is true that Hamlet dies because he postpones too long the killing of the king. But it is equally significant that Claudius dies because he postpones too long the killing of Hamlet' (p. xv). As Elliott admits, Claudius's delay is never given direct comment; nor as the play unfolds is it as clear as it is in hindsight that Claudius must kill Hamlet. Yet Claudius seems to be speaking from experience, as well as influencing Laertes, when he later says (in the Second Quarto only):

> That we would do
> We should do when we would, for this 'would' changes,
> And hath abatements and delays as many
> As there are tongues, are hands, are accidents . . . (4. 7. 101–4)

And he does make certain slight—but very important—delays. Although he had made up his mind to send Hamlet to England, he follows Polonius's advice to postpone action until after the playlet and a conference between Hamlet and his mother. Even after he has broken off the play and directed Rosencrantz and Guildenstern to prepare for the voyage, he delays in confining Hamlet, a nearly fatal pause which receives its visual symbol as he kneels attempting to pray during Hamlet's long deliberations. The King's inner deadlock is made explicit in his 'O, my offence is rank' soliloquy:

> Pray can I not.
> Though inclination be as sharp as will,
> My stronger guilt defeats my strong intent,
> And like a man to double business bound
> I stand in pause where I shall first begin,
> And both neglect.

He concludes:

> What then? What rests?
> Try what repentance can. What can it not?
> Yet what can it when one cannot repent?
> O wretched state, O bosom black as death,
> O limèd soul that, struggling to be free,
> Art more engaged!

As here, the arrestment of action is often because of moral inhibitions. In this phase the consciences of the characters are particularly tender. Hamlet aptly observes how 'conscience doth make cowards of us all' and just before, as the King and Polonius use Ophelia to bait their trap for the prince, they have a characteristic exchange:

POLONIUS   We are oft to blame in this:
  'Tis too much proved, that with devotion's visage
  And pious action we do sugar o'er
  The devil himself.
KING CLAUDIUS   O, 'tis too true.
  (*Aside*) How smart a lash that speech doth give my conscience.

> The harlot's cheek, beautied with plast'ring art,
> Is not more ugly to the thing that helps it
> Than is my deed to my most painted word.
> O heavy burden!
>
> (3. 1. 48–56)

Phase Two is the most distinctive part of *Hamlet*. Its features have often been taken as characteristic of the whole play. By its end, the two mighty opposites have found out one another's secrets, the detective story is essentially completed, and the action moves on to a new phase. Phase Three is less distinctive than the others; its features carry further earlier ones and put them together in a new way. The level of violence rises another notch. In Phase One the murder of King Hamlet was brought into the play in the form of verbal description by the Ghost. Although vividly recalled, its impact was less powerful than its treatment in Phase Two, where it was re-enacted, twice— first in dumb show and then as part of the spoken playlet. A key feature of Phase Three is that the play's conflicts become physical, although not so direct or extreme as they will be in Phase Four.

In general, the progression into violence is gradual. Yet the shift to a new phase is sharply pointed by the killing of Polonius, the first act of actual physical violence that we see. Even this, however, is modulated by the fact that Hamlet did not intend to kill him ('Is't the king?'). When he went to his mother's closet, indeed, Hamlet had determined to restrain his impulses towards physical violence, to speak daggers to his mother but use none. Ironically, her misplaced fear that he means her bodily harm ('Thou wilt not murder me? Help, help, ho!') cues Polonius's calls for help and Hamlet's fatal blow.

Elsewhere the violence, though growing, is less extreme. After he learns of Polonius's death, Claudius for the first time places physical constraints on the Prince and to himself resolves upon 'the present death of Hamlet'. Rosencrantz and Guildenstern no longer merely keep watch on the Prince but escort him to England. It is in keeping with this phase that the pirate attack should involve hand-to-hand combat. As described by Gertrude, Ophelia's drowning seems the least violent of violent deaths.

The killing of Polonius also precipitates the story of his family into a fully-fledged subplot. Its interweavings with the story of the Hamlet family, and parallels with it, now become more prominent than before, especially as the reactions of Ophelia and Laertes to their father's death resemble and differ from those of Hamlet to his father's death.

This is the phase in which the women in the two families release their hitherto pent-up feelings. Ophelia in her madness expresses her feelings of grief, her sexuality, and her disillusionment and sense of betrayal. Gertrude confesses to her son that he

> turn'st mine eyes into my very soul,
> And there I see such black and grainèd spots
> As will not leave their tint.

In this scene Hamlet relates directly to his mother the feelings about her betrayal that in Phase One he had expressed to himself in soliloquy. In Phase Two he had in part taken his suppressed revulsion out on Ophelia, and through the playlet pointed certain of its parallels towards his mother. Now he gives these feelings full vent, cannot seem to control them. Even after Gertrude breaks under his attack, he continues his charges.

Laertes in Phase Three in many ways recapitulates Hamlet's conduct in the first two phases. He is often taken as a contrast to Hamlet, the son who moves immediately and directly to the revenge of his father's death; and so he seems when he first storms in to see the King. But his momentum is soon halted, first—physically—by the Queen ('Let him go, Gertrude', Claudius twice directs) and then, as Claudius puts it, by the divinity that doth hedge a king. Spent in his own rodomontade, his rage is soon calmed, and he willingly becomes the King's 'organ'. His plotting with Claudius, however, goes beyond the detective work of Phase Two. As is appropriate to Phase Three, the two are intent on the death of Hamlet.

Phase Four begins, appropriately, in a graveyard. The escalation of physical violence begun in the previous phase continues. Hamlet and Laertes grapple in the graveyard, Hamlet with utter sang-froid tells Horatio how he contrived that Rosencrantz and Guildenstern be 'put to sudden death, / Not shriving-time allowed'. The final scene, of course, is a feast of 'proud death', as Fortinbras images it.

The most distinctive feature of this phase, however, is not the exceptionally large number of killings it depicts but the unexpected and sudden ways in which they come about. Perhaps the most surprising feature is Hamlet's new-found willingness to relax his compulsive drive to revenge his father's murder and 'let be'. This is Shakespeare's boldest twist to tradition. In Saxo Grammaticus and Belleforest, Amleth takes the initiative upon his return, not only killing his uncle but setting fire to the palace and destroying the courtiers. In *The Spanish Tragedy*, Kyd's Hieronimo suffers paralyses of action and speech that anticipate Hamlet's, but at the end he takes charge, proposing, organizing, and presenting the catastrophic play-within-a-play. Titus Andronicus is even more impotent than

Hieronimo; yet he is the 'cook' of the fatal banquet. Hamlet's change is subtler. We hear no more ringing vows and elaborate plans. His great opportunity comes about not through his own planning but through Claudius's machinations and the accidents of the moment. At the last minute, he regains the initiative he lost in the prayer scene and ends his prolonged conflict with Claudius in reckless haste. The first attempt at killing the King is the most instinctive kind of reflex to personal injury: 'The point envenomed too? / Then, venom, to thy work.' The second attempt, as he forces the King to drink the potion, is accompanied by his final curse: 'thou incestuous, murd'rous, damnèd Dane.' Each word adds a further area of villainy on Claudius's part, against the family, society, God, and the state. What began for Hamlet as an imperative for familial revenge has become an act of physical retaliation and then one of cosmic justice.

Claudius succeeds in killing Hamlet by proxy, as planned, but in a fashion which proves suddenly to be self-incriminating and self-destructive. Laertes, though it is almost against his conscience, completes his intended attack on Hamlet; yet its outcome is not, finally, the satisfaction of revenge but an exchange of forgiveness. In some sixty lines the play's prolonged main actions reach abrupt completion. Hamlet, Claudius, and Laertes all accomplish their purposes yet all have their acts of violence boomerang on themselves. Thus the three work out among themselves the whole cadence from resolution through frustration and standstill to growing violence culminating in an unexpected and disastrous fulfilment of their original goal.

The career of Fortinbras follows the four phases precisely. True to Phase One Fortinbras has set out to recover the lands lost in battle to King Hamlet, with 'mettle hot and full' and 'sharked up a list of landless resolutes'. In Phase Two this impulse has been halted and deflected towards Poland. In Phase Three we see him and his army and hear from his captain of the impending battle with the Polish garrison with its 'death and danger'. This incident widens the play's scope to become a tale of *three* families, for Hamlet in the soliloquy that immediately follows draws an explicit parallel between himself and Fortinbras. In Phase Four Fortinbras ends up unexpectedly, and without direct effort, with what he originally sought; indeed Hamlet bequeathes him the whole kingdom of Denmark.

The story of Prince Hamlet and its movement through the four phases thus provides the ground-plan for *Hamlet*. It always takes primacy over other features of the play. For the most part, of course, all of the units of the play work so well together that there is no question of primacy. This is especially true of the relation between the phases and the characterization of the Prince as he struggles against the King. So closely do the two coincide that the successive phases may be regarded as projections into Elsinore generally of moments in this struggle.

At certain points, however, Shakespeare's primary concern for his ground-plan shows through. Part of what seems so strange about the latter part of 1. 5 is that there the playwright shifts gears so abruptly from Phase One to Phase Two. In the following scene between Polonius and Reynaldo, too, he seems much more concerned with emphasizing the new notes of spying, deception, and mistrustfulness than with maintaining a consistent characterization of the King's councillor.

Shakespeare's interpreters should follow suit and give primacy to this ground-plan. Acting versions (beginning with the First Quarto, Olivier's film is another) have sometimes rearranged the order of events so that the 'to be, or not to be' soliloquy does not interrupt the flow from Hamlet's resolve that 'the play's the thing / Wherein I'll catch the conscience of the King' to the performance of 'The Murder of Gonzago'; by so doing, they have violated the halting rhythms that makes *Hamlet* unique. Critical interpreters have often been so struck by Phase Two that they have neglected features that distinguish the other phases and thus have missed the play's way of redefining itself as it moves through the successive phases.

Not that the ground-plan dictates a single line of interpretation. Which should be emphasized, the differences among the phases or their similarities? Should, for example, Polonius's advice to Laertes be played altogether in the idiom of Phase One as knowing, last-minute parental counsel or—in an anticipation of Phase Two—as the mistrustful maxims of a busybody? The lines permit either reading or some combination of the two. Should one phase be emphasized more than the others? Interpreters who wish to place such an emphasis are aided by the fact that features of one phase are often prepared for or followed through upon in other phases. Revenge, for example, is a major theme whether the play is treated primarily as a revenge story or as a detective story, a tale of two families, or a dance of death. Even in the plot, thus, the playwright provides guide-lines rather than hard and fast rules; none the less, it is in the plot that Shakespeare most clearly and definitely claims the playwright's share of *Hamlet*.

CHOREOGRAPHY

As it moves through its four phases, the play itself follows the prevailing rhythms of action and inaction that we have seen in the careers of Hamlet, Claudius, Laertes, and Fortinbras, proceeding from firm resolution through a period of frustration and standstill or misdirection to one of growing violence that culminates in an unexpected finale.

These rhythms are vividly bodied forth in the play's choreography. Hamlet's use of a sword is an example. There is no positive instance in Phase One, although stage Hamlets have often resolutely drawn their swords at 'Unhand me, gentlemen. / By heav'n, I'll make a ghost of him that lets me' (1. 4. 61–2). There is no doubt about the instances in Phase Two. Hamlet mistrustfully swears Horatio and Marcellus to secrecy 'upon my sword'. Later, when he is about to stab the kneeling Claudius, he halts his blow and concludes 'Up sword'. This interrupted gesture is deflected when he stabs Polonius behind the arras. His intent to kill Claudius is not completed until the finale, when, unexpectedly, he finds himself with the poisoned and unbated fencing foil in his hand and uses it to stab Claudius.

Within the play's choreography of arrested action, the moment of standstill is easily the most distinctive. The guards' cries of 'Stand' in the first scene sound the keynote, and the effect pervades the play, extending even to metrical gaps after 'Did nothing' in the Pyrrhus speech (itself a paradigm of arrested action) and Hamlet's 'Must give us pause'. Granville-Barker speaks of *Hamlet* as a 'tragedy of inaction', and R. A. Foakes points out that 'many of the "pictures" the play presents on stage, its direct images, are static or nearly so, like the pictorial effect of the dumb-show in the play scene, of Hamlet's contemplation of Claudius praying, of the pictures in the closet-scene, and of the skulls in the graveyard scene' (*Shakespeare Survey* 9, 1956, p. 36). Yet such terms as 'inaction' and 'static' do not do justice to the dynamic quality of the main moments of pause. Until flights of angels sing Hamlet to rest, there is no sense of real repose in *Hamlet*. Sleep is poisoned; graves are broken and violated. Even after Hamlet's 'rest, rest perturbèd spirit', the Ghost must return to whet his almost blunted purpose. Hamlet himself is not merely inactive but confined. He feels that Denmark is a prison; indeed, the world is one 'in which there are many confines, wards, and dungeons'. He fears being 'driven into a toil' and feels himself 'netted around with villainies'. On the ship to England, he 'lay / Worse than the mutines in the bilboes'. Thus confined, it is no wonder that he wants to put a stop to so many things—the King's wassail, marriage, overacting, 'honeying and making love over the nasty sty'—or that he tends to picture others in his own plight: he would shut the doors on Polonius 'that he may play the fool nowhere but in 's own house' and send Ophelia to a nunnery. He tells his mother, 'sit you down. You shall not budge.' He sets a 'mousetrap' for Claudius to 'unkennel his occulted guilt'. At the end, he cries, 'Let the door be locked!'

The effect of dynamic pause in *Hamlet* has been variously achieved in the theatre. As Gilder describes Gielgud's seated Hamlet (I. 2): 'He gives us at once, on our first sight of him, a picture of frustrated energy, of force held in check . . . he is motionless with the immobility not of repose but of arrested movement.'[2] When Horatio and Marcellus report seeing the Ghost, Kemble gave them his 'fixed, mute attention—not a finger moved'. Betterton must have caught something of this quality when Hamlet first sees the Ghost; Cibber tells us of his 'pause of mute amazement'. At this same point, Garrick and many other Hamlets doubtless overdid their dynamic 'starts'; but the essential effect—as Lichtenberg put it, Garrick stood 'rooted to the spot'—seems to me thoroughly in the rhythm of Shakespeare's own choreography.

Arrested movement is especially striking in the play's many delayed exits. Shakespeare's characters often begin to part and then pause to add an afterthought. But in *Hamlet* the name of action is again and again thus 'sicklied o'er with the pale cast of thought'. For a small instance, when Hamlet has broken loose and followed the Ghost, Horatio declares, 'Have after'; but then pauses to reflect:

> . . . To what issue will this come?

MARCELLUS
Something is rotten in the state of Denmark.

HORATIO
Heaven will direct it.   (I. 4. 66–8)

Only then does Marcellus return to the demands of the situation: 'Nay, let's follow him.' So the Ghost, after scenting the morning air, declares 'Brief let me be'; yet continues for thirty lines. So Laertes bids Ophelia farewell, only to add forty lines of admonition. So while Laertes' servants tend and 'the wind sits in the shoulder of his sail', Polonius chooses to deliver his few precepts and multiple blessings.

The effect of a delayed exit is intensified in later phases by repeated interruptions. The intensification is sharply marked at the beginning of Phase Two. After his 'adieu, adieu, adieu', the Ghost none the less

² Rosamond Gilder, *John Gielgud's Hamlet* (Oxford, 1937), 16.

lingers to give his repeated cries of 'swear' from the cellarage; in the same way, after he says farewell to Reynaldo, Polonius amusingly keeps adding further directions. Then, after Ophelia tells him of Hamlet's visit to her, Polonius immediately determines: 'Come, go with me. I will go seek the king'; yet it takes twenty lines and two more repetitions of 'Come' before they do so.

Claudius is a study in haste and pause. At first he is full of dispatch, sending off the ambassadors to Norway with 'Farewell, and let your haste commend your duty'. He seems less assured but still fully in control in his 'hasty sending' for Rosencrantz and Guildenstern and in his 'quick determination' to send Hamlet 'with speed to England'. After Polonius's death, there is something truly hectic about Claudius's haste in sending Rosencrantz and Guildenstern to catch Hamlet, while delaying their departure twice with afterthoughts. At this same point, he repeatedly tells Gertrude to 'Come'—each time interrupting their exit, however, by his further reflections. And while he knows that he should pretend 'to bear all smooth and even, / This sudden sending him away must seem / Deliberate pause', he plainly cannot wait for the party bound for England to be off with 'fiery quickness'. After that, he is all calm and patience, even after Hamlet returns. He is masterful in restraining Laertes, persuading him to 'keep close within your chamber' and controlling his outburst at Ophelia's grave. The funeral scene closes with the most sinisterly dynamic pause in the play; Claudius promises Laertes:

> This grave shall have a living monument.
> An hour of quiet shortly shall we see;
> Til then, in patience our proceeding be.   (5. 1. 295–7)

Hamlet makes many delayed exists. While others leave, he often remains on stage at the end of a scene, for a full soliloquy or a brief comment. After the Ghost episode, he shakes hands and parts from Horatio and Marcellus to 'go pray', only to return to swear them repeatedly to secrecy. He ends the scene characteristically, starting off ('Let us go in together'), but pausing for

> And still your fingers on your lips, I pray.
> The time is out of joint. O cursèd spite
> That ever I was born to set it right!   (1. 5. 188–190)

before concluding: 'Nay, come, let's go together.' In the 'get thee to a nunnery' episode, he again and again tells Ophelia 'farewell'. Even after the text calls for his exit, actors have effectively prolonged it. A. C. Sprague gives a number of instances.[3] Hazlitt was much taken

---

[3] A. C. Sprague, *Shakespeare and the Actors* (Harvard, 1944), 138–9.

by Kean's manner of 'coming back after he has gone to the extremity of the stage, from a pang of parting tenderness to press his lips to Ophelia's hand'. As Brereton adds, he then 'rushed off the stage'[4]— thus completely following the play's rhythm of arrested action. In the bedroom scene, Hamlet over and over bids his mother 'goodnight'. His most notable 'delayed exit' comes at his death, marked as it is by his 'I am dead, Horatio . . . Horatio, I am dead . . . I die, Horatio! . . . the rest is silence.'

Thus the element of delay in *Hamlet* is not just a debatable matter concerning the characterization of the Prince. The playwright has built delay into the plot and choreography.

LARGE PATTERNS OF SPEECH

The same may be said of the play's dialogue. It follows rhythms of arrested speech that parallel those of arrested action. The same kind of overarching irony that applies to the action applies to the dialogue. In the same sense that *Hamlet*—for all that happens in it—is about not acting, *Hamlet*—for all its more than 3,700 lines—is also about not talking. Like Laertes, many of the characters have in them a 'speech of fire'. Yet at first they cannot, will not, or dare not communicate it. Sometimes they are literally silent; sometimes they say everything but what they really have to say; sometimes they lie; sometimes they speak darkly, or to the wrong person, or to someone who chooses not to listen. With some, this speech of fire remains uncommunicated. With others, especially Hamlet, it finally blazes forth in an outburst all the more intense, and often extended, for its previous frustration. Of course, not all of the impulses to speak in the play are arrested. Far from it. No one in literature is quicker of tongue than Hamlet himself, and many of the other characters are notably articulate, in fact loquacious. Only the most important things are held back.

Every step in transmitting the truth about King Hamlet's death is marked by delay. The Ghost must appear twice to the guards, silent himself and distilling them to speechless fear, before they go to Horatio, whose ears are fortified against their story. Again, the Ghost is dumb (and dumbfounding to Horatio, who has to be urged to speak) but seemingly about to speak when the cock crows. When it appears to Hamlet, speech is again arrested on both sides. Hamlet vows to speak to the Ghost 'though hell itself should gape / And bid me hold

---

[4] Austin Brereton, *Some Famous Hamlets from Burbage to Fechter* (London, 1884), 34.

my peace'. Yet stage practice has often and convincingly delayed utterance. Like Betterton, Garrick was not only transfixed by the Ghost but struck mute—with his mouth open! When he then got out 'Angels and ministers of grace defend us!' it was at the end of a breath, as Lichtenberg reports, and another pause traditionally followed before the long invocation to 'answer me'. Still the Ghost does not speak until Hamlet declares: 'Speak, I'll go no further.'

The Ghost is forbidden to reveal the secrets of its prison house, and thus holds back the account 'whose lightest word / Would harrow up thy soul, freeze thy young blood, / Make thy two eyes like stars start from their spheres.' But the tale it does tell is almost as harrowing. For fifty lines after learning the name of the murderer, Hamlet says nothing. Not until after the Ghost's exit does he break his silence with an extended and extravagant protestation that his father's 'commandment all alone shall live / Within the book and volume of my brain'. Yet communication of the Ghost's message to Hamlet is still not complete. The Ghost was well advised to insist that Hamlet 'lend thy serious hearing' and 'list, O, list!' For he does not finally take the Ghost's word until he has grounds more relative.

The central instance of arrested speech is that of Hamlet towards Claudius meanwhile has built a court of concealment and lies, in the sun', Hamlet has nothing whatever to say to his uncle; every subsequent speech in this scene is pointedly addressed to his mother. In his first soliloquy, he expresses to himself contempt for Claudius, calling him a satyr, 'no more like my father / Than I to Hercules'. After the Ghost reveals that Claudius is a murderer, Hamlet denounces to himself that 'smiling, damnèd villain!' and seems on the verge of telling Horatio and Marcellus his 'news' immediately. It may be that he is about to say it when he begins 'There's ne'er a villain dwelling in all Denmark', only then to catch himself short and add, 'But he's an arrant knave'.

The pressure to speak out is a dominant concern of his 'rogue and peasant slave' soliloquy. Reflecting on how the First Player with his cue for passion would 'cleave the general ear with horrid speech', Hamlet lashes himself that he 'can say nothing'. For now, he merely storms to himself. His recourse to the play-within-a-play, on the assumption that 'murder, though it have no tongue, will speak / With most miraculous organ', is full of dramatic irony: for although Claudius's reaction to the play does proclaim his malefactions, at least to Hamlet and Horatio, Hamlet by putting it on also 'speaks' for the murder, putting Claudius in a position to know that the Prince knows about the crime. The players cannot, indeed, keep counsel;

they tell all. The play-within-a-play is thus still another way in which Hamlet tries to express his speech of fire.

Even after his secret is this much in the open, Hamlet continues to hold back his protests against the King. Before, he had hinted darkly about 'bad dreams' to Rosencrantz and Guildenstern, and thrown out to Ophelia, for the benefit of the hidden Claudius, 'Those that are married already—all but one—shall live'. Now his implications are clearer and more.pointed. When he sings of 'A very, very—pajock', he holds back from the rhyming 'ass' but Horatio gets the point. To Rosencrantz and Guildenstern, his self-interrupted proverb 'While the grass grows . . .' clearly implies the rest: 'the horse starves'. To his mother, Hamlet goes furthest, calling Claudius 'A murderer and a villain'; but he is interrupted by the appearance of the Ghost. To the King's face, he wishes him gone to hell (4. 3. 34). But direct denunciation he withholds until the moment of Claudius's death.

Claudius meanwhile has built a court of concealment and lies, founded on the 'forged process' of King Hamlet's death. 'Give thy thoughts no tongue', Polonius advises Laertes, and suggests perfectly the atmosphere at Elsinore. There is a progression in falsity, as the King's secret contaminates his own life and that of his court. At first, the one key lie having already been told, it is a matter of tacit concealment and smiling hypocrisy. As Hamlet takes malicious delight in demonstrating, Claudius has surrounded himself with yes-men. Then in the service of his purposes his subjects (even Ophelia) begin to engage in small deceptions. His own out-and-out lies do not come until the end, when, with truly extraordinary presence of mind, he declares that Gertrude merely 'swoons to see them bleed' and—his last words—'I am but hurt'. Although he suffers keenly from the gap between his deed and his most painted word, his cry for 'light' at the end of the play-within-a-play is as far as he ever goes towards the kind of public confession of guilt which, with its consequences, would allow him to pray for forgiveness. For all his easy public address, Claudius in the speech which most concerns him remains in effect mute:

> My words fly up, my thoughts remain below.
> Words without thoughts never to heaven go.   (3. 3. 97–8)

Claudius's refusal to listen to the rest of the play—ironically, a clear communication to Hamlet that Hamlet has communicated to him—is the least open expression that any speech of fire receives. Usually, when these speeches come, they overflow in extended and extravagant utterances that would seem as mad or false to us as they do to their hearers if it were not for our sense of the powerful and long-suppressed pressures behind them. What Hamlet did not say to Ophelia in that wordless visit in which he looked as though 'he had been loosèd out of hell / To speak of horrors', bursts out in the 'get thee to a nunnery' episode. Ophelia, meanwhile, continues to hold back her feelings of betrayal by Hamlet, which do not find expression until she sings her mad, bawdy songs. In part, of course, Hamlet is taking out on Ophelia the revulsion he feels toward his mother. So intense is this revulsion that, in his first soliloquy, he cannot bring himself to so much as say 'married with my uncle' until he has given vent to repeated parenthetical protests; yet he holds it in ('But break, my heart, for I must hold my tongue') until his prolonged and bitter sermon in the bedroom scene. Laertes' grief for Ophelia is a perfect instance of the play's rhythm of arrested speech. He has a compelling desire to give it expression (it is a 'speech of fire that fain would blaze'); yet it is at first suppressed, drowned with tears. Only when the priest denies Ophelia the requiem and other burial rites does it blaze out in a 'phrase of sorrow', as Hamlet put it, which 'conjures the wand'ring stars and makes them stand / Like wonder-wounded hearers'.

Hamlet's one-line denunciation of the dying Claudius is necessarily brief, but it is for that reason all the more powerful. In contrast to his earlier, private mouth-curse ('Bloody, bawdy villain! / Remorseless, treacherous, lecherous, kindless villain!') in which his drab-like terms of abuse come to his tongue as much for their sound as for their sense, his final, public denunciation is tersely meaningful and comprehensive: 'thou incestuous, murd'rous, damnèd Dane.' Though still sibilant and assonant, these sound effects are no longer excessive and the dentals at the end add bite.

Unlike Amleth in the legend, Hamlet is not allowed to deliver a final, explanatory public oration. To the end, his communication of what he most wants to say is arrested:

> You that look pale and tremble at this chance,
> That are but mutes or audience to this act,
> Had I but time—as this fell sergeant Death
> Is strict in his arrest—O, I could tell you . . .   (5. 2. 286–9)

And it is left to Horatio to report him and his cause aright. It is fully in the rhythm of arrested speech that Horatio's own report to the yet unknowing world should be promised and adumbrated but deferred.

The play's large patterns of speech work together with its choreography to create a distinctive way of life. The rhythms of arrested action and speech reinforce one another. The moments of silence and inaction tend to be one, and the same loquaciousness that postpones what really needs saying, postpones what really needs doing. These rhythms also interwork endlessly with other major elements: the play's images of hidden disease jibe with the prevailing sense of fatally suppressed deeds and words; its revelations of evil petrify not only Hamlet but Claudius and Laertes; its constant questionings result from the atmosphere of secrecy created by arrested speech. Above all, the dramaturgy of delay interpenetrates with the theme of death. Hamlet is acutely aware of both the fixity and the silence of death: dead Polonius will 'stay' for the guards and that prating knave 'Is now most still, most secret, and most grave'; Yorick's smile is fixed on his grinning skull and his gibes will no longer set the table on a roar. It is at the end that death is most in the rhythm of the play; that fell sergeant is most strict in his arrest.

CHARACTERS

As is evident from the discussion thus far, the characters enter into these common phases and patterns in richly individual ways. Or is it that the phases and patterns enter into the characters? When Shakespeare is at his best, both are true. For an extended example, consider the ways in which Prince Hamlet puts his own touch on the general modes of certainty and uncertainty.

Hamlet is the most searching of the play's questioners, especially as to whether the Ghost is truly that of his father, both before and after he sees it with his own eyes. In his independence of mind, he is often inclined to 'inquire too curiously', breaking out of the prevailing modes of certainty. About the past, he lacks the security and reliability that the others show. In particular, he seems obsessed with maximizing his mother's guilt, repeatedly shrinking the time before her 'o'erhasty' remarriage ('the funeral baked meats / Did coldly furnish forth the marriage tables') and even implicating her in the murder ('as bad, good-mother, / As kill a king and marry with his brother'). About the future, on the other hand, he is nothing short of prescient, divining his uncle's guilt ('O my prophetic soul'), the plot against his life in England, and the fatality of the fencing match.

About present conduct Hamlet is a generalizer. Where the other characters are tirelessly sententious, he characteristically extends particular instances to fresh universals, as he reflects upon his mother's frailty or Yorick's skull. He seems impatient with formulaic thinking ('There are more things in heaven and earth, Horatio, / Than are dreamt of in our philosophy') and suspicious of it. The immediate occasion of his outburst against Ophelia is her Polonius-like saw: 'Rich gifts wax poor when givers prove unkind.' Hamlet's response is: 'Are you honest?'

Like the others, Hamlet believes he knows how life should be lived. No character is so generous in his praise, nor so harsh in his blame. He is a sermonizer. Fortunately, he knows it. He engagingly cuts short his fulsome tribute to Horatio with 'something too much of this' and concludes his preacherly exhortation to his mother:

> Confess yourself to heaven;
> Repent what's past, avoid what is to come,
> And do not spread the compost o'er the weeds
> To make them ranker. Forgive me this my virtue . . .
>
> (3. 4. 140–3)

What chiefly redeems this trait is Hamlet's way of turning his searching questions and admonitions upon himself. He is not alone in this—Claudius, Gertrude, and Polonius all have such moments—but no other character comes close to such self-castigation as occurs in the soliloquies that begin 'O what a rogue and peasant slave am I' and 'How all occasions do inform against me'.

In a compliant society Hamlet stands out by his intransigence. He does not take orders well, however graciously they may be phrased. When Rosencrantz and Guildenstern transmit the biddings of the King and Queen, Hamlet replies at first with irony ('We shall obey, were she ten times our mother'), which turns to derision ('to be demanded of a sponge—what replication should be made by the son of a king?'). Under the guise of his antic disposition, he by innuendo insults and commands the King. When Claudius demands, 'Where is Polonius?' Hamlet replies: 'In Heaven. Send thither to see. If your messenger find him not there, seek him i'th' other place yourself.'

In the last scene, Hamlet generally speaks with a new assurance. He still asks questions, but they are now mostly incidental ('wilt thou hear me how I did proceed?'). Even 'These foils have all a length?' seems casual. His most significant questions now are rhetorical questions:

> . . . is't not to be damned
> To let this canker of our nature come
> In further evil?
>
> . . . since no man has aught of what he leaves, what is't
> to leave betimes?
>
> . . . Is thy union here?

In further ways, he speaks with a new certainty. Instead of self-blame he now speaks in self-defence; it is his madness, not himself, that he rebukes: 'Was't Hamlet wrong'd Laertes? Never Hamlet.' As he mocks Osric, he seems as sure as ever as to how others should act and speak. And he is never more prescient that towards the end, confessing to 'such a kind of gain-giving as would perhaps trouble a woman'. At the very end, Hamlet speaks with the commanding assurance of a king, as he denounces the usurper and names his successor.

So dialogue and characterization serve to enhance one another. A thorough analysis of how characterization in this play interworks with other dramatic elements would require a book of its own. None the less, one can differentiate among these elements as to their relative definitiveness. As it happens, there is at hand a shortcut to estimating how much of the characterization in *Hamlet* the play-wright claims as his share and how much he leaves to his interpreters. Prince Hamlet is himself much concerned with characterization as he puts his own construction on his own tragedy. Since Hamlet's *Hamlet* is by no means just the same as Shakespeare's *Hamlet*, Hamlet's version of the various characters can provide a useful comparison with Shakespeare's treatment of them.

From Hamlet's first soliloquy it is easy to see that he exaggerates in his estimates of people, that he glorifies those he loves, defames those he does not. So he compares his father to Hyperion and his uncle to a satyr. His comments on his mother illustrate another trait. When disappointed in someone, he can swing from one extreme to the other. His use of the expression 'she, even she' testifies to an earlier high estimate he had of her; Jenkins in the New Arden Edition glosses it as 'suggesting that better had been expected of her than of other women'. Now, however, she is in Hamlet's eyes even worse than her new husband. If Claudius is bestial enough to be compared to a satyr, Gertrude is not even bestial: 'a beast that wants discourse of reason / Would have mourned longer.' Soon Ophelia will have swung from 'the celestial and my soul's idol' to a wanton who belongs in a nunnery. With Rosencrantz and Guildenstern Hamlet's disillusionment is more gradual, but eventually those 'excellent good friends' become 'adders fanged'.

Hamlet's Polonius and Shakespeare's have interesting points of similarity and difference. In Phase One Polonius appears to be a highly valued councillor of the King and a concerned parent. The King tells Laertes:

> The head is not more native to the heart,
> The hand more instrumental to the mouth,
> Than is the throne of Denmark to thy father. (1. 2. 47–9)

Polonius's warnings to Ophelia about Hamlet seem appropriate, all the more because they second those that Laertes had just given her. His precepts to Laertes may be ill-timed (It is a 'double blessing' at a time when Laertes already fears 'I stay too long'), but they are not necessarily bad pieces of advice for a young man on his way to Paris.

It is in Phase Two that Polonius's foolishness is emphasized, first with Reynaldo and then with the King and Queen when—helplessly caught up in his own rhetorical flourishes—he expounds his theory about the cause of Hamlet's lunacy. The Queen understandably asks for 'More matter with less art', and the King is now more guarded in his appreciation. When Polonius asks if there has been a time 'That I have positively said " 'Tis so" / When it prov'd otherwise?', the King responds: 'Not that I know.' But it is the Prince who chiefly brings out Polonius's folly. He makes no comment on the councillor in Phase One, but in this phase he calls Polonius a tedious old fool (2. 2. 220) behind his back and to his face refers to him as a 'great baby . . . not yet out of his swathing-clouts' (2. 2. 384); to Ophelia he advises that the doors of his home should be shut upon him 'that he may play the fool nowhere but in 's own house'. Although he warns the players to 'mock him not', he himself delights in doing so at length and with growing contempt, especially of his intrusive attempts at dramatic criticism; when Polonius says of the First Player's speech, 'This is too long', Hamlet retorts: 'It shall to the barber's, with your beard. Prithee, say on. He's for a jig or a tale of bawdry, or he sleeps' (2. 2. 501–3).

If Hamlet's Polonius is an utter fool, Shakespeare's Polonius is more complex than that. Most of Polonius's foolishness has to do with his notion that it is his daughter's rejection of Hamlet that accounts for the Prince's strange behaviour. Like Hamlet we have the unfair advantage over Polonius of knowing the secret about the Prince's 'antic disposition'. Yet Polonius's surmise is not without basis nor is it altogether mistaken: Hamlet plainly *is* upset by Ophelia's rejection. Polonius's folly is of a special sort: it is that of a man with a theory that becomes an obsession, a theory whose applicability he exaggerates and persists in, ingeniously straining the evidence to fit it even after the King has astutely set it aside. Like Malvolio with his M.O.A.I. puzzle, his ingenuities are to us transparently self-advancing. How perfectly the theory suits his hopes! How satisfying to be the one who has solved the question of the hour (his rhetorical flourishes serve to prolong his moment of glory)! How better might he ensure his position as councillor to the new King? And for his own daughter to be the object of the Prince's desire! And for he himself to have played his roles as father and subject with such circumspection! In Polonius's position, one need not be very foolish to succumb to his obsession.

Moreover, Shakespeare's Polonius is wise enough to admit that he is a bit of a fool. In Phase Two Shakespeare allows the audience, but not Hamlet, to hear Polonius acknowledge to himself that in his youth he 'suffered much extremity for love', very near the love-madness he sees in Hamlet; to Ophelia he acknowledges his own over-solicitude:

> I am sorry that with better speed and judgement
> I had not quoted him. I feared he did but trifle
> And meant to wreck thee. But beshrew my jealousy!
> By heaven, it is as proper to our age
> To cast beyond ourselves in our opinions
> As it is common for the younger sort
> To lack discretion.   (2. 1. 112–118)

In his determination to find out the truth about Hamlet's transformation 'though it were hid indeed / Within the centre' (2. 2. 160–1), Polonius also seems more of a threat than Hamlet allows.

Instead of Hamlet's simple caricature, Shakespeare thus offers the actor of Polonius opportunities for a subtly shaded portrait of some complexity. The actor must depict a man who is astute enough credibly to hold a position of trust at court yet be capable of silly prolixity concerning the cause of Hamlet's lunacy. Within these limits, Shakespeare gives the actor considerable liberty to weight the various elements in Polonius's personality. That said, it must be recognized that Hamlet has a way in the end of being basically right about people. When it matters most, in Phase Three, Polonius is foolishly super-solicitous. Claudius has already determined to send Hamlet to England when Polonius persists in his plan to eavesdrop on the Prince and his mother and proves himself, as Hamlet terms him, a 'wretched, rash, intruding fool' (3. 4. 30). It is as though Hamlet could sense at the outset how Polonius was going to be relevant to his tragedy and responds accordingly throughout. The same can be said concerning a number of other characters.

Hamlet understands a great deal about Claudius. His 'prophetic soul' intuits the King's guilt and the designs on his life that the King intends in sending him to England. Although Hamlet rightly gives Claudius credit for having a conscience and knows how to play upon it, Hamlet's Claudius is essentially a 'smiling, damned villain'.

Through the first two phases of the play, Shakespeare's Claudius is a much more sympathetic figure, a responsible ruler, a loving husband, and a self-tormented sinner. In Phases Three and Four, however, Claudius more and more becomes what Hamlet always took him to be. With the King as with Polonius, Hamlet's prophecies are self-fulfilling: he helps to drive these men to what they become. Yet his influence is never to pervert but only to catalyse qualities already present.

Is Hamlet's harsh judgement of Rosencrantz and Guildenstern similarly prophetic? Perhaps. He himself talks and acts as if it were and as if they were complicit in the plot to have him executed in England. Although Horatio seems to have some reservations ('So Guildenstern and Rosencrantz go to't', (5. 2. 57), the two are not near Hamlet's conscience. Shakespeare, however, does not allow the audience to be so sure. They do make love to their employments by the King, but we never hear him take them into his confidence about the sealed commission to England. Why would Shakespeare leave the matter ambiguous? One reason may be that our uncertainty—and its discrepancy from the Prince's sureness—helps to emphasize Hamlet's sense in Phase Four of being in the service of ordaining powers, powers whose influence enables him to act in dubious circumstances that might have given pause to others (or to himself in an earlier phase).

About Ophelia there is still greater uncertainty. Is Hamlet justified in treating her as if she were a prostitute? In the same scene in which he challenges her honesty (3. 1. 105), she does prove dishonest, lying to Hamlet about the whereabouts of her father. In her madness she sings a bawdy song:

> Then up he rose, and donned his clothes,
>   And dupped the chamber door;
> Let in the maid, that out a maid
>   Never departed more.   (4. 5. 51–4)

Is it in some sense autobiographical? Does it thus confirm the prescience of Hamlet's earlier treatment of her? Perhaps. Shakespeare allows that possibility, but he does not allow us to be sure about it, one way or the other. And our uncertainty about Ophelia is compounded by uncertainty about Hamlet's feelings towards her, especially when at her graveside he experiences an apparent change of heart and declares his unbounded love for her.

A similar turn-about—or more precisely the same continuation of love despite powerful feelings of revulsion—can be seen in Hamlet's relationship with his mother. He thinks the worst of her, accusing her at one point of killing his father (3. 4. 28), yet he never seems to give up hope for her better nature. In the closet scene, his harsh words to her are not simply denunciations of past misconduct but exhortations to improvement. His hope for her is vindicated at the end, when she warns him about the poisoned drink.

About Laertes Hamlet has nothing at all to say until Phase Four. During his outburst in the graveyard, he treats Laertes as if he were a rival, the 'bravery' of whose grief for Ophelia (he 'rants' and 'outfaces' Hamlet by leaping in her grave) somehow competes with his own feeling for her. Even there, however, he protests to Laertes, 'I loved you ever'. And later he confides to Horatio his regret that 'to Laertes I forgot myself / For by the image of my cause I see / The portraiture of his'. He expresses this fellow-feeling to Laertes himself before the fencing match, when he asks his pardon:

> Sir, in this audience,
> Let my disclaiming from a purposed evil
> Free me so far in your most generous thoughts
> That I have shot mine arrow o'er the house
> And hurt my brother. (5. 2. 186–90)

Despite Laertes' treachery, there is truth in Hamlet's sense of their brotherhood, as is brought out when Laertes warns that 'the King's to blame' and, just before he dies, offers to exchange forgiveness with Hamlet.

About himself, Hamlet shows all of the tendencies he displays in estimating others. At first, in Phase One, he overrates himself; the true Prince knows not seems and will sweep to his revenge 'with wings as swift as meditation'. In Phase Two he then swings to the other extreme and exaggerates his own failings. In soliloquy he doubts his own mettle; he warns Ophelia against himself: 'I could accuse me of such things that it were better my mother had not borne me.' In later phases, as he continues to delay and light-heartedly does away with Polonius and Rosencrantz and Guildenstern, the truth in his self-denigration is confirmed. None the less, he continues to have great expectations of himself. The context of his self-rebuke is characteristically not of denunciation (as towards Claudius) but exhortation (as towards his mother). And these expectations are borne out in the end when, at long last, he succeeds in killing the King.

Hamlet is in a way the first interpreter of Shakespeare's play. As has been discussed, he can be brilliantly right in his judgements about himself and others and thus serves to underscore and often foreshadow essential features in Shakespeare's characterization. On the other hand, his lurid highlighting is characteristically partial (both incomplete and biased) where Shakespeare's *Hamlet* is more fully and evenly lit. And the positiveness of his judgements often seems cocksure amid the complexities, uncertainties, and multiple possibilities which Shakespeare emphasizes. Although many subsequent interpreters have largely followed Hamlet's lead, he himself is the first to admit his own unreliability, both because of his personal change of disposition (so that 'the paragon of animals' seems to him 'this quintessence of dust') and because of the general relativeness of values ('there is nothing either good or bad but thinking makes it so'). The discrepancies between Hamlet's *Hamlet* and Shakespeare's thus help to bring out the openness and variability that the playwright builds into his delineation of character. Although the analysis of the plot, choreography, and large features of the dialogue can provide some guidance, the area of characterization remains—as usual in Shakespeare—highly and properly subject to interpretation.

THEMES

In the course of *Hamlet* Shakespeare as usual invites the audience to consider a complex of ideas unique to that play. The story is not, however, in the service of the ideas but the other way around. The topics considered and discussed by the characters derive immediately from their developing circumstances. It is easy to see why in what eventually becomes a Tale of Three Families, family relationships are a concern; why—in the wake of the deaths of King Hamlet, Polonius, and Ophelia—characters express feelings of conscience and grief; why Hamlet and Laertes have a good deal to say about honour and revenge; why—in a court filled with secrets—there should be talk about deception and detection; why—in a nation with a new ruler and a border-dispute threatening to come to a head—guards should be nervous and others talk much of military affairs; why—when the ghost of a dead king has appeared and matters of life and death at the highest levels of society are at stake—the characters speak of fate, providence, and the supernatural. It is notable how many of the play's recurring topics are introduced in early scenes of Phase One. Talk of physical disease, crime, and murder does not come, however, until the Ghost's speeches when it comes all at once; that is part of their power. It is notable, too, how Hamlet addresses all of these topics in a more philosophical way than do the others, freely and speculatively pursuing their widest and deepest reaches.

Like the characters, the audience can scarcely avoid reflecting upon these various topics, but for the most part it does so without special urging from the playwright. The issue of proper conduct is an exception. It is true that the misconduct of the King and Queen in their incestuous and overhasty marriage and the antic misconduct of their heir apparent provide occasion for some of Elsinore's interest in proper conduct. But this interest ramifies in regard to other characters and into talk of proper manners and speech in a way that exceeds its occasion in the story. The playwright seems thus to have encouraged the critical response the play has received, for to a remarkable degree the interpretative search for meaning in *Hamlet* has concentrated on ethical issues as to what the characters (especially Prince Hamlet) do or do not do. Why does he delay? Is he to be praised or blamed for his delay? When he does take various actions, is he justified in doing so? The playwright poses these questions, but he makes answering them very difficult indeed.

Brilliant answers to these questions have been proposed, but they have focused too exclusively on Prince Hamlet. As the preceding analysis suggests, his conduct is best understood as it relates to the 'world' of Elsinore. It is a place in which direct action and speech are extremely difficult, almost impossible. Actions are not to be carried through without the utmost persistence, the most desperate measures, and the most extraordinary luck—and even then they may well miscarry. Communication is at best minimal and dubious. The inhabitants of Elsinore are subject to attacks of paralysis at crucial moments, followed by fits of wild activity and speech. In this nightmare world, Hamlet's difficulties in acting and speaking are nothing unusual. He delays because he suffers in their most acute form from maladies endemic in human life as it is lived in Elsinore.

It is true that Hamlet has his distinctive susceptibilities to this prevailing condition, one of which is his own awareness of it. In diagnosing these susceptibilities, however, interpreters have often extended to his whole career an explanation that fits only certain phases of it, especially the initial ones. Goethe and Coleridge provide the most famous instances.

Wilhelm Meister sees in Prince Hamlet 'a lovely, pure, noble and most moral nature, without the strength of nerve which forms a hero' who 'sinks beneath a burden which it cannot bear and must not cast away'.[5] This view applies well to the first part of the play, especially Phase Two; but it does not take into account Hamlet's later

---

[5] Johann Wolfgang von Goethe, *Wilhelm Meister's Apprenticeship and Travels*, trans. T. Carlyle (New York, 1882), Book 4, ch. 14, p. 185.

toughening of spirit or, indeed, his successful carrying out of the 'great action' which he is supposedly 'unfit' to perform.

Coleridge, too, throws most light on the Hamlet of Phase Two. Instead of 'instant action' Shakespeare shows us:

> endless reasoning and hesitating—constant urging and solicitation of the mind to act, and as constant an escape from action; ceaseless reproaches of himself for sloth and negligence, while the whole energy of his resolution evaporates in these reproaches. This, too, not from cowardice . . . but merely from that aversion to action which prevails among such as have a world in themselves.[6]

In Coleridge's view of Hamlet 'every incident sets him thinking', and he calls attention to this trait in his wassail speech; Bradley finds it also in his instructions to the players. Yet in neither instance does his speculative thought impede his action. As already noted, his 'to be or not to be' soliloquy does interrupt the flow of his thought towards using the playlet to catch the conscience of the King, but it does not deflect him from that purpose. Only when he has an opportunity to kill the kneeling King do his thoughts delay his impulse to act. But these thoughts are not of the philosophical sort Coleridge has in mind; they are the calculations of a revenger who wants eternal damnation for his enemy. It is in the last act that Hamlet's penchant for dallying speculatively on the verge of important events is most pronounced. When every moment before the ambassadors arrive should count, Hamlet is delighted to spend his 'interim' matching wits with a gravedigger and having some fun with a fop. Yet because of his new-found willingness to 'let be', these moments of prolonged distraction from his task do not seem as outrageously frivolous as they otherwise would. Instead they seem instances of the 'wise passiveness' that characterizes Hamlet's attitudes in Phase Four.

An understanding of Hamlet's delay, thus, needs to take into account his whole career, and furthermore to recognize that his motives are complex, changing, conflicting, and subject to a range of interpretations. There is good reason, for example, to find that Hamlet delays because he is either overmotivated or undermotivated or something of both. At the end of Phase One he vows utter devotion to the ghost:

> thy commandment all alone shall live
> Within the book and volume of my brain
> Unmixed with baser matter.

Yet fewer than a hundred lines later, at the beginning of Phase Two,

---

[6] *Coleridge on Shakespeare*, ed. T. Hawkes (Harmondsworth, 1969), 178.

he expresses contrary feelings: 'O cursèd spite / That ever I was born to set it right!' Later in this phase, he is torn between these contrary pulls. A crucial moment comes when Hamlet decides not to kill Claudius 'at prayer' lest he send him to heaven not hell. If we take the Prince at his word, this is an ultimate example of his *excessive* dedication. Literally honour-bound, zeal here postpones what ordinary duty would have accomplished. But many interpreters have seen this passage as a piece of rationalization in which Hamlet disguises a *deficient* acceptance of his role as a revenging son. On the other hand, if we take the Prince at his word in the 'rogue and peasant slave' soliloquy he has been culpably negligent in upholding his family's honour; yet his lines can also be read as the self-lacerations of an over-conscientious son. The performer of the role is thus given wide latitude for emphasizing one pull or the other, or a combination or sequence of the two.

Fully considered, the ethics of Hamlet's actions and inactions do not lend themselves to a philosophical meaning for the play. He most berates himself for his inaction. Whether he is seen as overmotivated or undermotivated, there is an excessiveness about his acceptance or non-acceptance of his duty that might be seen as a shortcoming, an excessiveness that in both respects is reduced in the course of the action in a way that seems to aid his ability to act. Still, it is hard to see excessive zeal as a 'tragic flaw'. If he resists his assignment, it should be remembered what an awe-inspiring charge he has been given: to kill his king, uncle, step-father. Further mitigations are a commendable felt need to test the Ghost's word, the fact that difficulty in carrying through actions is a prevailing condition in Elsinore, and the fact that he at last does perform the long-awaited deed.

Contrary to his own estimate, certain of his actions seem more culpable than his inaction. Hamlet has only the briefest of compunctions about his killing of Polonius and none at all about sending Rosencrantz and Guildenstern to their deaths; he never acknowledges any degree of responsibility for Ophelia's death. If he has more to answer for than he acknowledges, there are also—as already analysed—special circumstances about his part in these deaths that preclude simple condemnation. Indeed, a hardening of the Prince's heart is arguably a necessary precondition for his final killing of the King. Such ethical complications work against extracting any single clear or simple 'moral of the story'.

The circumstances and attitudes that conduce to Hamlet's final 'readiness' to kill the king have often been felt to be full of meaning.

Here the difficulty is that there are so many factors involved. Is it his mature assessment of his own strengths and weaknesses?:

>   I do not know
> Why yet I live to say 'This thing's to do',
> Sith I have cause, and will, and strength, and means,
> To do't.   (4. 4. 34–7; in the Second Quarto only)

Is it a greater willingness on Hamlet's part to accept the burden assigned him, and his own shortcomings in bearing it? He explains to his mother:

>   heaven hath pleased it so
> To punish me with this, and this with me,
> That I must be their scourge and minister. (3. 4. 157–9)

Is it that his imperative for action has become less his father's injunction and more his own? Compare his explicit motivations before his departure for England (as he berates himself for saying nothing):

>   . . . no; not for a king
> Upon whose property and most dear life
> A damned defeat was made.   (2. 2. 570–2)

with those after his return:

> Does it not, think'st thee, stand me now upon—
> He that hath killed my king and whored my mother,
> Popped in between th'election and my hopes,
> Thrown out his angle for my proper life,
> And with such coz'nage—is't not perfect conscience
> To quit him with this arm?   (5. 2. 64–9)

Before, Hamlet was fulfilling a role, chiefly on his father's behalf, avenging 'a' king. After, he is acting on his own behalf, retaliating for a wrong done to 'my' king and 'my' mother. Further, he is no longer merely the son of the King but the Crown Prince, incensed at the successful rival who 'popp'd in between th'election and my hopes'.

As the play proceeds, still further factors enter into Hamlet's final 'readiness'. His new-found willingness to 'let be' is one factor. Another is his mother's death, which frees the constraints of his sexual problems where she is concerned. At the end Hamlet is fighting directly 'for my proper life'. He does not act against Claudius until he is physically attacked and Laertes and the Queen have confirmed that it is the King's doing. There is something to be said for each of these options. Their very multiplicity, however, works against singling out one or the other of them as *the* meaning that Shakespeare intended.

The play is not, however, a study in futility, as may be shown by comparison with modern absurdist theatre. Certainly, the allusion to Hamlet in *Waiting for Godot* seems very much at home. Indeed, Vladimir's remark in the course of 'raising Pozzo'—'But that is not the question. What we are doing here, *that* is the question'—helps to confirm that the whole sequence parodies *Hamlet*'s rhythm of arrested action, including as it does:

1. The intense declaration of purpose—'Let us not waste our time in idle discourse! (Pause. Vehemently.) Let us do something, while we have the chance.'

2. The arrestment of action—involving deflection (Vladimir drifts from resolution to speculation, ignoring Pozzo's renewed calls for help) and total standstill (particularly in the 'long silence' that comes when both Vladimir and Estragon have themselves fallen).

3. The final, sudden, almost inadvert success that seems to come of itself—Pozzo simply says 'Let me go!' and orders Lucky 'Up!' When Pozzo offers two hundred francs for help, Vladimir's response could hardly be more Hamletesque: 'Come, let's get to work! (He advances toward the heap, stops in his stride.) In an instant all will vanish and we'll be alone once more in the midst of nothingness! (He broods.)'

'Waiting on Hamlet' is clearly an important part of the effect of Shakespeare's play. Yet equally clearly that is not the whole of it. Even in the worst productions, the finale is always strangely satisfying—chiefly, I think, because the impulse towards significant action which we see in the course of the play sputtering, jerking, veering, backing, stalling towards its modern failure, ultimately reaches fulfilment.

Still closer to absurdity are *Hamlet*'s arrestments of communication. One can imagine an Ionescan production of the play which would make the most of Hamlet's talking past his foes, Horatio's obtuseness (he would often be on the verge of saying ''Twere to consider too curiously, to consider so'), Laertes' rant. The last scene would stress the court's uncomprehending cries of 'Treason! treason!' when Hamlet stabs Claudius, and Laertes would die (as the stage direction suggests) before Hamlet manages to return his words of forgiveness. If Claudius then died just before, rather than just after Hamlet delivered his long-deferred denunciation, the effect of non-communication would be complete.

The point, of course, is that in *Hamlet* it isn't complete—quite. The special quality of Hamlet's heroism is that, confronted—within and without—by all the modern impediments to significant action and communication, he has the pluck and luck to achieve both.

As here, it is in the plot and in large features of the dialogue that the playwright's share in *Hamlet* is most clear-cut and definite. As here, these dramatic elements can provide guidance as to the less clearly defined elements of characterization (the Prince is finally heroic) and meaning (his career is not finally futile). The latter elements are left much more open to interpretation, within the rough outlines and options that the playwright provides. Duly weighted and taken together, these various indicators reveal enough for us to discern the role as playwright that Shakespeare the theatre-poet assigned himself in *Hamlet* and thus to understand the theatre-poetry of his interaction as playwright with the players and playgoers.

THE THEATRE-POETRY OF *HAMLET*

At the end of *Hamlet* Fortinbras asks to see 'this sight'. When he has seen the carnage, he exclaims:

> This quarry cries on havoc. O proud death,
> What feast is toward in thine eternal cell
> That thou so many princes at a shot
> So bloodily hast struck!   (5. 2. 318–21)

'Quarry' means the dead deer gathered after the hunt; 'havoc', the signal to an army for indiscriminate killing and destruction. As the audience surveys the newly dead bodies of Laertes, the Queen, the King, and the Crown Prince, and adds to them the off-stage dead— Polonius and Ophelia, Rosencrantz and Guildenstern—we may well conclude with Fortinbras that 'such a sight as this / Becomes the field, but here shows much amiss'.

Throughout the play this is the sight on which the muse of *Hamlet* 'sits on brood'. It is a morbid muse. Like its hero it is inclined to make things out to be even worse than they are. After all, not every death is violent, or the work of human hands. Shakespeare knows better and fills in a larger view in the graveyard scene; but that is a verbal backdrop to the slaughter actually shown. The *Hamlet* muse grieves to the verge of madness for what it does, especially over the death of fathers; but it has a sardonic streak too. It makes us laugh at its grisly handiwork, grin—like Yorick's skull—at the realization that in Elsinore, as with 'the noble dust of Alexander' (5. 1. 199–200), all roads lead to a bung-hole.

It is a sly muse as well. It tricks its hero into thinking Claudius is praying, then, behind his back, immediately reveals to the audience (with a wink) that he is not. It works its wiles on us as well. By the time 'this sight' is finally shown, we like Fortinbras find ourselves wishing to see it, or are at least ready to do so. Until then Shakespeare the theatre-poet like so many of his characters must work by indirection; for how many of his spectators would at the outset think that they could be led to bear, or even wish, to see such a thing? So he lets his cosmic joke dawn slowly, very slowly.

The length of *Hamlet* is of its essence. It is Shakespeare's longest play, half again the length of an ordinary Elizabethan play. Productions which cut and trim the text are shirking the play's challenge, a practice which Shakespeare seems to condemn in advance. When Polonius says of the Player's speech, 'This is too long', Hamlet retorts: 'It shall to the barber's, with your beard. (*To First Player*) Prithee, say on. He's for a jig or a tale of bawdry, or he sleeps' (2. 2. 501–3). For full effect the play should be done in its entirety—or its 'eternity' as the backstage joke goes. The joke is apt, for *Hamlet* should not only *be* long but *seem* so. The Prince not only has the most lines of any Shakespearian character but he seems talkative. He is never boring yet much given to expatiating on set topics. The play itself seems equally long-winded because it puts off for so long what it promises to do. There is irony in the Prologue that Shakespeare provides for 'The Murder of Gonzago':

> For us and for our tragedy
> Here stooping to your clemency,
> We beg your hearing patiently.   (3. 2. 142–4)

For Shakespeare's marathon tragedy comes close to exhausting its audience's patience. We want to have done with it. That is one way Shakespeare wins acceptance for his finale.

For his marathon tragedy Shakespeare created the least provokable of antagonists. He gives us a Prince who will not enter into direct conflict with his enemy until the eleventh hour and fifty-ninth minute, who will not for the sake of another kill his mortal enemy in face-to-face combat whether in hot blood or cold, who will not even kill in self-defence but posthumously—only after he has been fatally wounded by his enemy's confirmed agent; who will not until the very last minute so much as stand up to his enemy verbally, but will only do so when speaking indirectly or when wearing a mask. His antagonist the King is no more inclined toward direct confrontation and conflict. Not until all who have gone between these mighty opposites have been killed off will the two come to decisive conflict.

Shakespeare supposes in his audience a comparable unwillingness to enter into violence. As we have seen, he introduces it into his play very slowly and escalates its level very gradually.

As theatre-poet, Shakespeare makes the audience doubt his ability as playwright to bring his play to a successful completion. It is a doubt that he may have felt himself in trying to bring coherence to his very disparate materials. Geoffrey Bullough observes:

It may well be that in taking over the old *Hamlet* and preserving its outlines Shakespeare was much less interested in explaining the delay inherent in the story than in the many interesting scenes to be presented during it. His problem was given the variegated material which we have discussed . . . how to pull it together and make it happen credibly to the avenger so as to occupy his mind and time until the catastrophe—and our minds too.[7]

Michael Goldman has suggested an analogous problem for the actor who plays the Prince:

the interpretive problems which confront the actor who plays Hamlet are very similar to those which confront the Prince in making sense of life at Elsinore . . . The difficulty of making sense out of action, one's own action and other people's, is a central motif in the play, and it is echoed, refined, and kept before us by the accomplishment of any actor who succeeds in finding and expressing an inner coherence adequate to the major role.[8]

Although the parallel between actor and Prince seems to me sound, I myself would question whether the realization of such a parallel is an important part of the audience's experience, especially that it is 'kept before us' as a conscious awareness.

This crisis in confidence develops gradually. At first, in Phase One, the play moves along at a stately yet steady pace. Painting on a wide canvas the playwright introduces us to the court at Elsinore in all its variety. The importance of the Prince's story is not at first apparent. Typically the connection of an episode to Prince Hamlet does not emerge until the latter part of it. Yet progressively the story lives up to its title: *The Tragedy of Hamlet, Prince of Denmark*. We in the audience feel that we can place our confidence in the story-teller.

In Phase Two, this confidence is called into question. The certainties of Phase One are no longer secure. For the audience as for

---

[7] *Narrative and Dramatic Sources of Shakespeare*, ed. G. Bullough, 8 vols. (London and New York, 1973), vii. 52.

[8] Michael Goldman, 'Acting Values and Shakespearean Meaning: Some Suggestions', *Mosaic*, 10, iii (1977), 53.

the hero, the reliability of the Ghost is shaken by Hamlet's doubt ('The spirit that I have seen / May be the devil'). Like the characters, the audience is thus engaged in a search for truth and like them enters into the play's characteristic rhythm, in which a strong purpose is brought to a total standstill or deflected before it reaches its unexpected fulfilment. The audience is almost as eager as the Prince to test the Ghost's word: 'the play's the thing.' Yet this impulse is halted by the 'to be, or not to be' soliloquy and diverted, first to the nunnery episode with Ophelia and then to Hamlet's theory of drama. Although we strongly desire to see the mousetrap set, these interruptions of that impulse are not simple frustrations. Each of them is so fascinating in itself that we too are caught up in them. It is a matter of interpretation whether or not the audience can be as sure as Hamlet is that Claudius's reaction to the play-within-a-play confirms his guilt. Absolute confirmation comes unexpectedly, and totally, when we hear the King trying to pray.

In Phase Two, the flow of action also bogs down, eddies, veers. Like Hamlet, Shakespeare seems to dwell on secondary matters to the neglect of primary ones. With 'The Murder of Gonzago', however, it appears that the hold-ups will be broken through and the play brought to a decisive conclusion. This is after all about the time when an Elizabethan playwright would normally be bringing his tragedy to a close. Not so Shakespeare, who instead brings his action to a complete halt. Claudius tries to pray and Hamlet decides against stabbing. This is a Grand Pause with a vengeance!

It is in Phase Two that Hamlet's instructions to the Players are especially apt for the actors of *Hamlet*. For they must give full expression to the extra intensities of energy the play calls for—antic, hectic, manic—yet without seeming themselves as performers to be tearing a passion to tatters. At the same time, neither must they be too tame. For the effect of standstill must be conveyed without seeming dull.

In Phase Three Shakespeare brings up reinforcements. Claudius at long last goes into action. Laertes comes storming back. There is even reason to harbour hopes that Hamlet will come through. Before this phase is over, we will have seen that he has the ability to act in his killing of Polonius, however impulsively, heard him again exhort himself into action ('How all occasions do inform against me'), and heard about his physical courage in boarding the pirate ship. The fact that the stakes are now raised, to plotting death to adversaries, also reinforces the impression of conflicts coming to a conclusive head.

As the parallels with the Polonius family ramify, the scope and relevance of the action fall more into place. What had seemed to be incidental and peripheral in this larger context gains relevance as part of the Tale of Two Families. Shakespeare's waiting game begins to bear fruit. Our resistance to violence gives way to a desire for some kind of action, whatever its nature. Thus he wins readier acceptance for the increased violence of Phase Four.

By Phase Four, Shakespeare supposes in his audience a degree of the 'patience' the Prologue to 'The Murder of Gonzago' bespoke for his play. If for no other reason than exhaustion, we are invited to relax our imperatives for action and, with Hamlet, be willing to 'let be'. Our patience is rewarded when Hamlet at long last does what he and we have been waiting for through most of the play—he kills the King.

This analysis of *Hamlet* illustrates how, from a weighted analysis of its parts, the playwright's distinctive share in a play may be discerned. The last pages of the chapter show as well how this distinctive share can enter into the theatre-poetry of the whole play.

The next three chapters will turn from the playwright to focus on the players and on the guidance that Shakespeare the theatre-poet provides for them in rehearsal and in performance. Instead of sifting the text for the largest and most definite evidences of the 'playwright in the play', the reader will now be invited to enter the realms of Shakespeare's art that are most problematical, especially those of characterization and detailed line-readings. Of course, as playwright, Shakespeare has provided a script that stipulates what words are to be spoken and in what order; and he has outlined the principal features of the characters, through what they say and do and through the reactions they provoke in other characters. When one goes beyond regarding the text as a script—sketching an imaginary world—to see it as a guide to enactment, one finds that Shakespeare, as theatre-poet, has provided abundant help to his performers as to how his words are to be spoken, how his outlined characters may be fleshed out and brought to life. Indeed, one's first impression is of a bewildering superabundance, an infinite variety of interpretative possibilities. Further consideration, however, reveals that the variety, though great, is in fact finite. In these realms Shakespeare's presence is to be felt, and the players' function defined, by surveying the widest range of valid possibilities that the text leaves open to interpreting performers, by marking the outer limits of these possibilities, and by considering the pros and cons of the principal options within them. The theatre-poet's voice may be heard in the very range and nature of these options, just as the performer's contribution may be understood in terms of the choices he or she makes from among them. Since in real productions this trial-and-error process of exploration and selection takes place during rehearsals, the next two chapters have taken the form of imaginary 'rehearsals'.

7

The Theatre-Poet and the Players:
Four Rehearsals
(As You Like It, Henry V, Macbeth, Hamlet)

THE rehearsals in this chapter are imaginary in more ways than the
obvious one that they never actually took place, except in my mind.
Only to a degree are they meant to be like actual rehearsals. My
players are not concerned with lighting, costume, set, and the rest of
the features that actual players need to incorporate in their performances. They can concentrate on the movements of mind and
body that express the relationships of the characters and the progress
of the action. Even here I have not felt it necessary to give a complete
'blocking' of their movements but only so much as to indicate
especially significant developments. More than would ever become
explicit in actuality, I provide an account of the currents of thought
and feeling that run—in a given interpretation—beneath and between
the words. Whether or not Shakespeare or Burbage or an Elizabethan
groundling would have been conscious of a Stanislavskian subtext,
any coherent interpretation seems to me to require that such
undercurrents be imagined by everyone involved.

The main way in which my rehearsals differ from actual ones is that
my players are concerned solely with making a fresh and valid
interpretation of the script whereas for actual players such a concern
is only one factor among many and—quite properly—not the primary
one at that. For an actual performance, the players owe their first
loyalty to their audience. They must employ their particular talents,
at a particular time and place, in such a way as to give a particular
audience the best time in a particular theatre that they possibly can.
Obviously the script is a key means to that end. Indeed, it is my own
conviction that Shakespeare's theatre-poetry is such that his text is
the best guide a performer could have in giving his audience the best
possible performance. Yet fidelity to the text as such is not the
ultimate concern.

For my players, on the other hand, such fidelity is the prime
concern. For through these imaginary rehearsals I seek to explore the
nature of Shakespeare's presence to actors in rehearsals, as if what is

implicit in his text became audible. He certainly provides more than the raw material to be shaped by performers, as a potter shapes clay. On the other hand, his directions for performance are less precise than those to be found in a musical score. Within broad outlines, he provides options for interpretation. And beyond that he is a dynamic presence where details are concerned, suggesting some choices and resisting others.[1]

The texts to be rehearsed are arranged in ascending order of difficulty. The discussion of each begins with an analysis that is as uninterpreted as I can make it, bringing out notable features that will be worked into the various narrative interpretations explored in rehearsal. The narratives are followed or accompanied by 'commentaries' which weigh the pros and cons of the options involved. Each discussion concludes with an attempt to hear the 'Voice of the Theatre-Poet' implied in the text.

1. A PASSAGE: *AS YOU LIKE IT* (4. 1. 48–68)

ROSALIND Nay, an you be so tardy, come no more in my sight. I had as lief be wooed of a snail.

ORLANDO Of a snail?

ROSALIND Ay, of a snail; for though he comes slowly, he carries his house on his head—a better jointure, I think, than you make a woman. Besides, he brings his destiny with him.

ORLANDO What's that?

ROSALIND Why, horns, which such as you are fain to be beholden to your wives for. But he comes armed in his fortune, and prevents the slander of his wife.

ORLANDO Virtue is no hornmaker, and my Rosalind is virtuous.

ROSALIND And I am your Rosalind.

CELIA It pleases him to call you so; but he hath a Rosalind of a better leer than you.

ROSALIND Come, woo me, woo me, for now I am in a holiday humour, and like enough to consent. What would you say to me now an I were your very, very Rosalind?

ORLANDO I would kiss before I spoke.

---

[1] For comparable studies, see Judith Milhous and Robert D. Hume, *Producible Interpretation: Eight English Plays, 1675–1707* (Carbondale, Ill., 1985); Philip C. McGuire, *Speechless Dialect* (Berkeley, 1985), especially 'Open Silences and the Ending(s) of *King Lear*'; and John Barton, *Playing Shakespeare* (London, 1984), especially 'Rehearsing the Text: Orsino and Viola' and 'Exploring a Character: Playing Shylock'.

Analysis

This passage comes near the beginning of the make-believe wooing scene between Rosalind and Orlando, with Celia kibitzing under her assumed name of Aliena. In it Rosalind keeps up her disguise as a boy Ganymede, who in turn at various places pretends to be a make-believe Rosalind. Earlier, Ganymede has offered to cure Orlando of his love by impersonating an impossibly difficult mistress (3. 2. 390 ff.). Accordingly, Orlando greets Ganymede as 'dear Rosalind', and it is the make-believe Rosalind who roundly rebukes him for being late. Even after he has asked her pardon, she continues her rebuke, telling him she would as soon be wooed 'of a snail' as by a tardy lover.

In the passage itself, a number of things happen for the first time. Orlando here first breaks off the impersonation, stepping out of the imagined situation by declaring 'my Rosalind is virtuous'. This is his first and most confident use of the expression 'my Rosalind'. His next break-off line—'I would not have my right Rosalind of this mind'—is the expression of a hope, and his final one is the uncertain 'But will my Rosalind do so?'

Rosalind's line—'And I am your Rosalind'—is the first place in which she may be thought to speak in her own person instead of (or as well as) playing the role of Ganymede or the make-believe Rosalind. There are a dozen or so other places of that sort in the scene, but this is the most explicit of them. She may be thought perverse not to abandon all disguise and reveal her true self at once. She herself seems frequently drawn towards such a revelation. Yet on further thought one can see some powerful appeals for her in maintaining her disguise. She understandably needs to assure herself of Orlando's love and worth. He was tongue-tied when they first met in their own persons, his love-poetry is conventional (if prolific), he doesn't look as though he is suffering from love's wounds. In worldly terms, he is not the most eligible of suitors; he is not bringing her a jointure. Moreover, she is able through her impersonation to express and explore her own feelings about him. Her role-playing, for example, allows her to give vent to her real impatience at Orlando's lateness. And it allows her in his presence to imagine their whole relationship, beyond wooing to marriage to child-breeding. In passing, she pictures him 'out of his apparel'. Beyond all this, what a luxury to be wooed, and exactly to one's liking, yet without having to make committed response!

Celia's line—'It pleases him to call you so; but he hath a Rosalind of a better leer than you'—represents the first and only time in the scene that she intervenes on her own initiative. Her intervention seems intended to keep the impersonation going. She has good reason to do so. For her friend's sake, she knows that Rosalind is enjoying the game she is playing and is helping to keep her from undoing it. For her own sake, Celia wants to retain her friendship with Rosalind as long as possible; she is feeling a bit left out as it is, and if Rosalind reveals herself immediately, she will be left out altogether.

This evidence suggests that something noteworthy happens at this point, but it is not easy to decide exactly what. Why does Celia intervene? Is it to keep the two lovers together? or to keep them apart?—at least enough to sustain the impersonation? How strongly does Orlando in 'my Rosalind is virtuous' protest the implied insult to the virtue of the real Rosalind? How strongly does he break off the impersonation? Why doesn't he say something in reply to 'And I am your Rosalind'? To what degree, if at all, does Rosalind say 'And I am your Rosalind' in such a way as to suggest her own voice?

Rehearsal

To explore these questions, let us first imagine a reading which emphasizes a break between Orlando and Ganymede.

Scenario 1. Make-believe Rosalind likes to say unexpected, intriguing things that will engage Orlando's interest and provoke a response. So she has introduced the superiority of a snail to Orlando as a lover and now enlarges on the invidious comparison: 'Besides, he brings his destiny with him.'

Good-humouredly drawing out his pretty new friend, Orlando responds, 'What's that?' Her reply is witty. 'Why horns', was predictable, perhaps; but she goes on to put the blame on husbands, such as Orlando, for the loss of reputation that attends their wives' infidelity. How much more considerate is the snail, who, by already wearing his horns at marriage, forestalls any slander of his wife.

Orlando, however, is not amused. It's the honour of his beloved Rosalind that by implication Ganymede is besmirching, and he will have none of it. 'Virtue is no hornmaker, and my Rosalind [unlike your version of her] is virtuous,' he protests. A very mocking make-believe Rosalind might assume an exaggeratedly pious pose, hands held in prayer, at 'And I am your Rosalind'. At any rate, Orlando turns heel and starts off.

Celia then as Aliena tries to gloss over the break, 'It pleases him to call you so'; he is anything but pleased! Does she hurry after him to bring him back? Taking his side in the dispute, she adds: 'He [presumably] hath a Rosalind of a better leer than you.' Or, as an aside in her own voice to the real Rosalind, she might with these words rebuke her friend for 'misusing their sex' (as she will put it at line 201) and imply that Rosalind is being too off-putting for her own good.

Make-believe Rosalind takes her point and progressively coaxes Orlando back: 'Come, woo me, woo me.'

Scenario 2. An alternative reading might emphasize 'And I am your Rosalind' and her desire to break through her impersonation and speak in her own voice.

After 'prevents the slander of his wife', Orlando has had enough of this impersonation, and is not about to stand still for even playful aspersions on his beloved's virtue: 'Virtue is no hornmaker, and my Rosalind is virtuous,' he roundly declares.

As she shows to the audience but not to him, the real Rosalind could not be more pleased, to be 'his' Rosalind and have him stand up for her good name. She cannot help herself saying in her own voice, 'And I am your Rosalind'. Their eyes meet, and (as at their first meeting) Orlando finds himself struck dumb. He is at once enchanted and bewildered by the strange charm of this boy he has met in the forest. They seem about to embrace.

Seeing this, Celia hurries to intervene. 'It pleases him to call you so,' she says as Aliena. But then drawing her friend apart, she reminds her that she is not exactly looking her best.

Rosalind takes her advice to the extent of returning clearly to role as make-believe Rosalind, motioning Orlando to her, 'Come, woo me', but her mood continues from their near embrace. When Orlando is still unable to speak after the second 'woo me', she adds encouragement: 'for now I am in a holiday humour, and like enough to consent.' And when he still does not speak, she steps out of her role as make-believe Rosalind and prompts him as Ganymede: 'What would you say to me now an I were your very, very Rosalind?' Secretly she is still very very much relishing being 'his' Rosalind. Only now does Orlando speak, but his words carry over from his earlier feeling: 'I would kiss before I spoke.' At which Rosalind almost obliges with a kiss. Stopping herself as much as him with 'Nay', she then turns the impulse aside with 'you were better speak first . . .'.

Scenario 3. A third alternative might combine both Orlando's impulse to break off the impersonation and Rosalind's to break through it.

After 'slander of his wife', Orlando gives Ganymede a half-serious push, as a way of saying, 'You're speaking of the woman I love' before adding with sincerity: 'and my Rosalind is virtuous.' He turns and starts to walk away until Rosalind says, in her own voice, 'And I am your Rosalind.' This brings him to a halt and strikes him dumb. As he tries to collect himself and find words, Celia intervenes. After the bewildering experience of wanting to kiss this boy who for a moment magically seemed to become Rosalind, Orlando with a little coaxing by make-believe Rosalind ('woo me') returns and regains his composure. Indeed he is self-possessed enough to turn his disturbing impulse around and threaten Ganymede with a kiss, just to see how cleverly the boy can talk his way out of it.

Commentary

All three of these alternatives are within the range of valid interpretation. In one way or another all three contribute to the dramatic tension of the passage, which—like that of the whole episode—depends on whether the multiple impersonations will be sustained. The first is the least interesting of the three because it denies Rosalind an active role in the exchange; she merely reacts to what Orlando does. If Orlando is very displeased with Ganymede's insult, this version requires a special, reverse reading of Celia's 'It pleases him to call you so'. The second alternative gives Rosalind an active role, but at the expense of Orlando. And her breakthrough to her own self overly anticipates later ones in the scene, especially at the mock-wedding. Some version of the third alternative, combining and moderating the other two, seems to me the most attractive.

The Voice of the Theatre-Poet

This passage illustrates several typical features of Shakespeare's presence to actors in rehearsal. He provides a highly flexible script, as with 'Come, woo me, woo me' in which the repeated clauses and the possible pauses between them allow the performers of Rosalind and Orlando to fine-tune the amount of coaxing she gives and he requires. When the words and situation are given their full due, Shakespeare's presence tends to moderate and enrich the more extreme and simplified versions of the first two alternatives. Orlando does to a degree break off the impersonation, Rosalind may well to a degree break through it. By playing the two off against one another, Shakespeare keeps either from becoming too heavily dominant. 'Keep it light,' he seems to be saying to the actors, 'don't lock into a single tone, stay flexible.' Thus the audience may savour the piquancy of the impersonation. It doesn't want it broken off but can enjoy its precariousness, secure in the knowledge that Celia is there to set things to rights if necessary.

2. A PASSAGE: *HENRY V* (4.8. 58–73)

KING HARRY
>   Here, Uncle Exeter, fill this glove with crowns
>   And give it to this fellow.—Keep it, fellow,
>   And wear it for an honour in thy cap
>   Till I do challenge it.—Give him the crowns.
>   And captain, you must needs be friends with him.

FLUELLEN   By this day and this light, the fellow has mettle enough in his belly.—Hold, there is twelve pence for you, and I pray you to serve God and keep you out of prawls and prabbles and quarrels and dissensions, and I warrant you it is the better for you.

WILLIAMS   I will none of your money.

FLUELLEN   It is with a good will. I can tell you, it will serve you to mend your shoes. Come, wherefore should you be so pashful? Your shoes is not so good. 'Tis a good shilling, I warrant you, or I will change it.

>   *Enter [an English] Herald*

KING HARRY   Now, herald, are the dead numbered?

Analysis

Stage movements and gestures are as open to interpretation as is the dialogue, if not more so. For often, as in this passage, a key stage direction is missing from all surviving texts. Except for Williams's one line 'I will none of your money', the text gives no direct indication of how he responds when the King offers him the glove filled with crowns and then Fluellen offers him a shilling. The questions for interpretation are: what are the valid options for his response? What are the pros and cons of these options? What possibilities should be ruled out?

The passage comes towards the end of the 'band of brothers' phase of the action, discussed in Chapter 2. In it the King follows through on the altercation he had with Williams on the eve of battle, when he was in disguise as Harry Le Roi. This episode amounts to an elaborate practical joke, designed by the King (and Shakespeare) to tie up a loose end. The King may feel it a point of personal honour to clear the air of the challenges—and the exchange of gloves—that occurred during the earlier altercation. In the scene just before this one, the King had encountered Williams, still wearing the King's glove in his cap; they had discussed the niceties of honour as to settling the dispute (suppose Williams's 'enemy is a gentleman of great sort, quite from the answer of his degree', what then?); and the King had set up arrangements for Williams's confrontations, first with Fluellen and then with himself.

When the King reveals to Williams that ''Twas I indeed thou promised'st to strike', their exchange is as follows:

WILLIAMS   All offences, my lord, come from the heart.
Never came any from mine that might offend your majesty.
KING HARRY   It was ourself thou didst abuse.
WILLIAMS   Your majesty came not like yourself. You appeared to me but as a
common man. Witness the night, your garments, your lowliness. And what
your highness suffered under that shape, I beseech you take it for your own
fault, and not mine, for had you been as I took you for, I made no offence.
Therefore I beseech your highness pardon me.

(4. 8. 47–57)

Rehearsal

Let us look closely at the 'gloveful of crowns' passage and imagine the options it affords for interpretation.

Scenario 1. Williams accepts the King's largesse and eventually accepts Fluellen's shilling as well. The understanding King not only 'pardons' his outspoken subject but royally rewards his mettle for thinking so well on his feet. It takes a little while for Exeter to fill the glove with crowns, during which time Henry tells Williams to keep the glove. The repeated word 'fellow' has a strong note of 'fellowship' in it. Not putting too fine a point on questions of honour, Williams good-naturedly accepts the King's gift in the spirit of reconciliation in which it is given and as a compensation for the practical joke played upon him. He silently accepts the gift after 'Give him the crowns', his acceptance being the cue for the King's 'And captain, you must needs be friends with him'. Note the word 'And'.

Williams is still angry with Fluellen because of their recent altercation and put off by the officiousness of his sermonizing; hence he declares, 'I will none of *your* money'.[2] But he is finally won over by Fluellen's assurance that the shilling is offered 'with a good will' and by his solicitous promise that it is a good coin or he will change it.

Scenario 2. Williams is abject in his acceptance of the crowns and the shilling. He has made a very cogent defence of his conduct, which was essentially complete at 'for had you been as I took you for, I made no offence' (4. 8. 55–6). Why, then, does he go on to say, 'Therefore I beseech your highness pardon me'? Is it because the King seems unresponsive to his logic and threateningly remote? There are a

[2] Herbert Coursen suggests this emphasis in *The Leasing Out of England* (Washington, DC, 1982), 205.

number of reasons to think so. In the speech just before, the king had
used the royal plural: 'It was ourself thou didst abuse.' When, shortly
before, the King had revealed himself as his antagonist, Williams had
stopped referring to the King as 'my liege' and begun addressing him
as 'your majesty' or 'your highness'. In their first dispute, Williams
expatiated on his feeling of the overwhelming power of the King as
compared with that of a common soldier:

That's a perilous shot out of an elder-gun, that a poor and a private displeasure
can do against a monarch. You may as well go about to turn the sun to ice with
fanning in his face with a peacock's feather . . .   (4.1. 196–200)

The strict path of honour had been fully spelled out by Fluellen and
with the King's confirmation (4. 7. 117–49). When Williams explained why he was wearing a glove in his cap, the King asked
Fluellen, 'Is it fit this soldier keep his oath?' Fluellen opined that 'He
is a craven and a villain else'. When the King raised the supposition
that 'his enemy is a gentleman of great sort, quite from the answer of
his degree', Fluellen maintained that 'Though he be as good a
gentleman as the devil is, as Lucifer and Beelzebub himself, it is
necessary, look your grace, that he keep his vow'. The King concluded: 'Then keep thy vow, sirrah, when thou meetest the fellow.'
(Note the deprecating 'sirrah'.) Williams apparently had no hesitation
in asseverating, 'So I will, my liege, as I live'.

In the event, however, Williams does not keep his vow. It makes a
difference when the case is not hypothetical but real and the 'gentleman of great sort' the King. Instead, Williams 'beseeches' the King's
pardon, perhaps on his knees. The King's gift thus rewards Williams's
humbled acceptance of his role as subject.

Williams's initial refusal of Fluellen's shilling may in part represent
a taking-out on the captain of the pride he has had to swallow with the
King. When reminded of his poverty (the hole in his shoes), however,
Williams at last accepts the shilling, thus anticipating Pistol's
subjugated acceptance of Fluellen's groat in the next scene.

*Scenario 3. Williams at first resists taking the crowns as well as the
shilling: eventually he accepts the crowns but may or may not accept
the shilling.* The sequence of the King's commands—'give it to this
fellow.—Keep it, fellow' (referring in this reading to the grammati-
cally antecedent 'glove with crowns'), and the repeated 'Give him the
crowns'—reflects a self-respecting holding back on Williams's part.
Perhaps he at first accepts the crowns, then starts to give them back

(his integrity is not to be bought), thus occasioning the King's 'keep it, fellow', but is finally overborne by the King's insistence.

Williams again starts to accept Fluellen's coin because Fluellen says '*There* is twelve pence' rather than '*Here* is twelve pence'. He then gives it back with 'I will none of *your* money'.

A subvariant within this scenario would turn on whether Williams finally accepts or refuses the shilling, the latter choice of course making a stronger statement about his independence.

Scenario 4. Williams keeps neither the King's crown nor Fluellen's shilling. His emphasis in 'therefore I beseech your highness pardon me' falls on *therefore*, following logically from 'had you been as I took you for, I made no offence'. 'Beseech' is a form of earnest request rather than of imploring, the 'pardon' sought is for an imputed wrongdoing rather than a real one. The King's line 'And captain, you must needs be friends with him' is a blandly worded call for reinforcement in the face of Williams's recalcitrance. His staunch resistance may prompt Fluellen's expression of grudging admiration, 'the fellow has mettle enough in his belly'.

As in Scenario 3, Williams may at first accept, then return the crowns; but in this scenario, he stands firm in his refusal of the shilling. Having maintained his resistance to the King's offer, he would scarcely be at all receptive to Fluellen's. His 'I will none of your money' thus applies to his rejection of both offers. Fluellen still doesn't give up, but Williams is spared his further importunities by the arrival of the herald.

Commentary

As different as they are, all four of these scenarios seem to me within the range of valid interpretation, options that Shakespeare has built in to his text. What can be said for and against each?

Scenario 1 is the one that has most commonly been performed. It comes closest to the King's own way of looking at the incident—as a bit of comic relief after the strains of battle. 'I will none of your money' does give a jolt to the King's plan, but its reference can be localized to Williams and Fluellen, with the King at a considerable distance. Williams, for example, might be shown to be not only 'blunt' (4. 7. 174), but with a temper, as shown in the initial dispute. Fluellen could be very officious and condescending in his 'pray you to serve God, and keep you out of prawls and prabbles and quarrels and dissensions'. Their earlier contention might be very fierce. Even this flare-up might be rapidly reconciled by Fluellen's more caring comments in his next speech.

This scenario strongly favours the King. Although his treatment of his subordinates may seem high-handed (not only towards Williams but towards Fluellen, whose loyalty and trust he imposes upon without apology or compensation), rank has its privileges. The King's conduct can be seen as a bit of rough-and-ready horseplay with his men, which he earlier takes commendable care to keep from getting out of hand (4. 7. 167–80).

The scenario would suit best a king who clearly used the expression 'band of brothers' only as a manner of speaking and in which its breaking up would receive the least possible attention. In general, it would go along with a light reading of the lines, passing over the suggestions in the text of the deeper preoccupations of the play. In particular, it would play down the resonance of Williams's forthright integrity. This is the chief shortcoming of Scenario 1, for Williams's integrity is a dramatic value that is powerfully established in the initial philosophical debate on the eve of battle and is reaffirmed by his thoughtful defence here that 'all offences come from the heart'.

So far as I know, *Scenario 2* has not previously been seen as an option, either by performers or critics. It is severely critical of both the King and Williams. It would ask a great deal of both the audience and the actor of Williams. In order to realize that Williams is failing to 'keep his vow', the audience needs to recall his exchange on the subject with the King and Fluellen in the previous scene. And this realization would run counter to our general impression of Williams as an unusually self-respecting personality. His performer would have to make his 'mettle' clear while showing that under supreme duress it might none the less give way. The King's largesse, in turn, would come across as a reward to his subject for knuckling under.

Disturbingly, the effect would be that of a practical joke that had gone too far and gone sour (as with the excessive humiliation of Malvolio). The upshot would be a heavy indictment of the King, who—far from elevating his comrades-in-arms to nobility and even brotherhood—would have succeeded only in reducing Williams to 'a craven and a villain'.

Scenario 3 gives Williams an opportunity to act on his convictions to an extent, since he shows a self-respecting capacity to resist blandishment. But it also somewhat compromises his integrity, since he ultimately accepts the King's conscience-money. The King is also treated more subtly. He has his way in the end but is more discomfited than in Scenario 1. This is the most complex and evenly balanced of the options. It is my personal favourite because it reflects most fully and sensitively the mixed evidence I find in the episode. But unless it is strongly enacted it may lack clarity and impact.

Scenario 4 strongly favours Williams and makes the King's shortcomings stand out in contrast. It requires, however, some special reading of lines having to do with Williams's ability to stand up to the King.

In this scenario Fluellen might play an especially important role. While *he* feels that 'Your grace does me as great honours as can be desired in the hearts of his subjects' (4. 7. 157–8), Fluellen's words, for us, unwittingly underline the King's lack of sensitivity towards his subjects. Just before Henry launches into the elaborate duplicities of his practical joke, Fluellen declares 'I need not to be ashamed of your majesty, praised be God, so long as your majesty is an honest man'. 'God keep me so' is the King's response. 'In my conscience' is of course a habitual expression of Fluellen's that resounds in this passage; it is turned towards the King when Fluellen asks the King's support: 'I hope your majesty is pear me testimony and witness, and will avouchment that this is the glove of Alençon that your majesty is give me, in your conscience now' (4. 8. 36–9). The King does not reply. How could he and keep up the appearance to Fluellen of being an 'honest man'?

This scenario makes it very clear that the band of brothers has broken up, and that it is in large part the King's own doing.

What are the limits of interpretation? To my knowledge, no one has thought that Williams might refuse the King's crowns but accept Fluellen's shilling, or even be undecided about accepting it. Those theoretical possibilities, it seems to me, can be ruled out. As a practical example of a mistaken scenario, consider in detail the staging of the incident in the 1975 Royal Shakespeare Company production, with Alan Howard as Henry V and Dan Meaden as Williams. The footnotes to the published text give a particularly thoughtful ventilation of the issues involved, but the choices made in performance seem to me none the less wrong:

On 'Keep it, fellow', Williams refuses the money. Henry then tips the money (in a pouch) out of the glove, and on 'And wear it for an honour in thy cap', taps Williams with the glove on both shoulders, as if to knight him. 'Give him the crowns' becomes almost humorous. Having established his integrity, the money could be accepted by Williams, and was.

Director Terry Hands finds the 'semi-knighting' 'over-elaborate', but Alan Howard argues in its defence that the King is here making a final test of Williams's integrity:

Henry for a start uses selfconsciously insulting terms—'fellow', he says to Williams, twice. Exeter fills the glove with crowns; Henry urges Williams to accept it. But what exactly happens between this line and the next—'And wear it for an honour in thy cap . . .' Is Williams supposed to put the glove, plus crowns, into his cap? Clearly not. Something else is suggested. Particularly since Henry then repeats the 'Give him the crowns'. Why would he need to repeat this if Williams had accepted the money? These textual ambiguities, together with the fact that Shakespeare has already deliberately introduced the subject of knighting with Williams 'I warrant it is to knight you, Captain' seem to me clear evidence that Henry (who likes testing people) is testing Williams at this point. Williams refuses the money and earns Henry's respect. He knights him, or prefers him, for this reason. The accepting of the money then carries no moral implications. It can be a joke.[3]

How appealing, and ingenious, Howard's solution is! The 'semi-knighting' allows Williams to keep his integrity without compromise and the King to follow through on his band of brothers promise of ennoblement. It lets Williams have his gloveful of crowns and the King have a successful joke. It is what everyone would very much like to have happen. But it neatly resolves a situation that the text—at least to a degree—leaves hanging, with the arrival of the Herald. And it maintains the fraternal community that, in every other respect, we see the King moving away from. Howard's solution is thus not only 'over-elaborate' but it provides the incident with the happy ending that Shakespeare went out of his way to frustrate.

The Voice of the Theatre-Poet

Comparison of the RSC version with the four valid scenarios I have sketched can help us to hear Shakespeare's voice, even within the interpretative options his text allows. The RSC version relaxes the tension we feel towards both Williams and the King whereas all four of the other scenarios sustain a tension, whether towards one or the other or both. 'Whatever you do', Shakespeare seems to be saying, 'keep some tension there.' One can see how it is to his larger purpose to do so. For the tension not only maintains dramatic interest but helps to make us aware—in one way or another—that the band of brothers is disbanding.

---

[3] *The Royal Shakespeare Company's Production of Henry V*, ed. S. Beauman (Oxford, 1976), 210–11.

3. A SCENE: *MACBETH* (I. 7. 28–82)

Enter Lady Macbeth
How now? What news?

LADY MACBETH
He has almost supped. Why have you left the
chamber?

MACBETH
Hath he asked for me?

LADY MACBETH   Know you not he has?

MACBETH
We will proceed no further in this business.
He hath honoured me of late, and I have bought
Golden opinions from all sorts of people,
Which would be worn now in their newest gloss,
Not cast aside so soon.

LADY MACBETH   Was the hope drunk
Wherein you dressed yourself? Hath it slept since?
And wakes it now to look so green and pale
At what it did so freely? From this time
Such I account thy love. Art thou afeard
To be the same in thine own act and valour
As thou art in desire? Wouldst thou have that
Which thou esteem'st the ornament of life,
And live a coward in thine own esteem
Letting 'I dare not' wait upon 'I would',
Like the poor cat i'th' adage?

MACBETH   Prithee, peace.
I dare do all that may become a man;
Who dares do more is none.

LADY MACBETH   What beast was't then
That made you break this enterprise to me?
When you durst do it, then you were a man;
And to be more than what you were, you would
Be so much more the man. Nor time nor place
Did then adhere, and yet you would make both.
They have made themselves, and that their fitness now
Does unmake you. I have given suck, and know
How tender 'tis to love the babe that milks me.
I would, while it was smiling in my face,
Have plucked my nipple from his boneless gums
And dashed the brains out, had I so sworn
As you have done to this.

MACBETH   If we should fail?

LADY MACBETH   We fail!
  But screw your courage to the sticking-place
  And we'll not fail. When Duncan is asleep—
  Whereto the rather shall his day's hard journey
  Soundly invite him—his two chamberlains
  Will I with wine and wassail so convince'
  That memory, the warder of the brain,
  Shall be a fume, and the receipt of reason
  A limbeck only. When in swinish sleep
  Their drenchèd natures lies as in a death,
  What cannot you and I perform upon
  Th'unguarded Duncan? What not put upon
  His spongy officers, who shall bear the guilt
  Of our great quell?
MACBETH   Bring forth men-children only,
  For thy undaunted mettle should compose
  Nothing but males. Will it not be received,
  When we have marked with blood those sleepy two
  Of his own chamber and used their very daggers,
  That they have done't?
LADY MACBETH   Who dares receive it other,
  As we shall make our griefs and clamour roar
  Upon his death?
MACBETH   I am settled, and bend up
  Each corporal agent to this terrible feat.
  Away, and mock the time with fairest show.
  False face must hide what the false heart doth know.

                                        Exeunt

Analysis

As a result of his interchanges with Lady Macbeth in this scene, Macbeth must convincingly reverse his decision concerning the assassination from: 'we will proceed no further in this business' to: 'I am settled, and bend up / Each corporal agent to this terrible feat.' His inner change, however, is not as drastic as these words suggest. In his immediately preceding soliloquy and other speeches, Macbeth has clearly been of two minds about the matter. It is not as though his change is from an unreservedly favoured choice to a previously abhorrent one; he is attracted towards both alternatives. His initial declaration is thus the outcome of an agonized process. And even after his final reversal to the contrary choice he expresses some misgivings. His change of heart is not total on either side. But from here on his decision is irrevocable. This is the moment at which he crosses his Rubicon.

Macbeth's final pronouncement ('I am settled') signalizes an already accomplished fact. Exactly where the essential turning-point in his change of mind is reached Shakespeare leaves to interpretation. He does, however, give certain pointers. One can be sure that Macbeth is still maintaining his initial decision against the deed at 'I dare do all that may become a man'. 'If we should fail?' marks an important change of some sort. It is a question after a series of declarative sentences; it changes the subject from whether the deed should be done to whether it can be done successfully, if at all. After this question, Macbeth expresses no more resistance to the assassination. His next speech also marks a change. For the first time he expresses admiration for Lady Macbeth and enters positively into her line of thought, as he develops her plan to put the blame on the two chamberlains. But exactly where or why Macbeth's decisive change occurs is not specified. Perhaps there is no clear, single point of decision. By making Macbeth's speeches so short, Shakespeare protects the heart of his hero's mystery. It is never fully revealed why he kills Duncan.

The decision, however, is his. Lady Macbeth is without doubt the decisive influence upon his change. She leaves no question whatsoever about what she wants him to decide, but the line of decision is in his words. When he says 'We will proceed no further in this', she does not say, 'Oh yes we will' or words to that effect. Instead she goes to work to bring him to change his mind. She proposes but he disposes.

Macbeth moves at his own pace. Lady Macbeth always answers his questions; he never directly answers a single one of hers. His answers come at his own time and in his own way. When she asks, 'Why have you left the chamber?' he might have answered directly 'I've been having second thoughts about going ahead with this great business'. Instead of giving her a direct answer, he first follows his own line of thought, 'Hath he asked for me?' Her question does not receive its answer until he makes his pronouncement, 'We'll proceed no further . . .'.

She on the other hand responds immediately to his question: 'Know you not he has?' (Note his 'hath' in referring to the King and her, impersonal, 'has'.) She might have said simply 'Yes, he has' or 'Yes he has, more than once'. She might have said 'Of course he has' or she might have made the implied criticism stronger by making it explicit and called his question 'a foolish thought' (as she will do later); after all, it is a piece of wishful thinking on his part to imagine that the King would not have noticed or commented on the absence of his host and favourite. Or she might have said 'You know he has', thus indicating that he is intelligent enough in general to know that the question is unnecessary. What she actually says—'Know you not he has?'—implies that she would ordinarily have thought that he would not need to ask the question. Could she have been wrong in this high estimate? Could he be less intelligent and sensible than she had thought? 'I had thought better of you; can you really be less a man than I had believed?'—this is the general nature of her questions throughout the scene.

As challenging as Lady Macbeth's questions to Macbeth are, their tact should also be emphasized. It is true that she uses no endearments; yet neither does she go so far as to call him a fool, drunken boaster, coward, or beast. It is hope (not Macbeth) that she pictures as drunk; it must have been some beast (not Macbeth) that made him break this enterprise to her. She consistently employs euphemisms for the assassination ('this enterprise') and never refers to Duncan as King. She speaks at first in vague and general terms of achieving a desire, fulfilling a promise, not of assassinating a king. Throughout she is ultraresponsive to what Macbeth says and how he says it, picking up immediately not only on the content but the manner of his expression. She uses his image of wearing golden opinions in their newest gloss, to ask 'was the hope drunk / Wherein you dressed yourself?'

This last speech marks a point of change. It is Lady Macbeth's first venture into metaphorical language and also the first time she has associated her husband with contemptible qualities. Her next sentence ('From this time / Such I account thy love') stands out as a declarative sentence in the midst of questions. Note her change at this point and for the rest of this speech to 'thy'. Modern performers often make much of sex as a factor in Lady Macbeth's influence on her husband, yet this is her only explicit reference to romantic love in the scene.

Although this is a scene of high passion and a conflict of wills, there is a line of logic in it that should not be overlooked. In part, Macbeth changes his mind because Lady Macbeth introduces some important factors that he did not consider in his soliloquy. In general, what she does is put herself into this picture. (She is essentially left out of his preceding soliloquy; his 'we' there is an anticipatory royal 'we'.) The first new considerations are the consequences of *not* doing the deed. It would result in the loss of *her* golden opinion of him and of his love since his fidelity to his vows of love would be undermined by his infidelity to his vows of prowess; and (she goes on to emphasize) it would result in his own loss of self-respect: living a coward in his own esteem.

As usual, Macbeth does not respond directly to her questions when asked. He never does respond directly to her repeated charges of bragging and breach-of-promise. Yet his comment when it does come effectively replies to both of her main points: 'I dare do all that may become a man.' He is not worried about being a coward—either in his own eyes or presumably anyone else's, including hers—because he is convinced that anyone who dared to do more than he dares would be inhuman ('none').

After Lady Macbeth's string of questions, her next speeches shift to rational argumentation, in declarative sentences, using 'you'. Again very responsive both to the content and imagery of what few remarks Macbeth makes, she enters into his own logic: 'In that case it must have been some kind of beast (less than a man) that dared to break this enterprise to me since you now say that to do so would make a person not a man at all (none). Just what kind of beast was it?' She would thus reduce his logic to absurdity since he is not a beast. He could have argued back that his earlier thought *was* indeed bestial but that he was not yet reduced to a beast because there is a difference between a thought and an act. But she proceeds to argue that far from being bestial: 'when you durst do it, then you were a man'; and she goes on to challenge his assumption that such daring would destroy his manhood. Quite the contrary, it would enlarge his manhood: to be such a superman would not make him less but 'so much more the man'. You do not even have to be as daring as you thought you did (and were prepared to be). Circumstances have played into your hands. Yet now, instead of capitalizing on this advantage you let it 'unmake' you. She implies that he was merely boasting before and that now circumstances are conspiring to call his bluff. To sharpen her argumentative point, she has progressively strengthened her version of Macbeth's previous commitment; from a 'hope' it becomes 'this enterprise'; now it is a 'sworn' vow. Recurring to her idea of the loss of esteem, in his and her own eyes, she combines the two: if I had sworn to do something even more appalling (brain my nursing child), I would do so.

In a way, Lady Macbeth's extreme image undercuts her own argument, reduces to enormity the assumption on which she has been arguing: that any restraint from carrying out one's desire into action is cowardice. For the kind of determination she is advocating would here result in an act that is obviously unnatural and inhuman. Yet by plunging into Macbeth's imagistic way of seeing things, her words strike deeper than reasoned arguments at what he means by 'none'. His imagination of more than may become a man has paralysed his will to act. For his 'conscience' is of a special sort. He knows his crimes and sins for what they are and labels them as such to himself (assassination, murderous thought, murderer, sold my eternal jewel, etc.). What deters him from committing these acts, though, is not their proscription in a theological scheme but his realization of their social consequences and the horrors he experiences in imagining them, a physiological repulsion against something that goes against the use of nature. Hence the power for him of his image of Duncan's virtues pleading

> like angels, trumpet-tongued against
> The deep damnation of his taking-off,
> And pity, like a naked new-born babe,
> Striding the blast, or heaven's cherubin, horsed
> Upon the sightless couriers of the air,
> Shall blow the horrid deed in every eye
> That tears shall drown the wind.

Lady Macbeth's imagination of something still worse clearly does not have any such paralysing effect on her.

But in Macbeth it prompts: 'If we should fail?' This line is very much subject to interpretation. How is 'failure' to be understood? Failure at a certain stage of their effort?—if so which stage? Or failure in general, at any stage? In particular, is Macbeth wondering whether they have it in them to carry out the dreadful feat at all? Or is he weighing their chances of carrying it out successfully and going on to take the throne?—pondering 'what if something goes wrong?' Either choice breaks the line of discussion. The former is a crucial step back—before arguing about whether we should do it, we should be sure that we are capable of doing it at all; the latter is a very large step ahead—to anticipating problems and providing for contingencies. At any rate, Macbeth is certainly much affected by Lady Macbeth's image because his verbal response to it, 'Bring forth men-children only', which one might have expected earlier, perhaps after 'we'll not fail', is delayed until line 72.

Lady Macbeth's response, in contrast, is a surge of confidence. 'We fail!' may be read as a stoic looking in the face at the possibility of failure or as an incredulous denial of that possibility—if only Macbeth will maintain his courage. Either is tough-minded and affirmative. She then proceeds to introduce three enabling considerations:

1. She sets forth a concrete plan.
2. She proposes that they carry it out together. Macbeth had been unwilling or unable to act according to two previous possibilities: she had proposed that he leave it to her, that all he need do is disguise his

dark looks (he had been unable to do even this but instead withdrew altogether); nor could he decide to do it alone by himself (as his soliloquy indicates). Now she proposes a third method.

3. Perhaps most important, she has the idea of shifting the blame to the chamberlains, which at one stroke relieves him of all the social consequences of which he had expressed such fear.

It remains only for Macbeth to express his admiration for his wife's intrepidity ('Bring forth men-children only') and to second (as if it were his own idea) her proposal to blame the King's guards, adding a few embellishments (to use their very daggers and mark them with blood). As if recognizing the implausibility of the guards thus incriminating themselves, Lady Macbeth leaps to the solution of outdaring anyone—in the face of this *fait accompli*—to say otherwise. At this point Lady Macbeth's challenge becomes complete: If you cannot leave it to me or do it yourself, then you must either lose me or join me; but to join me you must be as undaunted and daring as I am: together we can outdare the world.

Macbeth can then make his conclusive-sounding declaration 'I am settled' and state his resolve to carry out 'this terrible feat' as if it were a fearsome test of his 'corporal agents' rather than an act of treachery and murder. However, his exit line ('False face must hide what the false heart doth know') betrays some remaining misgivings. In the event, he—and Lady Macbeth—will again withdraw early from their intended victim's presence before the King has gone to bed, and Macbeth will need the apparition of the bloody dagger to marshal his way to knavery.

From this analysis it is obvious that the relative strength of Macbeth and Lady Macbeth is a key factor in the interpretation of this scene. In general, the plot does much to define this matter. He must be strong enough to leave his wife behind, beginning with the murder (which he can bring himself to do and she cannot). Yet he must not be so strong that he could have done it without the valour of her tongue. She must be strong enough to make this crucial difference yet not so strong she cannot be progressively left behind. She must be able convincingly to faint at 2. 3. 119 (or to seem to do so) and to regain dominance one last time when Banquo's ghost temporarily unmans her husband. Within these limits, the exact balance and shifts of balance between the two remain to be explored in rehearsal.

Rehearsal

For this rehearsal section, and the remaining ones in this chapter, the reader is asked to imagine that we are assisted by some versatile actors. We will work our way through the passage under consideration, with the actors demonstrating various alternative interpretations while I provide a running commentary, criticizing what the actors have done and directing what they should do next. The present-tense narratives of the 'acted' portions are set off by indentation. Usually this scene is interpreted as one in which a domineering wife overbears a weak-willed husband. As a way of opening fresh alternatives, let us imagine a Macbeth who is as strong as the text permits:

> Macbeth is still lost in thought when Lady Macbeth hurriedly enters, seeking him out. He half-consciously comes back to reality with 'How now?' Then, fully functioning: 'What news?'
>
> She gives the shortest possible answer, with urgency: 'He has almost supped.' Soon the meal will be over and your absence will be even more awkward and noticed, may put Duncan on his guard. She never says: 'We must hurry back or we'll both be missed', but that is what her manner conveys. She takes her stand near the exit, waiting for him to join her. She is irritated with him. Just as he had done at Duncan's arrival, he has left her to do all the hosting; she is thinking: 'When, before, I urged you to beguile the time, that was all I asked you to do, and you're not even doing that.'
>
> When he does not respond, she asks, 'Why have you left the chamber?' even though she can guess the answer, having seen him brooding.
>
> He does not answer her question but proceeds on his own track: 'Hath he asked for me?' He had been desperate to escape an unbearable situation, thought he could slip out unnoticed, must have spent longer in thought than he had intended.
>
> Still irritated, she points out that this is wishful thinking on his part: 'Know you not he has?' Surely you know better than to think otherwise.
>
> To this point they have both stood their grounds.

Commentary

Clearly so large a distance between the two is wrong. It is too abrupt a change from their rapport in the previous scene, too much of an anticipation of the division between them that is shortly to come. A strong Macbeth could afford to come closer to Lady Macbeth if she met him half-way. Let us imagine a beginning in which they are closer together.

Lady Macbeth in her frantic looking does not at first see Macbeth brooding. The sound of her hurried steps causes him to come to. He sees her first: his 'How now?' causes her to turn to where he is, by which time he is quite self-possessed. He comes part of the way towards her with 'What news?' Thinking that he is going to go right back with her at her urgent 'He has almost supped' she makes as if to hurry back again. But seeing that he has stopped, she comes towards him and takes his arm, her irritation mixed with uncertainty and concern: 'Why have you left the chamber?' Perhaps he is ill? or even possibly making preparations for the dread business?

He does not answer her question but asks by way of confirmation, realizing that his longer-than-intended absence may look bad, 'Hath he asked for me?'

With a smile she softens the rebuke in her words and tone, 'Know you not he has?' With a shrug he acknowledges ruefully the wishful thinking of his question. Taking that as her cue she starts to draw him back to the feasting.

But the thought of this, and his physical revulsion at it (which has in part led him to withdraw in the first place) cause Macbeth to jump to the conclusion he had not quite reached in soliloquy. He stops short and declares 'We will proceed no further in this business'. This is my decision and these are my reasons. He doesn't expect her to like it, but there it is.

Commentary

So strong a declaration on Macbeth's part, announcing a unilateral decision, runs counter to his earlier promise 'We will speak further'. Also so positive a decision would be virtually impossible to alter in fifty lines. After the strong first line, the remaining lines in the speech admit, indeed invite, some softening of Macbeth's initial pronouncement, some inclusion of his wife in his thought process:

> We will proceed no further in this business.
> He hath honoured me of late, and I have bought
> Golden opinions from all sorts of people,
> Which would be worn now in their newest gloss,
> Not cast aside so soon.

As an exercise let us imagine the weakest possible rendering of these lines.

Far from looking Lady Macbeth in the eye, Macbeth turns his back on her, speaks 'We will proceed no further in this business' with bravado but little conviction, as though asking her to dissuade him and thus bear the guilt. He turns to her and offers the next two clauses not as explanation but as attempts at persuasion, almost as an appeal.

Commentary

Clearly this is too weak, even for the weakest Macbeth. In this reading Macbeth is already so close to abandoning his negative decision as to rob the rest of the scene of its dramatic conflict. How should Lady Macbeth respond to her husband's veto? with surprise? outrage? She can't be much surprised since from her first soliloquy it's clear that such qualms are just what she would expect from her husband. When she does speak, her words sound like an outburst, but perhaps she is in more control of her outrage than she might seem. Note that she refrains at this point from an obvious counter-argument to Macbeth's reference to 'golden opinions'. She might have said: 'If you enjoy the golden opinion of others as Cawdor, think what you would enjoy as king.' As elsewhere, however, she avoids mention of kingship, for she apparently senses that for Macbeth a divinity hedges it and such a reference might backfire, dissuading Macbeth from its violation. Let us imagine a third reading of Macbeth's veto, one that respects the integrity of Macbeth's decision but not to the exclusion of his wife.

Macbeth looks Lady Macbeth in the eye, 'We will proceed no further in this business.' She reels back at this pronouncement as if he had struck her. Is there a touch of play-acting in her reaction? Taken aback, he offers as explanation, 'He hath honoured me of late, and I have bought / Golden opinions from all sorts of people . . .'. When she turns her back to him at this, he continues as a concession: 'Which would be worn now in their newest gloss / Not cast aside so soon.' As if to say 'Not now but maybe later.'

Having announced the terms on which he will return to the King's presence, Macbeth starts for the door, and this time it is Lady Macbeth who stops him with her outburst, the need to head him off giving edge to her disappointment and anger. She is no longer worrying about the time, no longer speaking in short clauses: this is the time to 'have it out' with her husband. She lashes out, hitting hard. He is surprised, not expecting her to take it quite so hard. Also her words are puzzling at first. Only in successive clauses does the demeaning image emerge of his hope as a drunken braggart now eating his words. He has stopped and turned in puzzlement. At 'green and pale' the whole image at last clicks into place. He turns away from her.

She waits for a response to her questions after 'what it did so freely?' When he says nothing but starts out, she—to stop him—hits still harder, and below the belt: 'From this time / Such I account thy love.' The intimate 'thy' allows her a note of hurt as well as anger. He turns back to her to protest: this is unfair; I deserve some rebuke for raising your hopes and then changing my mind but there is no real connection between my hopes for the kingship and my vows of love to you.

Thinking, none the less, that she has scored a point, she hurries on: that's what I think of you; now what do you think of yourself?

Commentary

The remainder of her speech raises questions about why a strong Macbeth would not walk out on her at this point. Her words are stinging. One reason is that she is introducing considerations he hadn't pondered in the preceding soliloquy: the consequences of not carrying out the assassination. It might also be questioned why Lady Macbeth is repeating herself. She asks him twice in so many words whether he is really a coward and then compares him to the poor cat in the adage. Apparently, she is trying, repeatedly, to draw a response from him.

'Art thou afeard / To be the same in thine own act and valour / As thou art in desire?' Her question, softened by 'thou', makes no mention of killing a king but is couched in terms of fulfilling a desired aim. Drawing no reply, she tries again to prompt him to 'say it isn't so': 'Wouldst thou have that / Which thou esteem'st the ornament of life, / And live a coward in thine own esteem'? Again she judges the act strictly in terms of what he 'esteems' (she uses the word twice). She raises the stakes, questioning now not whether he is in these circumstances 'afeard' but whether he is intrinsically 'a coward'. Still drawing no reply, in her frustration she goes still further, comparing her husband to the poor cat in the adage.

At last, she has drawn blood. Macbeth cries, 'Prithee, peace.' He turns very deliberately to her to say with finality, 'I dare do all that may become a man; / Who dares do more is none.' He thus effectively answers all of her challenging questions. He is confident of his own valour.

Now neither of them is about to go. The issue is joined.

Commentary

Since Lady Macbeth does so much of the talking, she can easily seem
domineering. With a strong, silent Macbeth, however, her talk can
thus be seen as an attempt to draw him out. The same is true of the
next passage.

There is a sharp edge of sarcasm in Lady Macbeth's voice when
she asks: '*What* beast [exactly] was't then / That made you break
this enterprise to me?' He looks down, starts to admit that it was
bestial of him to be thinking in that way. But realizing that she
has struck too hard, that her sarcastic words may boomerang, she
changes her tone and starts glorifying him as he had been before:
'When you durst do it, then you were a man . . .' Still in a tone of
praise she continues trying to arouse his fighting spirit; 'Nor time
nor place / Did then adhere, and yet you would make both.' She
pauses a little, hoping he will say something, then goes on: 'They
have made themselves . . .' When he still doesn't respond but
instead seems paralysed, she ends quietly, more in sorrow than in
anger, with a wry play on words: 'and that their fitness now /
Does unmake you.' Having so far failed to win Macbeth over by
argumentation, or even to draw a response, she then suddenly
changes her tone, touches his arm. 'I have given suck,' she says,
glances at her husband who has now looked up, and with a slight
smile at her homely phrase, she tenderly invokes her love of 'the
babe that milks me', another homely expression. Still holding his
eye at 'Have plucked my nipple from his boneless gums', her
voice turns hard: 'And dashed the brains out . . .' Macbeth, who has
been picturing the domestic scene—she has invaded his way of
imaging things—and lowered his guard, winces as if struck. He
turns away as she concludes, 'had I so sworn / As you have done
to this'.

Commentary

Macbeth's 'If we should fail?' and Lady Macbeth's 'We fail!' are the
lines that are most subject to interpretation in the scene. A weak
Macbeth might essentially capitulate at this point and cravenly plea
for reassurance from his indomitable wife. By way of contrast, let us
imagine a very self-possessed Macbeth, who does not change his mind
until his wife has set forth a plan of action.

At 'And dashed the brains out', Macbeth starts to remonstrate,
realizing during her long pause before her next words that she is

not as shaken by her image as he, reflects that with her nerve to bolster his they might be able to manage it, but what if something went wrong? Then, musingly, he says, 'If we should fail?'

Exultant at his apparent agreement and with a kind of stoic glee at facing up to the worst, Lady Macbeth cries 'We fail!' But when Macbeth doesn't respond in kind, she recovers: 'But [however] screw your courage to the sticking-place / And we'll not fail'.

Commentary

Such a reading minimizes the impact on Macbeth of the horrific image of infant-braining and requires him to cover a great deal of ground, even allowing for pauses before and after the 'had I so sworn' clause. As an alternative, a more sensitive, less self-assured Macbeth might still retain his decision-making powers, the essential source of his strength in this scene. Also Lady Macbeth might not be quite so purely confident as she chooses to sound at this point. Perhaps there is a touch of bravado masking the weakness that will surface later when she can't bring herself to kill Duncan and in the sleep-walking scene. Although her words are vivid, perhaps she does not have so susceptible an imagination as does her husband. Or perhaps by an act of will (or with the help of the powers she earlier invoked) she is able to suppress her sensibilities.

At 'dashed the brains out' Macbeth is appalled at this pre-enactment of the atrocity. His heart is pounding, scalp creeping. When horrible imaginings have such an impact on him, how could he possibly bring himself to carry out the real thing? A fear is released that he had not previously allowed expression, even to himself: 'If we should fail?'

In the face of this fear but rejoicing that he is now talking in terms of 'we', Lady Macbeth must bolster his courage by a bold denial of the possibility of failure: 'We fail!' Out of the question! You need only keep *your* courage, as I have done, and *we* won't fail.

Immediately and with gusto she launches into her plan, walking about, in an ecstasy of confidence, playing on words, throwing in parentheses. She seems to have thought of every-thing—that Duncan (she dares to name him now, but not as king—just an assailable individual) will be not only asleep but *soundly* so; she waxes learned about the workings of the brain.

As she expatiates, Macbeth is in part getting over his shock and marvelling that she is unshaken, that she can 'behold such [imaginary] sights / And keep the natural ruby of your cheeks /

When mine is blanched with fear . . .' (3. 4. 113–15). Indeed she seems to be reveling in its wake! Furthermore, she is providing a detailed plan of action. Perhaps she and I together could manage it, he thinks. But what about the consequences, the bloody instructions that will come home to roost with us when our guilt is known? Blame it on the chamberlains! That solves it in one stroke. What a woman! 'Bring forth men-children only . . .' He joins in her planning: 'Will it not be received / When we have marked with blood those sleepy two / Of his own chamber and used their very daggers, / That they have done't?'

Lady Macbeth exults at his praise and complicity. She nevertheless sees and implicitly acknowledges the implausibility of the self-incrimination by the chamberlains. Her husband has, with enthusiasm and embellishments, seized upon the weakest part of her plan! But who would dare to challenge an accomplished fact? 'Who dares receive it other?' Then, with gleeful complicity at the practical joke the two of them can play on the fearful world, she adds: 'As we shall make our griefs and clamour roar / Upon his death?' That ties up the final loose thread, and Macbeth can declare: 'I am settled . . .'

Commentary

How should they exit? His 'Away, and mock the time with fairest show' may well be addressed to her ('fairest') and echo her advice of duplicity at the end of their first scene together. She would precede him off the stage, as he lingered to express to the audience and himself his sense of inner falsity: 'False face must hide what the false heart doth know.' This would suit a weak Macbeth, overborne, against his better judgement, by his strong-willed wife. At the other extreme, Macbeth's 'Away' might mean 'Let us away'. He might take the lead as they go off together, with him now resolving—as she had urged before—to keep up appearances. This, however, would lose the suggestion in the last line of remaining misgivings. Hence a third alternative, that includes both his independent commitment to the plan and his misgivings about the duplicity it entails:

> With Macbeth's '[Let us] Away', they start off together, and he resolves to 'mock the time with fairest show'. As he hears his own words, however, they cause him to pause and acknowledge with regret the falsity of his heart. Then at her touch, he recalls himself and, as he assumes a convincingly hostlike expression, they make their exit together.

The Voice of the Theatre-Poet

From this analysis and rehearsal, several features of the scene become clear. One is how much Shakespeare is willing to risk in order to maintain Macbeth's mystery and how much he counts on the audience's being intrigued by it. Unless Macbeth is to seem merely henpecked, Lady Macbeth must be careful to balance the fact that she does almost all of the talking by her verbal deference to his will, by her extreme responsiveness to what little he does say, and by her exhortation of his strengths—as she sees them—not just her scorn for his 'weaknesses'. Indeed, in most respects, unless extremely careful attention is paid to the text, a too weak Macbeth and a merely domineering Lady Macbeth are almost certain to result. If the scene is played simply as a struggle of wills, that will be the outcome. The subtler ways in which it is as well a struggle of minds, hearts, souls, psyches, nerves, and imaginations are clearly there in the text but need to be brought out in performance.

On the other hand, as was illustrated in the rehearsal, readings in which Macbeth excludes his wife from his process of decision are likely to lose additional dramatic values. Macbeth's initial veto is an example of how Shakespeare builds into his text opportunities for fine-tuning the degree to which Lady Macbeth is included in her husband's decision-making.

4. A SEQUENCE OF SCENES: HAMLET VS. CLAUDIUS (*HAMLET*, 3. 2. 218–3. 3. 98)

HAMLET (*to Gertrude*) Madam, how like you this play?

QUEEN GERTRUDE The lady protests too much, methinks.

HAMLET O, but she'll keep her word.

KING CLAUDIUS Have you heard the argument? Is there no offence in't?

HAMLET No, no, they do but jest, poison in jest. No offence i'th' world.

KING CLAUDIUS What do you call the play?

HAMLET *The Mousetrap*. Marry, how? Tropically, this play is the image of a murder done in Vienna. Gonzago is the Duke's name, his wife Baptista. You shall see anon. 'Tis a knavish piece of work; but what o' that? Your majesty, and we that have free souls, it touches us not. Let the galled jade wince, our withers are unwrung.

    Enter Player Lucianus

This is one Lucianus, nephew to the King.

OPHELIA You are as good as a chorus, my lord.

HAMLET I could interpret between you and your love if I could see the puppets dallying.

OPHELIA You are keen, my lord, you are keen.

HAMLET It would cost you a groaning to take off mine edge.

OPHELIA Still better, and worse.

HAMLET So you mis-take your husbands. (*To Lucianus*) Begin, murderer. Pox, leave thy damnable faces and begin. Come: 'the croaking raven doth bellow for revenge'.

PLAYER LUCIANUS
Thoughts black, hands apt, drugs fit, and time
    agreeing,
Confederate season, else no creature seeing;
Thou mixture rank of midnight weeds collected,
With Hecate's ban thrice blasted, thrice infected,
Thy natural magic and dire property
On wholesome life usurp immediately.
    He pours the poison in the Player King's ear

HAMLET A poisons him i'th' garden for 's estate. His name's Gonzago. The story is extant, and writ in choice Italian. You shall see anon how the murderer gets the love of Gonzago's wife.

OPHELIA The King rises.

HAMLET What, frighted with false fire?

QUEEN GERTRUDE (*to Claudius*) How fares my lord?

POLONIUS Give o'er the play.

KING CLAUDIUS Give me some light. Away.

[COURTIERS] Lights, lights, lights!
    Exeunt all but Hamlet and Horatio

HAMLET
    Why, let the stricken deer go weep,
      The hart ungallèd play,
    For some must watch, while some must sleep,
      So runs the world away.
Would not this, sir, and a forest of feathers, if the rest of my fortunes turn Turk with me, with two Provençal roses on my razed shoes, get me a fellowship in a cry of players, sir?

HORATIO Half a share.

HAMLET A whole one, I.
    For thou dost know, O Damon dear,
      This realm dismantled was
    Of Jove himself, and now reigns here
      A very, very—pajock.

HORATIO You might have rhymed.

HAMLET O good Horatio, I'll take the Ghost's word for a thousand pound. Didst perceive?

HORATIO Very well, my lord.

HAMLET Upon the talk of the pois'ning?

HORATIO I did very well note him.
    Enter Rosencrantz and Guildenstern

HAMLET Ah ha! Come, some music, come, the recorders,
  For if the King like not the comedy,
  Why then, belike he likes it not, pardie.
  Come, some music.

GUILDENSTERN Good my lord, vouchsafe me a word with you.

HAMLET Sir, a whole history.

GUILDENSTERN The King, sir—

HAMLET Ay, sir, what of him?

GUILDENSTERN Is in his retirement marvellous distempered.

HAMLET With drink, sir?

GUILDENSTERN No, my lord, rather with choler.

HAMLET Your wisdom should show itself more richer to signify this to his
  doctor, for for me to put him to his purgation would perhaps plunge him into
  far more choler.

GUILDENSTERN Good my lord, put your discourse into some frame, and start
  not so wildly from my affair.

HAMLET I am tame, sir. Pronounce.

GUILDENSTERN The Queen your mother, in most great affliction of spirit,
  hath sent me to you.

HAMLET You are welcome.

GUILDENSTERN Nay, good my lord, this courtesy is not of the right breed. If it
  shall please you to make me a wholesome answer, I will do your mother's
  commandment; if not, your pardon and my return shall be the end of my
  business.

HAMLET Sir, I cannot.

GUILDENSTERN What, my lord?

HAMLET Make you a wholesome answer. My wit's diseased. But, sir, such
  answers as I can make, you shall command; or rather, as you say, my
  mother. Therefore no more, but to the matter. My mother, you say?

ROSENCRANTZ Then thus she says: your behaviour hath struck her into
  amazement and admiration.

HAMLET O wonderful son, that can so astonish a mother! But is there no
  sequel at the heels of this mother's admiration?

ROSENCRANTZ She desires to speak with you in her closet ere you go to bed.

HAMLET We shall obey, were she ten times our mother. Have you any further
  trade with us?

ROSENCRANTZ My lord, you once did love me.

HAMLET So I do still, by these pickers and stealers.

ROSENCRANTZ Good my lord, what is your cause of distemper? You do freely
  bar the door of your own liberty if you deny your griefs to your friend.

HAMLET Sir, I lack advancement.

ROSENCRANTZ How can that be when you have the voice of the King himself
  for your succession in Denmark?

HAMLET Ay, but 'while the grass grows . . .'—the proverb is something musty.
      Enter one with a recorder
  O, the recorder. Let me see. (*To Rosencrantz and Guildenstern, taking them*

aside) To withdraw with you, why do you go about to recover the wind of me
as if you would drive me into a toil?

GUILDENSTERN O my lord, if my duty be too bold, my love is too
unmannerly.

HAMLET I do not well understand that. Will you play upon this pipe?

GUILDENSTERN My lord, I cannot.

HAMLET I pray you.

GUILDENSTERN Believe me, I cannot.

HAMLET I do beseech you.

GUILDENSTERN I know no touch of it, my lord.

HAMLET 'Tis as easy as lying. Govern these ventages with your fingers and
thumb, give it breath with your mouth, and it will discourse most excellent
music. Look you, these are the stops.

GUILDENSTERN But these cannot I command to any utterance of harmony. I
have not the skill.

HAMLET Why, look you now, how unworthy a thing you make of me! You
would play upon me, you would seem to know my stops, you would pluck
out the heart of my mystery, you would sound me from my lowest note to
the top of my compass; and there is much music, excellent voice in this
little organ, yet cannot you make it speak. 'Sblood, do you think I am easier
to be played on than a pipe? Call me what instrument you will, though you
can fret me, you cannot play upon me.

Enter Polonius

God bless you, sir.

POLONIUS My lord, the Queen would speak with you, and presently.

HAMLET Do you see yonder cloud that's almost in shape of a camel?

POLONIUS By th' mass, and 'tis: like a camel, indeed.

HAMLET Methinks it is like a weasel.

POLONIUS It is backed like a weasel.

HAMLET Or like a whale.

POLONIUS Very like a whale.

HAMLET Then will I come to my mother by and by. *(Aside)* They fool me to
the top of my bent. *(To Polonius)* I will come by and by.

POLONIUS I will say so.

HAMLET 'By and by' is easily said.   *Exit Polonius*
Leave me, friends.

Exeunt Rosencrantz and Guildenstern

'Tis now the very witching time of night,
When churchyards yawn, and hell itself breathes out
Contagion to this world. Now could I drink hot blood,
And do such bitter business as the day
Would quake to look on. Soft, now to my mother.
O heart, lose not thy nature! Let not ever
The soul of Nero enter this firm bosom.
Let me be cruel, not unnatural.
I will speak daggers to her, but use none.

My tongue and soul in this be hypocrites—
How in my words somever she be shent,
To give them seals never my soul consent.   *Exit*

3.3   *Enter King Claudius, Rosencrantz, and Guildenstern*

KING CLAUDIUS
I like him not, nor stands it safe with us
To let his madness range. Therefore prepare you.
I your commission will forthwith dispatch,
And he to England shall along with you.
The terms of our estate may not endure
Hazard so dangerous as doth hourly grow
Out of his lunacies.

GUILDENSTERN   We will ourselves provide.
Most holy and religious fear it is
To keep those many many bodies safe
That live and feed upon your majesty.

ROSENCRANTZ
The single and peculiar life is bound
With all the strength and armour of the mind
To keep itself from noyance; but much more
That spirit upon whose weal depends and rests
The lives of many. The cease of majesty
Dies not alone, but like a gulf doth draw
What's near it with it. It is a massy wheel
Fixed on the summit of the highest mount,
To whose huge spokes ten thousand lesser things
Are mortised and adjoined, which when it falls
Each small annexment, petty consequence,
Attends the boist'rous ruin. Never alone
Did the King sigh, but with a general groan.

KING CLAUDIUS
Arm you, I pray, to this speedy voyage,
For we will fetters put upon this fear
Which now goes too free-footed.

ROSENCRANTZ *and* GUILDENSTERN
We will haste us.   *Exeunt both*
     Enter Polonius

POLONIUS
My lord, he's going to his mother's closet,
Behind the arras I'll convey myself
To hear the process, I'll warrant she'll tax him home.
And, as you said—and wisely was it said—
'Tis meet that some more audience than a mother,
Since nature makes them partial, should o'erhear
The speech of vantage. Fare you well, my liege.
I'll call upon you ere you go to bed,

And tell you what I know.
KING CLAUDIUS   Thanks, dear my lord.

Analysis

What chiefly happens in this sequence is that both Hamlet and Claudius confirm decisively that the other is his mortal enemy and then react to this confirmation. Somehow Claudius's response to the talk of poisoning in the play-within-a-play shows to Hamlet's satisfaction the validity of the Ghost's account of the murder. In turn, since Hamlet makes it clear that he already knows the argument of the playlet, Claudius probably learns at the same time that Hamlet knows his secret. Even in his soliloquy, however, Claudius never explicitly draws this conclusion. What is positive and more important is that after the playlet he repeatedly speaks of Hamlet as a threat to his own life. Hamlet does, after all, identify the regicide Lucianus as the King's nephew.

One might expect that after this mutual confirmation of enmity, both antagonists would move with all possible speed to act upon it. Yet at the end of this sequence the two are shown in successive moments of utter standstill. Claudius is unable truly to pray and Hamlet decides not to kill the King while he thinks him at prayer.

The other high point of dramatic interest comes in the first part of the sequence. The play-within-a-play involves the two adversaries in an exciting war of nerves. Both are prompted by emotions that run very deep. With both there are important questions as to the degree to which their behaviour is under control. As Hamlet had hoped, and as will be confirmed later for the audience, Claudius's conscience is powerfully stirred. Against Hamlet's pressures, his problem is to keep his poise intact. Hamlet is so excitable, his problem is to keep his pressures on target. His volatility requires a strong cutting edge, lest it seem frivolous. There must be something dangerous in his wild manner that makes him seem capable of dealing with a wild situation where someone steadier might be merely bewildered. Claudius is the massive dam that has a point of weakness; Hamlet is the powerful jet of water that veers wildly yet tellingly across its surface.

Yet in the event the two could hardly have played their cards more skilfully if they had been coolly self-controlled throughout. In his free-wheeling way Hamlet succeeds in working up Claudius to just the breaking-point that reveals what he most wants to know. Claudius does not, however, give himself away to others apart from Horatio. There is no comment to that effect, and Hamlet seems to assume that his discovery is his alone, requiring Horatio's confirmation. For Claudius's conscience is not as strong as Hamlet had hoped. It is strong enough to betray his guilt to his enemy during the play, and—during his attempt at prayer—it causes him to leave himself open to his enemy's attack. Yet it does not prove strong enough to make him 'proclaim his malefactions' publicly; it merely makes him 'blanch'. Nor does it move him to genuine prayer; it merely makes him want to pray. In the end prudence wins out. After this there will be no more unequivocal indications that his conscience is active at all.

The main lines of Claudius's inner life are thus clearly indicated. Its interpretation chiefly requires decisions about matters of degree and timing. How concerned is he when he asks about the argument of the play? At what points does his agitation build towards his breaking it off?

There is much more room for interpretation concerning Claudius's public disclosure of his feelings. Shakespeare's indicators are spare:

1. Claudius asks if there is offence in the argument of the play. His way of asking 'Have you heard the argument? Is there no offence in't?' invites reassurance. After Hamlet's response, he still wants to know 'What do you call the play?' That way of putting it emphasizes Claudius's connection of the play with Hamlet personally.

2. He does something 'upon the talk of poisoning' that we learn a little later confirms his guilt to Hamlet and Horatio. Is this something evident to others on-stage? No one says as much. Is it evident to us in the audience off-stage? The text does not provide us with positive confirmation of his guilt until Claudius refers to 'a brother's murder' in his attempt at prayer.

3. He rises in a way that arouses the Queen's concern and causes Polonius to call off the play.

4. He says, 'Give me some light. Away.'

5. He withdraws, Guildenstern tells Hamlet, to his place of 'retirement marvellous distempered . . . with choler'. Shakespeare leaves it unclear exactly what happens off-stage after Claudius's departure. His focus at this point is on Hamlet, and upon the emissaries who soon are coming to him from behind closed doors. We are given incidental indications about what has been taking place in private. Guildenstern reports the displeasure of the King and Queen. His tone with Hamlet is firmer than usual, perhaps reflecting the tone of his superiors. Somehow it has been decided to proceed with the interview between Hamlet and his mother that Polonius had proposed earlier. The message from mother to son that Rosencrantz delivers— 'She desires to speak with you in her closet ere you go to bed'—has

become more urgent by the time Polonius arrives: 'the Queen would speak with you, and presently.'

There is nothing conclusive in the text to keep the most conscience-stricken of Claudiuses from giving vent to his anger to his Queen and then withdrawing into utter solitude, not to return until he receives the reports of Rosencrantz and Guildenstern. The King is said to be 'in his retirement'; the messengers say that they come from the Queen, specifically. All other evidence, however, suggests that he was accompanied in his 'retirement' by his Queen and confidants. Somehow Rosencrantz knows what his mood is. Later, Polonius will speak of how because of Hamlet's pranks the Queen has 'stood between / Much heat and him' (3. 4. 3–4), and she will tell her son that he 'has his father much offended'. It is the King who receives the emissaries' reports. All in all, it seems likeliest that Claudius has had no opportunity to be alone with his conscience until his soliloquy, the opening lines of which have the sound of a first expression of pent-up agony: 'O, my offence is rank . . .'

6. By the time of his conference with Rosencrantz and Guildenstern Claudius is certainly in enough control of himself to deal effectively with their reports and to contemplate countermeasures. Yet although he emphasizes haste in the English expedition to Rosencrantz and Guildenstern and hurries them off, he himself does not proceed immediately to prepare the necessary dispatches. Instead, as soon as Polonius leaves, he tries to pray.

As for Hamlet, his comments during the play-within-the-play establish an identification of him with it and it with him. He talks whenever there is no dialogue in the playlet. For the most part his comments at this point as in the earlier part of the scene are in response to what others say. But at the beginning of this sequence he takes the initiative in addressing a question to his mother.

When Claudius questions the suitability of the play, Hamlet offers reassurances that do not finally reassure: 'They do but jest' is followed by the stinger, 'poison in jest'. More subtly, he seems to assure the King that the connection with real life is with past events in Vienna, yet in doing so he is still emphasizing the idea of connecting the play directly with real parallels. His remarks grow more and more provocative. At first he says that there is no offence in the play, then he grants that it is 'a knavish piece of work' but not to the innocent. Finally, he dwells on the idea of letting 'the galled jade wince'.

When he then talks with Ophelia, his tone is much as it was before with her. He becomes provocative to Claudius only at the end, after 'leave thy damnable faces'. His next remarks, after Lucianus' speech, are probably addressed to Ophelia. The first and last are incendiary and seem clearly meant for Claudius to hear or overhear. The two between seem incidental.

After confirming Claudius's guilt, Hamlet is not at all inclined to follow up his advantage immediately but rather to celebrate his discovery. He sings or recites quatrains, congratulates himself on his thespian powers, calls for some music. At this point the full dramatic focus is on Hamlet. Yet when the royal emissaries begin to arrive, we realize that those who have gone off-stage have already been regrouping and starting countermoves, efforts which will more and more take the initiative away from him. For the rest of the scene, although Hamlet is at the centre-stage of our attention, we are aware too of his adversary in the wings. In addition to conveying his mother's invitation, the emissaries are also plainly concerned with keeping an eye on him, warding off further mischief, sounding out his 'distemper'. Against this Hamlet fights verbally. He easily wins all of the resulting little battles, all too easily since his interlocutors are not interested in winning them but in keeping him under surveillance. They do not go until he dismisses them. Even then Polonius may linger secretly. He does not report to Claudius until after Rosencrantz and Guildenstern have finished and is able to report that Hamlet is 'going to his mother's closet'.

In the course of these exchanges Hamlet's mood must shift from triumph to renewed and rising hostility. His tone with the emissaries is lightest at the beginning. He reserves his barbs for Claudius and his mother. Indeed, his response to Rosencrantz's pointed query about the cause of his distemper is more than usually forthcoming. Having confirmed that the King is a murderer and thus not a fit occupant of the throne, Hamlet now has good reason for feeling that as next in line he 'lacks advancement' and confides as much. Only in the latter part of their interview does Hamlet vent his hostility directly against Rosencrantz and Polonius. We begin to sense that Hamlet might drink hot blood before he tells us he could.

The movement of Hamlet's 'witching time of night' soliloquy is very much in the halting *Hamlet* rhythm. It begins with a resounding but generalized and relatively brief protestation of virulence. This is cut sharply off when he recalls that he must go to his mother. He checks an impulse which in this mood might lead to murder and modifies his hostility to the extent of restraining it to verbal violence. Thus Shakespeare tunes his hero to the exact emotional pitch required for his 'Now might I do it pat' speech. If he had gone off after his opening five lines, vowing to do 'such bitter business as the day / Would quake to look on', he could hardly have restrained his first impulse to kill Claudius. As it is, his mood at that point is specifically lowered below dagger use. Thus Hamlet is wrought up to just the point where he can credibly say his words, but not quite to the point at which he must act on them.

Rehearsal

As with *Macbeth*, the rehearsal will proceed through the sequence of scenes, exploring options along the way, with the 'acted' segments set off from my running commentary by indentation.

The key interpretative issues in the sequence are: how overtly does Hamlet threaten Claudius and how overtly does Claudius betray his disturbance? and how much is their behaviour a rational war of nerves and how much an emotional outbreak? To explore the range of possibilities, let us first imagine a rendering with maximum concealment and dispassion on both sides.

> At the lull in the play that comes after the Player Queen has left the stage and while the Player King sleeps, Hamlet crosses from his place with Ophelia to where the King and Queen, Polonius, and Rosencrantz and Guildenstern make a group. He wants to make sure that they watch the coming part and to check up on their attentiveness to what has gone before.
>
> As if making small talk during an interval, he asks Gertrude, 'How like you this play?' The Queen confirms that she has been attentive, indeed astute in her reactions: 'the lady protests too much, methinks.' Hamlet, who knows the script, replies, 'O, but she'll keep her word.'
>
> Since Hamlet has this inside information, Claudius wants to be reassured about the rest. In his philistine way, he has thought of the play as a harmless diversion for his worrisome nephew (3. 1. 25–6); yet it begins with talk of royal remarriage, to say nothing of the alarming dumb-show murder. And now it comes out that Hamlet already knows the play. 'Have you heard the argument? Is there no offence in't?'
>
> Hamlet obliges with the invited reassurance: 'No, no, they do but jest.' Very lightly he needles the King by dropping disturbing hints while ostensibly providing background details ('poison in jest', 'a murder'). He stresses that the story concerns a real-life event in Vienna, not Elsinore. Seeing Lucianus about to enter, he goes further with a stinger followed by a reassurance: ''Tis a

knavish piece of work; but what o' that?' While crossing to rejoin Ophelia, Hamlet addresses the auditors generally: 'This is one Lucianus, nephew to the King', thus resembling the 'chorus' that Ophelia then dubs him. While Lucianus makes his 'damnable faces', Hamlet exchanges some badinage with Ophelia, as before treating her as a wanton.

Commentary

Clearly such a rendering is too tame. At this rate, Claudius would never be agitated enough to break off the play, nor would Hamlet be excited enough to egg him on and then crow afterwards. Let us switch to the other extreme and imagine a performance playing for maximum passion and overtness.

Hamlet wants to catch the Queen's conscience as well as the King's. He has called out 'wormwood' at the Player Queen's line 'none wed the second but who killed the first'. After her couplet ('Both here and hence pursue me lasting strife / If, once a widow, ever I be wife.'), he has exclaimed 'If she should break it now!' Now during the lull after the Player Queen's 'Sleep rock thy brain, / And never come mischance between us twain', he crosses over to see if the Queen is getting the point.

'Madam, how like you this play?' he fishes.

The Queen's reply confirms that she has indeed been thinking about the lady's sincerity, but does she draw a parallel with her own? Hamlet seizes the opportunity to underline the moral: 'O, but *she*'ll keep *her* word.'

Alarmed by Hamlet's tone, and his drawing of a parallel with their own situation, Claudius rises, beckons Polonius: he is thinking of calling off the play. Who knows what the next parallel may be? How much does Hamlet know? He demands: 'Have you heard the argument? Is there no offence in't?'

Hamlet, alarmed that his trap may be interrupted, is all reassurance: 'No, no, they do but jest.' Or rather *almost* all reassurance, for he cannot forbear throwing in 'poison in jest', which is enough to make Claudius ask further: 'What do you call the play?'

Commentary

At this point it begins to be apparent that, with so overtly alarmed a Claudius, Hamlet would have to be very reckless indeed to risk saying 'poison in jest'. In the cat-and-mouse game he is playing with

Claudius, Hamlet must throw out hints that are tantalizing enough to keep the King watching and thus be subjected to the provocations of the play. Claudius plays along in order to find out how much the Prince knows, but he can't let Hamlet go so far that he reveals his crime to all. Strong feeling but more guarded disclosure of it is in order on both sides. In particular, for the King to rise at this point over-anticipates the climactic moment later when 'the King rises'.

> When Claudius asks 'have you heard the argument?' there is urgency in his question but he does not rise. His way of asking 'Is there no offence in't?' invites reassurance.
>
> Hamlet cannot resist the parenthesis 'poison in jest', but he emphasizes 'no offence i'th' world'. Even though Gertrude touches his arm calmingly, Claudius still enquires further: 'What do you call the play?' Hamlet's image of the play as a trap is a bit disturbing but the rest of his answer is disarmingly bizarre: 'Marry, how? Tropically.' At this Claudius may look puzzlingly at Polonius, who might silently signal 'far gone, far gone'.
>
> Hamlet's tone becomes matter-of-fact. He drops the hint that a murder is to come but denies local application: 'This play is the image of a murder done in Vienna. Gonzago is the Duke's name, his wife Baptista. You shall see anon.' Seeing Claudius relax a bit, and Lucianus about to make his entry, Hamlet then goes further. He now grants that the play may be offensive to some ('Tis a knavish piece of work') but only to the guilty: 'your majesty, and we that have free souls, it touches us not.' And he gives his thrust a second twist: 'Let the galled jade wince, our withers are unwrung.'
>
> He then heads back to his place by Ophelia, pausing to make his introduction of Lucianus. For the first time he reveals that the murderer is a member of the royal family, an identity that is doubly alarming to Claudius—as an exposure of his crime and a threat on his life by his nephew.

Commentary

The exchange between Hamlet and Ophelia represents a drop-off in intensity. Ophelia initiates it. It may be simply a distraction. Except for the speeches addressed to his mother, all of Hamlet's speeches in this episode are tendentious reactions to what the King and Ophelia have to say. On the other hand, all of the other exchanges play into his hand, and this may too, providing an opportunity for Hamlet to lower the heat on Claudius a bit.

At 'This is one Lucianus, nephew to the King', Claudius signals to Polonius to come over to him. Hamlet, fearing that he has gone too far too soon in alarming Claudius, welcomes Ophelia's 'You are as good as a chorus, my lord' as an opportunity to subside into his earlier, less threatening manner. His badinage with her is very much like their earlier exchange, except this time the King and Polonius are listening closely. Polonius may take 'It would cost you a groaning to take off mine edge' as further evidence of Hamlet's love-sickness for Ophelia.

The actor of Lucianus has either been waiting for the Prince to finish or, as in the dumb show, has been lifting the crown from his sleeping prey, kissing it, and making his damnable faces. After a final shot at his mother ('So you mis-take your husbands'), Hamlet suddenly turns up the heat on Claudius: 'Begin, *murderer*.' And in words that must seem cryptic to everybody else but directly—even physically—threatening to Claudius: 'Come: "the croaking raven doth bellow for revenge".'

Commentary

How should Claudius finally reach his breaking-point? The text suggests several options. The Folio gives the stage direction that Lucianus 'Pours the poison in his ears'. This with Hamlet's 'A poisons him i'th' garden for 's estate' might constitute 'the talk of poisoning' to which Hamlet attributes Claudius's revelation of his guilt. The Quarto editions do not include this stage direction. Following them, the most susceptible of kings might succumb strictly to the *talk* of poisoning. Or the least susceptible of kings might require still greater incitement than the pouring of the poison. Taking his cue from Lucianus's last line that the poison 'On wholesome life usurps immediately' and recalling the Ghost's vivid account of the effect of the poison, the sleeping victim might writhe in agony while Hamlet puts his signature on the re-enactment: 'A poisons him i'th' garden for 's estate. His name's Gonzago. The story is extant, and writ in choice Italian. You should see anon how the murderer gets the love of Gonzago's wife.' To whom is this last speech addressed? Should Hamlet confront Claudius eye-to-eye? If so, he has the problem that the second and third sentences relapse into inconsequential background information. It seems more likely that Hamlet is talking directly to Ophelia as before but keenly aware that the King is listening, and thus dropping more and more telling details amid the incidental information.

What should Claudius's reaction be? It is most unlikely that

Claudius should make an anguished cry for 'light' and rush off, as in the stage tradition and the Olivier film. So overt a reaction runs contrary to Hamlet's repeated seeking of Horatio's confirmation of the break, the fact that the audience has been prepared to watch for a subtle indication ('if he but blench'), that Claudius has time for several lines before his exit, and that most evidence suggests that Claudius was very much in control of himself off-stage afterwards.

Claudius's reactions may be divided into three distinct moments:

1. his involuntary revelation of guilt 'upon the talk of poisoning';
2. his decision to rise;
3. his decision to leave.

The sight of the Player King writhing in agony while the Prince explains 'A poisons him i'th' garden for 's estate' is too much for even Claudius's self-control. He winces, perceptibly to Hamlet and Horatio but not to others on-stage, perhaps not even positively to the audience off-stage. Hamlet continues with his chatter to Ophelia, and then drops another bomb: 'You shall see anon how the murderer gets the love of Gonzago's wife.'

Claudius in the mean time has regained his self-control. As the court reacts with shock to the Prince's scandalous words, he sees his opportunity to break off the play before Hamlet, who has somehow found out all these details of his crime, makes his charges still more explicit.

'The King rises', Ophelia tells Hamlet, who exclaims: 'What, frighted with false fire?' as if he were now going to fire his *real* ammunition.

The King glares at Hamlet. He can see that he will have to silence him immediately, would like in fact to choke him then and there. His agitation is evident enough to cause the Queen to ask 'How fares my lord?' and for Polonius to command that the play should be stopped. Thinking fast, Claudius wonders if he should take charge and have the madcap Prince confined but decides instead that he can sooner break up Hamlet's audience than silence the Prince. In high dudgeon, he calls for 'some light' and stalks out: 'Away.'

Commentary

For the actor playing Hamlet the rest of the scene requires an extended set of transitions. Although his victory over Claudius is almost certainly not the public rout it is in the Olivier film, he still can give full manic expression to his elation, while Horatio, by his brief understatements, tries to calm him. Hamlet, however, must be able to return to full self-possession by his line to Guildenstern, 'I am tame, sir. Pronounce.'

Hamlet's first exchanges with Guildenstern are very much in the wake of what has gone before. His hyperresponsiveness to any sign of guilt in Claudius carries over to his hyperresponsiveness to Guildenstern's words. His good mood also extends into the playfulness of his interruptions and pretended misunderstandings. Guildenstern, on the other hand, is quite put out by these shenanigans. He gives up in disgust when his demand that Hamlet make him 'a wholesome answer' is met by the reply 'Sir, I cannot'. Rosencrantz then takes over, or tries to do so: 'What, my lord?'

Commentary

To whom is Hamlet's following speech addressed?: 'Make you a wholesome answer. My wit's diseased. But, sir, such answers as I can make, you shall command; or rather, as you say, my mother. Therefore no more, but to the matter. My mother, you say?' Frustrating Rosencrantz's attempted interposition, Hamlet might continue to address his remarks to Guildenstern. Or he might have some fun with the change-over, turning back and forth from one to the other in mock bewilderment as to which of them he is supposed to be addressing.

When Rosencrantz instead of Guildenstern responds, 'What, my lord?' Hamlet still directs his answer to Guildenstern: 'Make you a wholesome answer. My wit's diseased.' Then to Rosencrantz: 'But, sir, such answers as I can make, *you* shall command.' Then to Guildenstern: 'or rather, as *you* say, my mother.' Then, as if putting an end to his joke, 'Therefore no more, but to the matter', only then to continue to frustrate the change-over by saying to Guildenstern, 'My mother, you say?' until Rosencrantz, in a no-nonsense manner, takes charge: 'Then thus she says . . .'

Hamlet's tone towards Rosencrantz continues to be friendly enough. When Rosencrantz recalls that 'you once did love me', he replies: 'So I do still', although modifying his affirmation by a double-edged oath: 'by these pickers and stealers.'

Not until after the arrival of the Players with recorders does his tone change decisively.

Commentary

What exactly is going on during Hamlet's speech? 'O, the recorder. Let me see. To withdraw with you, why do you go about to recover the wind of me as if you would drive me into a toil?' To whom does Hamlet say 'To withdraw with you'? To Rosencrantz and Guildenstern, as the *Oxford Shakespeare* editors surmise? or to a Player? The Quarto and Folio editions do not say. What occasions Hamlet's hunting metaphor? As Jenkins explains in the Arden Edition: 'To *recover the wind* is to get to windward. The quarry is allowed to scent the hunter, so that it will run in the opposite direction and into the net (toil).' Something at this point triggers a much more hostile mood in the Prince. Let us imagine that Hamlet addresses 'To withdraw with you' to a Player and starts to leave with him.

> Guildenstern moves to head them off. Part of his assignment is to keep the Prince under surveillance. Hamlet stops short and says to Guildenstern, who is obstructing his path: 'Why do you go about to recover the wind of me?' Guildenstern is apologetic but firm: 'O my lord, if my duty be too bold, my love is too unmannerly.' It is Guildenstern's overt move that provokes Hamlet's eventual 'Why, look you now, how unworthy a thing you make of me!' Even now, however, his tone is one of remonstrance. It is against Polonius, who then appears, that Hamlet aims his most direct attack, ridiculing the self-serving way all three have been humouring his antics. ' "By and by" is easily said' and the heavily ironic 'Leave me, friends' have a sharper edge than any of his previous words to the three.

Commentary

Even with so strong a flow of hostility to build on, the actor playing Hamlet must make a large leap to be ready to 'drink hot blood'. Do bells once more toll the eery 'witching time of night' while the Prince works himself up by thoughts of yawning graves and hell breathing out contagion to this world? Does he draw a dagger at 'do such bitter business' and put it back at 'let me be cruel'? In one way or another the actor of Hamlet must sustain a pitch of intensity that will remain in the memory of the audience during his absence from the stage.

The actor of Claudius has problems that are remarkably similar to those of Hamlet. After the play-within-a-play, he too has had to reach a wrought-up condition that will remain in the audience's memory after his exit. And now, again like Hamlet, he has to suggest a developing mood beneath more superficial exchanges with Rosencrantz and Guildenstern and Polonius. What he desperately wants to do is to withdraw and release his sense of guilt: 'O, my offence is rank!' Instead he must hear out Rosencrantz's extended reprise of Guildenstern's already fulsome expression of loyalty. There are abundant opportunities during this speech for Claudius to show impatience. None the less, the King seems emboldened by their extended declarations of fealty to disclose the threateningness of his intentions, as he urges them at the end to 'Arm you' in order to put fetters upon this fear.

Claudius's Soliloquy

　　　O, my offence is rank! It smells to heaven.
　　　It hath the primal eldest curse upon't,
　　　A brother's murder. Pray can I not.
　　　Though inclination be as sharp as will,
　　　My stronger guilt defeats my strong intent,
　　　And like a man to double business bound
　　　I stand in pause where I shall first begin,
　　　And both neglect. What if this cursèd hand
　　　Were thicker than itself with brother's blood,
　　　Is there not rain enough in the sweet heavens
　　　To wash it white as snow? Whereto serves mercy
　　　But to confront the visage of offence?
　　　And what's in prayer but this twofold force,
　　　To be forestallèd ere we come to fall,
　　　Or pardoned being down? Then I'll look up.
　　　My fault is past—but O, what form of prayer
　　　Can serve my turn? 'Forgive me my foul murder'?
　　　That cannot be, since I am still possessed
　　　Of these effects for which I did the murder—
　　　My crown, mine own ambition, and my queen.
　　　May one be pardoned and retain th'offence?
　　　In the corrupted currents of this world
　　　Offence's gilded hand may shove by justice,
　　　And oft 'tis seen the wicked prize itself
　　　Buys out the law. But 'tis not so above.
　　　There is no shuffling, there the action lies
　　　In his true nature, and we ourselves compelled,
　　　Even to the teeth and forehead of our faults
　　　To give in evidence. What then? What rests?
　　　Try what repentance can. What can it not?
　　　Yet what can it when one cannot repent?
　　　O wretched state, O bosom black as death,
　　　O limèd soul that, struggling to be free,
　　　Art more engaged! Help, angels! Make assay.
　　　Bow, stubborn knees; and heart with strings of steel,

> Be soft as sinews of the new-born babe.
> All may be well.
> *He kneels.*

Analysis

In his soliloquy Claudius 'pours his heart out' only at the beginning and the end. After his initial outburst, he testifies to a feeling of inner deadlock, but then most of the speech is given over to a rational inner debate. In his wish for release from his guilt, Claudius makes plausible, theologically sophisticated arguments designed to make it possible for him to pray, after which, with utter candour, he acknowledges the impossibility of these arguments. At first he asks a series of rhetorical questions about the power of prayer, to which the answer is 'yes' (or would be if the sinner were truly repentant), leading Claudius to conclude: 'Then I'll look up.' But this impulse is immediately countered by a series of questions to which the answer is 'no'. These comprise the bulk of the speech. Claudius then vacillates much more rapidly from the one impulse to the other. His earlier deadlock gives way to a feeling of entrapment. Finally comes his desperate plea for aid, 'Help, angels!' and a bit of wishful thinking, 'all may be well', as he finally succeeds in forcing his knees to bend in attempted prayer. The total effect is of emotion breaking momentarily through rational control but not finally overwhelming it, as is confirmed in the couplet that concludes the scene.

Rehearsal

The problem for the actor playing this speech is to make its complicated patterns evident to an audience. As an exercise, let us imagine a Claudius who is semaphorically demonstrative of his psychic movements.

> He throws himself on his knees for 'O, my offence is rank!' He gets up at 'Pray can I not', walks a little away from the place where he has knelt, faces the audience. He gestures with one hand in the direction he was walking at 'my stronger guilt', and with the other towards his place of prayer at 'strong intent'. At 'stand in pause' he locks his hands together. Looking at his doubled hands, he pictures his 'cursèd hand . . . thicker than itself with brother's blood', then gestures towards the 'sweet heavens' that can wash it white as snow. His next few lines carry him literally as well as figuratively back towards his place of prayer. He kneels again at 'Then I'll look up. My fault is past.' He tries

silently to pray. He rises and walks further and further from his kneeling place as all the considerations that attend retaining the offence come to his mind. He stops at 'What then?' and turns back towards his place of prayer at 'Try what repentance can'. He quickly stops short, however, at 'what can it when one cannot repent?' and stands still in torment for 'O limèd soul that, struggling to be free, / Art more engaged!' He rushes back to his place of prayer at 'Help, angels!' and pleads with his knees and heart to pray as he finally kneels.

Commentary

The exaggerations are obvious. The King begins by saying that he cannot pray, that his knees are stubborn. In general his effort is not to keep praying but to start doing so. Nevertheless, this cartooned choreography may help us to imagine a rendering that will restrain its exaggerations but keep its clarity.

Claudius hurries towards the altar with 'O, my offence is rank!' He starts to kneel but finds he cannot. He extends his right hand towards his guilt, his left hand towards his strong intent, clenches both fists at 'double business bound'. He looks at his right hand at 'cursèd hand' and then briefly but longingly up at 'sweet heavens'. After justifying doing so, he then fully implores cleansing mercy and pardon: 'Then I'll look up. My fault is past.' He again tries to kneel but turns away at 'but O, what form of prayer / Can serve my turn?' He then paces back and forth during the many lines until his final rush to the altar and successful effort to bend his knees (if not his heart) in prayer.

Hamlet's Soliloquy

HAMLET Now might I do it pat, now a is praying,
  And now I'll do't,
     [*He draws his sword*]
           and so a goes to heaven,
And so am I revenged. That would be scanned.
A villain kills my father, and for that
I, his sole son, do this same villain send
To heaven.
O, this is hire and salary, not revenge!
A took my father grossly, full of bread,
With all his crimes broad blown, as flush as May;
And how his audit stands, who knows save heaven?
But in our circumstance and course of thought
'Tis heavy with him. And am I then revenged

To take him in the purging of his soul,
When he is fit and seasoned for his passage?
No.
He sheathes his sword
Up, sword, and know thou a more horrid hint.
When he is drunk asleep, or in his rage,
Or in th'incestuous pleasure of his bed,
At gaming, swearing, or about some act
That has no relish of salvation in't,
Then trip him that his heels may kick at heaven,
And that his soul may be as damned and black
As hell whereto it goes. My mother stays.
This physic but prolongs thy sickly days.   *Exit*
KING CLAUDIUS
My words fly up, my thoughts remain below.
Words without thoughts never to heaven go.   *Exit*

Analysis

When Hamlet happens upon Claudius kneeling, he realizes that now
he might do it pat, resolves that he will do't, and then speaks as if he
had already done so: 'and so a goes to heaven, / And so am I revenged.'
At some point in these lines he has drawn his sword. He then,
however, stops himself. He ponders the fact that to kill his enemy
while in the holy act of prayer would send him to heaven, whereas
Claudius had killed his father with his sins upon him. He decides not
to kill him. Instead, he puts up his sword, deciding to wait until his
enemy is 'about some act / That has no relish of salvation in't', and
thus send his soul to hell.

The most notable prosodic features of the speech are the two
incomplete lines, metrical gaps which often in Shakespeare signal an
unspoken event in the interim. Also the parallel rhetorical structure
of 'now a is praying, / And now I'll do't' and 'And so a goes to heaven, /
And so am I revenged' suggests parallel movements, whether physical
or spiritual.

A particular problem of the diction is that Hamlet, who is always
hyperresponsive to language and never more so than in the scene just
before, seems slow to catch the implication of his own words 'now a is
praying . . . and so a goes to heaven'.

Many interpreters have felt that Hamlet is rationalizing in this
passage, not giving his real reasons for postponing the killing of
Claudius. Two main considerations do make one wonder about the
validity of his words. One is that Hamlet has hitherto glorified his
father; now for the first time he dwells upon his sins, which fit very

neatly indeed into his argument. The other is that Claudius after Hamlet's exit reveals that he was not praying at all, thus immediately undercutting Hamlet's decision and suggesting that he may be self-deceived. Neither of these considerations, however, is conclusive. We have heard the Ghost tell Hamlet of his sins. And the ironic point that appearances are deceiving need not have the further implication that the one deceived wishes to be deceived. In the long run, Hamlet's parting shot at Claudius proves true: 'This physic but prolongs thy sickly days.'

Rehearsal

Let us take the Prince at his word, accepting that he genuinely wants to kill Claudius but decides to wait for a more suitable occasion. The actor of Hamlet thus has a problem in sincerity that is parallel to that of the actor of Claudius in his soliloquy. Each must persuade his audience that he truly wants to do something (pray, kill the King) that his reason tells him he cannot or should not do and that in the event he does not do.

Much depends on when exactly Hamlet draws his sword from its scabbard and when and why he decides to put it back (neither stage direction in the quoted edition is definitive). Let us first imagine a Hamlet who, while genuinely wanting to kill the King, has the least possible determination to do so and who most readily talks himself out of completing the act.

Hamlet hurries across the stage, bound for his interview with his mother. He catches sight of Claudius kneeling with his back to him. He sees his opportunity ('Now might I do it pat') and draws his sword. He starts to strike the King after 'And now I'll do't' but something holds him back from doing so. His next sentence is a piece of exhortation to himself to follow through on this impulse: 'and so a goes to heaven, / And so am I revenged.' Again he starts to strike yet checks himself. Looking ahead has made him see a hitch. He pauses, reflects: 'That would be scanned.' He changes his mind, lowers his sword, explains, ironically: 'A villain kills my father, and for that / I, his sole son, do this same villain send / To heaven.' During the remaining beats of the unfinished line, he laughs; then 'O, this is hire and salary, not revenge.' 'No' confirms his decision not to send Claudius to heaven. During the nine-syllable pause, he starts to return his sword to its scabbard, completing the act with 'Up, sword'. He then goes on to foresee a time when the King might be cut off in the midst of his sins and his damnation assured.

Commentary

Let us now imagine a more determined Hamlet who is less ready to be self-dissuaded from acting now.

He sees his opportunity ('Now might I do it pat'), walks closer ('now a is praying, / And now I'll do't'). He draws his sword and with 'and so a goes to heaven, / And so am I revenged' he prepares to strike. He has played down the words about 'a-praying' and 'goes to heaven', using each respectively as the preliminary to the strongly emphasized 'And now I'll do't' and 'And so am I revenged'. He pauses ('That would be scanned') and as if he had said 'How's that again?' he sums up the hitch that his surprise and excitement have made him a bit slow to realize: 'a villain kills my father, and for that / I, his sole son, do this same villain send / To heaven.' He laughs, then 'O, this is hire and salary, not revenge'. His further thoughts lead him to say 'No' to the idea of sending his foe to heaven, but he does not put up his sword until he obviously has the further idea, during the silent beats that follow, of sending him to hell. It is this additional idea that clinches Hamlet's decision: 'Up, sword, and know thou a more horrid hint.'

Commentary

The second Hamlet is perhaps less quick-witted than the first in seeing the hitch in killing his enemy at prayer. But the second seems much more sincere, even though the differences in the two versions are subtle. Indeed the first Hamlet might well be seen as merely rationalizing his procrastination.

The Voice of the Theatre-Poet

Although sustaining the continuity in a sequence of scenes is always a problem for actors, Shakespeare in this sequence gives the actors of Hamlet and Claudius particularly difficult challenges. In particular, during the aftermath of the play-within-a-play, they are required to sustain a presence *in absentia*. Shakespeare provides some help. He keeps the absent King before us through his henchmen's colloquies with the Prince; and, in turn, Hamlet is kept before us immediately thereafter because the King and these same henchmen talk of nothing else but the absent Prince. He gives Claudius his 'Give me some light' and Hamlet his 'drink hot blood'—memorable lines that stay in the audience's memory. But none of this will succeed unless the actors have previously created so intense a struggle between their two characters that it can continue even when one and then the other of them is off-stage.

This prolongation of their struggle continues through the two soliloquies that follow, again without direct interaction. Indeed, looking back to the play-within-a-play one sees how little direct interaction it need include between the King and the Prince, since both are working behind masks, the one of innocence and the other of 'idleness'.

How then is their struggle to be brought to the necessary intensity? Stage tradition from Edmund Kean to Olivier has successfully done so by making Hamlet dominant and largely adopting Hamlet's point of view: allowing him to be very overt in his challenge (Kean 'openly stalked his prey . . . he crawled upon his belly toward the King . . . and insolently scrutinized Claudius, as if bullying the King into confusion') and Claudius to be very overt in his self-exposure.

Yet the 'analysis' and 'rehearsal' sections above suggest just the opposite approach. Far from making the conflict as open as possible, Shakespeare seems to want to keep it for the most part tantalizingly submerged though felt, even as the King and the Prince are doing for their own purposes. This mutual concealment demands acute awareness on both sides. The audience, too, is challenged to the attentiveness it might bring to a staring-match, where a single blink tells all. Shakespeare thereby builds suspense for the moment of disclosure at the talk of poisoning, maintains suspense for when the conflict may flare out again, seems suddenly to offer a total resolution of the conflict when Claudius is trying to pray, only to end with another prolongation: 'This physic but prolongs thy sickly days'. Such an approach is very much to Shakespeare's long-term purposes. For the enmity between the two has by now become so mortal that much open conflict at this point would end his play in mid-course!

Nor does Shakespeare encourage Hamlet's total dominance. As in the other rehearsals, the values of the text best come through when each role is given its independent due. Indeed, as already shown, the King and the Prince find themselves in remarkably similar circumstances. During the playlet they both must deal with a tricky, mortal enemy, while maintaining a public mask and trying to control powerful drives within themselves. Immediately after the playlet, they must in turn deal with the same intermediaries and with inner impulses that halt their ability to act. Small wonder, then, that one finds these roles presenting their performers with very similar problems.

As usual Shakespeare provides passages through which the performers may make fine-tuning adjustments in their interpretations. Claudius's repeated questions to Hamlet about the play allow him to show precisely the desired amount of alarm. Hamlet's 'drink hot blood' speech allows him to heat then cool the degree of his ferocity. His 'Now might I do it pat' speech functions as another such passage, bringing him to a somewhat higher pitch of intensity for his scene with his mother than he reached at 'I will speak daggers to her, but use none'. For the Queen must soon fear that her son means to murder her, and he must soon, by stabbing Polonius, commit his first act of violence.

Here, as in the other rehearsed passages, Shakespeare thus serves actors not only as a guide to broad outlines and sets of options but—if one attends to subtleties in the text—as a dynamic and inspiring presence in the working out of crucial details.

8

The Role of Othello

FROM the very outset, the role of Othello is an enormously demanding one. Its performer must not only render his character's struggles with an alien world (he is the Moor of Venice) but meet extraordinary challenges within the workings of the performance-ensemble.

Soon after his first entry, Othello must have established enough authority to give the brief, cool command, 'Keep up your bright swords or the dew will rust 'em' and be obeyed by his foes as well as his friends. The audience's acceptance of this authority must be achieved without the help of a famous name (like Julius Caesar) or preliminary words of praise (as for Macbeth). Far from it. Up to that point the playwright has chosen to let us hear of Othello only in derogatory terms, as 'thick lips' and 'an old black ram'. If the actor is strong, the derogatory contrast will make Othello seem all the stronger; but the power must be there, and in abundance. Furthermore, he is not allowed a positive show of strength; his authority must be earned through his powers of restraint, of himself as well as others.

Othello speaks with a distinctive, pre-Miltonic eloquence that can help to give epic scope to what happens in his life. But this epic style constantly runs the danger of becoming mere grandiosity. At the Duke's hearing, for instance, the actor must be sure to match the outward deference he receives from the Duke and the Senators with an inner dignity and poise or his 'courtly' diction will seem merely pompous. Throughout, the actor must deal with a problem very like that confronting his character: of maintaining an elevated view of himself and his experiences despite circumstances which tend to undermine it. When the time comes, however, he must portray an Othello who has lost his self-control entirely, dissolving into half-coherent babble ('Noses, ears, and lips! Is't possible? Confess? Handkerchief? O devil!') and falling into a trance.

Without the actor in the least showing his technique, Othello's degeneration must be artfully graduated and timed. The actor must rise to one peak of vengefulness ('Arise, black vengeance, from the hollow hell', 3. 3. 451), then surge to another even higher ('I will chop her into messes', 4. 1. 195); yet immediately before actually killing

Desdemona he must, without anticlimax, completely change the nature of the progression he has been building. The roaring avenger must become, at least in his own eyes, a hushed and sorrowing agent of transcendent justice ('It is the cause', 5. 2. 1)—only to degenerate at last, in the face of Desdemona's resistance, into a desperate wife-murderer, fearful of being caught.

From the onset of Othello's jealousy, the actor has the difficult problem of convincing the audience of the sincerity of his character's belief and feeling, even though we know them to be the product of delusion. Our response must exceed the 'understanding' that we extend to the insane, reminding ourselves that, to them, their tormenting fantasies are real. Othello's conviction must be such that we may need to remind ourselves that his fantasies are *not* real. If the actor falters in this respect, his moments of pathos can very easily drop to bathos, particularly because his plight in any case borders on farce—that of a foolish husband who, in his mistaken jealousy, becomes the butt of a clever knave.

Of course, the chief external challenge to the actor of Othello is represented by the character of Iago—and the actor who portrays him. The struggle for dominance between the Moor and his ensign is concealed by Iago and unrecognized by Othello. The audience, however, can see that it is thoroughgoing, involving the conflict not only of wills but of whole ways of viewing the world. As has often been observed, Othello constantly tends to glorify or magnify what happens while Iago's tendency is to denigrate and reduce. The romantic 'story of my life' with which Othello wooed Desdemona becomes in Iago's mouth 'bragging . . . fantastical lies . . . prating'. Shakespeare plays the two views off against one another, putting the audience—like Othello—in a quandary as to what and who to believe. For a time Iago takes control. Othello himself becomes slave not only of Iago's slanders but of his whole way of thinking. His once epic world becomes inhabited solely by 'goats and monkeys'. At the end, however, Othello returns to his former self. On the whole, neither view prevails. Instead, paradoxically, they come to seem complementary as well as contradictory, as if they were aspects of a single personality.

The relationship between Othello and Iago is remarkably intimate, much more so than between Othello and Desdemona. It is hard to imagine the one man without the other. Each needs the other to work out his destiny. The result is a combination of unacknowledged rivalry and mutual dependence between the characters. A parallel relationship cannot be avoided by the actors who play the two roles. It was knowingly exploited in the nineteenth century when two leading actors would alternate the roles on successive nights.

As so often in this play, the playwright's treatment of this relationship gives the actor of Othello an uphill effort. The actors of Iago often steal the whole show, and through much of it Shakespeare aids and abets the theft. He gives Iago more total lines than Othello, and more soliloquies. From the first scene he shows us a series of characters (Roderigo, Brabanzio, the Duke) whose excessive trust in appearance and tendency to leap to conclusions on insufficient evidence alert us to the very errors in judgement that will prove Othello's undoing. Iago, in contrast, knows full well how deceiving appearances can be and never tires of demonstrating the fact, for his own entertainment and ours.

Shakespeare does invite us to admire Othello in his glory—as the military man-of-the-hour in Venice and the successful wooer of the much sought-after Desdemona. Yet he is an outsider to us as to the Venetians. Bradley is probably right in suggesting that the same is true of his creator, that there is less of Shakespeare in Othello than in the other tragic heroes. By contriving the coincidences involving the fateful handkerchief, the playwright seems yet again to work against his hero. And he never invites us to do more than look on—perhaps a bit enviously—at the happiness Othello at first shares with Desdemona, for we are denied their intimacy. Contrast the love-duet that Verdi and Boito give them early in *Otello*. In Shakespeare we do not see the two alone together until the middle of Act 4 when they are hopelessly far apart.

The actor of Othello cannot, thus, expect that his audience will immediately 'identify' with his character or extend unmixed sympathy to him either in his joy (which we see only from the outside) or his sufferings (which we see to be unnecessary). We may indeed take a certain satisfaction in his downfall. Of course, most tragedies offer the audience the secret pleasure of witnessing 'how the mighty hath fallen' and reflecting that 'pride goeth before a fall'. It is not unnatural that the ordinary people who make up the majority of an audience should take satisfaction in confirming that those who have in one way or another risen above ordinary humanity may prove in the end to be no better (and no better off) than the rest. The special touch that Shakespeare places on this satisfaction in *Othello* is his emphasis on disenchantment, the poignant discovery that those we thought to be genuinely superior beings are in fact subject to ordinary frailties.

Disenchantment is one of the central experiences that the audience shares with the leading characters. Othello is disenchanted with

Desdemona (however mistakenly) and she with him. Although she does her best to believe otherwise, Desdemona must at last admit that Othello is susceptible to faults: 'We must think men are not gods', she reminds herself (3. 4. 146). In the very process of his disenchantment with Desdemona, Othello causes the audience to become disenchanted with himself. And our own enchantment with Desdemona is lessened when we hear her twice lie to Othello about the handkerchief. Othello is of course finally disenchanted with 'honest' Iago, as are we. It was one thing to go along with him in a daring and clever plot against Othello's domestic tranquillity; it is another when Othello in his passion converts it into murder and Iago does not resist but instead volunteers to become a full partner. In the end Iago isn't even a successful villain. For all his supposedly superior intellect and resource, his plot against Cassio goes wrong and his whole scheme unravels.

For some in the audience the shared experience will go beyond disenchantment to iconoclasm. We resent those who disappoint us. Moreover, discovering that those we admire are less than perfect can lead us to regard them as worse than they are, and—in that exaggerated disappointment and resentment—make us want to strike back accordingly. For example, Iago never accuses Desdemona of infidelity with anyone other than Cassio, yet Othello imagines her having intercourse with his whole camp, 'pioneers and all'. It is against this imagined 'cunning whore of Venice' that he retaliates. When Iago reduces his former lord to his slave, indeed his ass to be led by the nose to his destruction, it may seem to some no more than justice that Othello should have done deliberately to him by Iago what he is himself unwittingly doing to Desdemona.

There is still another way in which Shakespeare invites us, to a degree, to share Iago's drives. He is absolutely heartless, so much so that he cannot feel fully his own grievances. Hence his repeated asseverations that he hates the Moor and his multiplication of reasons to feel sexual jealousy. In part, we may surmise, Iago drives 'greathearted' Othello to extremes of jealousy in order to experience vicariously—or voyeurlike at least to witness—something he is incapable of experiencing himself. Few in the audience may have so absolute a shortcoming in this respect as does Iago. Yet few in the audience could 'let themselves go' in so all-out a way as does Othello, and there is a satisfaction in having our inhibited feelings thus given full sway.

It is precisely here that the actor of Othello can make an irresistible claim on our sympathies. If he has it in him, he should release a torrent of feeling so compelling that—as if we were watching a volcanic eruption—the members of the audience can take a positive satisfaction in the sheer extremity of it, however destructive it may be. Otherwise we will feel merely cruel in being at all a party to the suffering he undergoes and inflicts.

As usual this opportunity for the actor is accompanied by hazards. Othellos tend to become mere roarers. To avoid monotony, the expression of unadulterated, barely articulate emotion ('Blood, blood, blood') must be balanced by subtle blends of complex attitudes. His jealousy must ebb as well as flow; his desecration of Desdemona must alternate with his adoration of her, each rendered with such conviction that the change from the one to the other reflects at any given moment only the strength of the dominant impulse, not the weakness of the other.

Some of Othello's emotional appeals to the audience are of a low kind. He is something of a one-man crowd. Emrys Jones draws many parallels between his behaviour and Gustave Le Bon's analysis of the *Psychology of Crowds* (1895). Like Othello, a crowd is 'credulous', 'open to influence'; its 'feelings are always very simple and very exaggerated. It knows neither doubt nor uncertainty but goes at once to extremes.' As part of a theatre crowd, we may thus find Othello the agent of our worst collective instincts. The actor of the role must be careful to show the Moor as the victim as well as the exponent of these traits.

For it is in his utter vulnerability that Othello makes his chief claim on our sympathies. In the extremity of his suffering he reveals a depth in his love for Desdemona that reaches to the very springs of his own identity. And it is the depth of his sense of loss that prompts us to feel the pity of this love-tragedy, for his sake as well as for Desdemona's. Since Othello himself feels 'the pity of it', his actor will be well advised not to let Othello feel so sorry for himself that the audience won't feel the need to do so.

These, then, are the daunting challenges that the player of Othello must face. Shakespeare provides him with a rich set of options with which to do so. At the centre is the temptation scene (3. 3), which I should like to use as the focus for detailed analysis of the role of Othello.

The scene may be divided into four phases. Each begins with an expression of love and trust by Othello towards Desdemona. The first phase begins at line 91: 'Perdition catch my soul / But I do love thee!' The second begins at line 230: 'I do not think but Desdemona's honest.' The third begins at line 282: 'If she be false, O then heaven mocks itself!' The last begins at line 389: 'I think my wife be honest, and think she is not.' Each of these phases, moreover, contains a passage in which Othello gives credence to Iago's insinuations. The first is during the lines immediately following Iago's speech beginning, 'She did deceive her father, marrying you' (l. 210). The second is during Othello's soliloquy beginning, 'This fellow's of exceeding honesty' (l. 262), especially: 'She's gone. I am abused, and my relief / Must be to loathe her' (ll. 271–2). The third is during Othello's absence from the stage, as signalized by his returning line, 'Ha, ha, false to me?' (l. 338). The final one is his line, 'Now do I see 'tis true' (l. 449). During which of these four phases does Othello decisively bite on Iago's bait? There is something to be said for each.

Some may feel that the question is academic since in any case Othello may be seen to be 'easily jealous', having succumbed to these slanders in a single interview, with no more of a case than Iago presents. To take this view is to mistake the nature of the scene, which condenses into a single episode a sequence of psychological states that in a realistic novel might be spread over a number of separate interviews. Because of this dramatic concentration, it does make a difference at which point Othello essentially succumbs.

On the other hand, the importance of the scene should not be exaggerated. It marks only the first stage of Othello's response to Iago's slanders. Whatever Othello's protestations about being like to the Pontic Sea, he will waver in his determination and not at all act on his deluded beliefs until he has actually seen Bianca return his handkerchief to Cassio. And he will not actually commit the murder of Desdemona until he believes that Iago has set the example by killing Cassio. His initial belief thus does not reach the point of providing a basis for action until more time has elapsed and more support of his belief has materialized.

It should be acknowledged as obvious that in analysing the four phases and their significance, one is largely weighing matters of emphasis. Factors that are given special prominence in any given phase may well enter into a portrayal of the Moor in which one of the other phases is seen as decisive.

None the less, the exact moment in 3. 3 at which Othello believes Iago does make a crucial difference in the interpretation of the role. An Othello who succumbs at the first likely point is significantly different from one who does not do so until the last likely point, and to a lesser extent the same is true of the intermediate options. I should like thus to distinguish carefully between these four Othellos, defining Othello One, Two, Three, and Four according to the qualities emphasized in the phase in which he is thought to succumb.

Othello One believes Desdemona unfaithful very soon after he hears his ensign's advice to 'Look to your wife. Observe her well with Cassio'. Of course, Iago has from the beginning of their interview been hinting that something is going on between Cassio and Desdemona. But he has not made his innuendoes explicit until this point, and Othello One's immediate credence needs to be clearly accounted for. Certainly it is not because of any prior distrust of Cassio; Iago's first feelers sought unsuccessfully to find opportunities in that quarter. It is only when the focus shifts to Desdemona that Othello One proves vulnerable.

Iago never has to make the full, direct charge that Brabanzio did (and that Iago's use of the expression 'look to't' recalls): 'Look to her, Moor, if thou hast eyes to see. / She has deceived her father, and may thee' (1. 3. 292–3). He first represents adultery as a generic trait of wives in his country: 'In Venice they do let God see the pranks / They dare not show their husbands.' Othello's response is the first of a series of very brief expressions (never as much as a full line) which follow Iago's warning: 'Dost thou say so?' He may well emphasize *thou*, as actors sometimes have, to bring out the trust that he places in his ensign as a 'man that's just', whose every word and hesitation deserve to be given due weight. Iago then enlarges on Desdemona's deception of her father ('She that so young could give out such a seeming, / To seel her father's eyes up close as oak, / He thought 'twas witchcraft'). He then breaks off, perhaps seeing that Othello is much affected: 'But I am much to blame.' The likeliest place for Othello's conversion to be put into words is with 'I am bound to thee for ever'.

To give way so immediately, Othello One's love for Desdemona cannot be deep enough to provide a firm basis in trust. It may be virtually as superficial as he himself earlier painted it in his formula: 'She loved me for the dangers I had passed, / And I loved her that she did pity them' (1. 3. 166–7). It will thus contrast sharply with that of Desdemona's, which is at once more spiritual than his ('I saw Othello's visage in his mind', 1. 3. 252) and more physical ('I did love the Moor to live with him', 1. 3. 248). Here again Othello emphasizes his wife's accomplishments and traits more than her person:

> 'Tis not to make me jealous
> To say my wife is fair, feeds well, loves company,
> Is free of speech, sings, plays, and dances well.
> Where virtue is, these are more virtuous . . .

In the shallowness of his love, Othello One may show some mild irritation with Desdemona's importunities on Cassio's behalf at the beginning of the scene. 'Our general's wife is now the general', Iago had told Cassio (2. 3. 307–8). Rightly or wrongly, Othello One may fear that she thinks that such is the case. He might be a bit put out with her, stressing 'Prithee, no more' (l. 76) and 'leave me but a little to myself' (l. 86) and thus occasioning her rebuked 'What e'er you be, I am obedient' (l. 90).

Othello One is bound to seem quickly deceived, whether because the Moor is especially subject to delusion or because his ensign is especially deceptive or both. His powers of judgement may well seem notably weak, all the more because he protests so much about their strength:

> I'll see before I doubt; when I doubt, prove;
> And on the proof, there is no more but this;
> Away at once with love or jealousy.

To himself, these lines express a firm executive authority; to us they may sound cocksure and beneath that, insecure. We have just seen Othello's irritability when faced with Iago's pretended reluctance to disclose his suspicions. It is reminiscent of Othello's rising passion when frustrated in gathering evidence about the fight between Cassio and Montano. Instead of taking time for a full investigation, Othello One in both cases leaps to an immediate decision.

Othello One may, indeed, have a strong *self*-deceptive and masochistic streak which prompts him to believe what he fears most. Desdemona's departure at the beginning of this episode causes him not only to express his love for her ('Perdition catch my soul / But I do love thee!') but also to add: 'and when I love thee not, / Chaos is come again.' Why does he so immediately think of its loss and its consequences?

Both the Moor and Iago, though, see Othello as being easily deceived primarily because he is excessively trusting, whether of Desdemona or Iago. Othello One's bond with Iago is very close: in the first part of the scene they exchange strong expressions of love for one another.

Iago One will need to be skilfully manipulative. The first part of the scene provides him with abundant opportunities to demonstrate his skill, as he—by disingenuous self-deprecation of his own suspiciousness—at once prepares a line of retreat for himself if necessary and at the same time works up Othello's emotions. He introduces his slander by at first warning against jealousy in general before airing his particular suspicions concerning Desdemona and Cassio.

Othello One's moment of conviction may well be largely unspoken. It may occur in some silent indication of his response that causes Iago to observe that his words 'hath a little dashed your spirits'. His repeated comments—'I see you're moved'—help to focus attention on Othello's unspoken responses. For Othello One, the rest of the scene develops the consequences of this moment of decision. As he broods—and with occasional waverings—his feeling of being abused grows as does his impulse towards retaliation. His vows at the end of the scene crystallize the consequences of his earlier decision.

Othello Two takes somewhat longer to succumb and more factors enter in. He is not nearly so transparent as is Othello One. We cannot feel sure that he has taken Iago's bait until his soliloquy at line 262. He is shocked by his ensign's warning, but Iago Two's lines concerning how moved he is are more in the nature of probes (and suggestions that he *should* be very upset) than reflections of emotional changes in Othello of which Iago and the audience may be sure. His rendering of 'I am bound to thee for ever' may mean no more than that he greatly appreciates his loyal subordinate's overcoming his scruples and confiding his suspicions. By line 230, Othello has recovered enough from the shock to deny that he is much moved and to declare, 'I do not think but Desdemona's honest'.

Iago wastes no time in trying to undermine this declaration, however: 'Long live she so, and long live you to think so!' At which Othello goes on to muse, 'And yet how nature, erring from itself—'. Iago Two had heard the disguised insecurity behind Othello's earlier declaration:

> Nor from mine own weak merits will I draw
> The smallest fear or doubt of her revolt,
> For she had eyes, and chose me.

He therefore plays tellingly on Othello Two's feeling that Desdemona was unnatural in not marrying a man 'Of her own clime, complexion, and degree' and on his fears that in time her exotic taste may change. These thoughts are as much as he can bear for one interview. He bids Iago 'farewell', asks him to continue to keep him informed of further developments, and directs him to 'Set on thy wife to observe'. But, within, Othello Two already feels that 'This honest creature, doubtless, / Sees and knows more, much more, than he unfolds'. He thus sees Iago not only as 'a man that is just' but one who is loving in a protective way, as someone like himself who does not wear his heart upon his sleeve.

In his soliloquy he finally pours out his feelings, and these confirm

our surmises. In the first phase Iago had claimed only limited special
expertise ('I know our country disposition well'), but here Othello
Two accords him much greater authority: his ensign 'knows all
qualities, with a learned spirit / Of human dealings'. He reviews Iago's
specifics:

> Haply for I am black,
> And have not those soft parts of conversation
> That chamberers have . . .

Then he adds the difference in age (which Iago had not mentioned): 'or
for I am declined / Into the vale of years.' Yet even as he denies the
importance of his age ('yet that's not much'), he is swept to his key
moment of accepting the truth of Iago's warning. Just seven lines
before he had been cautious enough to say '*If* I do prove her haggard';
but now, he concludes:

> She's gone. I am abused, and my relief
> Must be to loathe her.

He goes on to generalize his sufferings as the product of 'marriage' and
'destiny'. As with Othello One, the rest of the scene shows the
consequences of Othello Two's decision. But Othello Two has
foreseen such consequences even before his decision was final; he
vows that if she is guilty he will 'whistle her off ' (send her away).

Othello Three was shocked by Iago's warning and then half
concealed his growing suspicions of Desdemona. He is, however,
recalled from his premature condemnation of her by her entry: 'If she
be false, O then heaven mocks itself! I'll not believe't'. This is not as
strong an affirmation as it might be. He does not quite declare that she
is true but rather that if she is not, nothing is. He does not quite say, 'I
don't believe it' but rather that it is a matter of choice and he chooses
not to: 'I'll not believe't'. Still, her attraction for him is strong enough
that simply her entry is enough to sway Othello Three in her favour.

After his private expression of faith in Desdemona, the Moor then
speaks to her only in very short speeches. Clearly he is upset. Even
Desdemona, who is in general slow to discern his real feelings, can tell
that. Do Desdemona's speeches then allay his distress or add to it?
How does he 'hear' her concern for his dinner, the waiting islanders,
his headache? Does he find a note of officiousness in it that recalls the
persistence of her earlier entreaties for Cassio? Othello One might.
His 'I am to blame' might reflect his feeling that she is finding fault
with him. Othello Three—with his strong attraction towards
Desdemona—seems more likely to hear simple solicitude for his own
welfare. His 'I am to blame' may blame himself not only for his

neglect of the islanders but for his suspicion of her. He may bask in her wifely ministrations as they go off together.

However that may be, something then happens off-stage that causes him to leave her and that turns Othello Three decisively against her. Does she again bring up Cassio? Or is it, as Iago thinks, the inevitable working of his poisonous slander?:

> The Moor already changes with my poison.
> Dangerous conceits are in their natures poisons,
> Which at the first are scarce found to distaste,
> But, with a little act upon the blood,
> Burn like the mines of sulphur.

In his eyes Othello has here reached the point of no return. When the Moor then enters, Iago feels sure that no medicine 'shall ever' restore to his victim the sweet sleep he had enjoyed before.

Ironically, if it is Desdemona's appearance in person that at first influences Othello Three in her favour, it is also her person that helps to turn him against her. Perhaps it is the resurgence of his own physical desire for her and her 'sweet body' that causes him to extend these desires to her and to her imagined lovers. Earlier he had lamented 'That we can call these delicate creatures ours, / And not their appetites!' Now the Moor goes further; his Desdemona is indiscriminately lustful. In his fantasies, 'the general camp, / Pioneers and all' have 'tasted her sweet body'. He thus resolves his conflicting feelings of desire for Desdemona and loathing of her in the single image of a whore.

For Othello Three, the essential moment of decision occurs while he is off-stage. His first line on his return expresses a foregone conclusion: 'Ha, ha, false to me?' His first reaction is focused on himself. The word 'me' might well be emphasized. He tells Iago: 'Thou hast set me on the rack.' His self-pity has a surprising irony, suggesting the sophistication that comes from dwelling on a grievance: 'I swear 'tis better to be much abused / Than but to know't a little.' He is preoccupied with the consequences to his own being: it is essentially a personal chaos that is come again with the destruction of his romantic conception of himself as a heroic warrior.

His trust in the military verities thus shaken, the general then turns on his subordinate: 'Villain, be sure thou prove my love a whore.' He becomes openly, probably physically, threatening, a hazard that Iago surmounts only by piously rebuking himself:

> take note, take note, O world,
> To be direct and honest is not safe!

He may start to leave, thus prompting Othello's self-restraint: 'Nay, stay. Thou shouldst be honest' (l. 386). Othello's later 'Now do I see 'tis true' (l. 449) may acknowledge to Iago that his ensign has—as ordered—proved his love a whore.

The first three Othellos are passionate because they are deceived; Othello Four is deceived because he becomes passionate. He is at last won over because it drives him out of his reason to picture his wife in the arms of another man and to hear that she has given his love-token to her supposed lover, who uses it to wipe his beard with. Only then does he conclude: 'Now do I see 'tis true.'

Earlier in the scene he had been momentarily swayed against Desdemona by Iago's warnings as his passions were progressively stirred. But in each case he had made a return to a better balanced judgement, each successive swing of the pendulum, however, involving a more heavily qualified expression of trust in his wife. In this final phase Othello can at best muster only a half-trust in either Desdemona or Iago:

> I think my wife be honest, and think she is not.
> I think that thou art just and think thou art not.

Othello Four is less simply under the influence of Iago than are the other three. He explicitly takes the initiative away from Iago. When the latter asks, 'You would be satisfied?' Othello replies, 'Would? Nay, and I will.' Earlier in the scene, there are many opportunities to suggest that Iago is doing little more than fanning to a blaze suspicions and fears that Othello already harbours. Iago Four is thus as much a sado-masochistic partner as a confidence-man. Together they may share a voyeur's lust to ogle a couple as 'prime as goats, as hot as monkeys, / As salt as wolves in pride'. Note how Iago dwells on the idea; and since such ocular proof is not possible he substitutes Cassio's supposed dream of 'sweet' Desdemona, alertly echoing Othello's earlier image of her 'sweet' body.

Othello Four is the least easily jealous of the options. To convince him finally that Iago's suspicions are true, it takes the effect of factors that have accumulated in the preceding phases, plus Iago's highly provocative account of Cassio's dream and the master-stroke of the handkerchief. On the other hand, his immediate response is much more violent than before. It is not to loathe Desdemona and turn her out but to 'tear her all to pieces'. And for the first time Cassio has been added as the object of his wrath: 'O that the slave had forty thousand lives! / One is too poor, too weak for my revenge.'

For all four Othellos the very end of the scene (from line 449 on) represents a fifth phase that moves beyond the process of decision (with its waverings) to formal declarations of revenge and command. Their renderings of it may well reflect the emphases that have come before. With Othello One we may be especially reminded of the extreme manipulativeness of the ensign and manipulableness of the general. Iago One's assurance that he is ready to do whatever 'bloody business' he is commanded may cue Othello's command to kill Cassio; his 'but let her live' may cue Othello's determination to kill Desdemona. With Othello Two we may be especially reminded of the general's penchant for self-dramatization and 'keeping up a front'. His 'Like to the Pontic Sea' speech may well ring a bit hollow since in the future Othello will in fact waver in just the way he here so ringingly declares he will not. With Othello Three we may well reflect that his occupation is no longer gone, since he so self-consciously now assumes the role of revenger. His reference to his wife as 'the fair devil' may recall his sensual attraction/loathing towards her person. With Othello Four, 'O blood, blood, blood!' may be the key, as his passionate flood of feelings demands outlet in ceremonial forms and plans for action. Iago Four may be genuinely counselling restraint when he says of Desdemona, 'but let her live', only to be overborne by Othello Four's tendency to rush ahead of his tempter. In any case, his intimate partnership with Iago Four here reaches a new development. He not only supplants Cassio with Iago as his lieutenant but makes Iago the object of the bounteousness he had hitherto extended to Desdemona. In return Iago Four may give special ironic weight to his final line: 'I am your own for ever.'

Each of these four Othellos seems to me within the range of valid interpretation. What are their relative strengths and weaknesses, not only in this scene but in the reading of the entire role that they suppose?

For Othello One, deception is the key, whether it is deception exposed (supposedly in Desdemona) or masterfully perpetrated (by Iago) or self-imposed (by Othello). This emphasis is supported by a general deception-motif in the play, which could be played up as a context. Desdemona's real and presumed deceptiveness would be particularly important. She did, after all, pull the wool over her father's eyes, disguising her courtship with Othello and successfully eloping. Her father's words of warning to Othello would be given full weight. Perhaps they would not be spoken in a bitter tone but ruefully, as though facing an ugly fact of his daughter's nature. Desdemona's repeated lie about the handkerchief to Othello would be stressed as would Emilia's lie to her about it. Her lying to herself about Othello's invulnerability to jealousy would put an ironic twist on this motif and be capped by her loving lie in her last words denying Othello's guilt. Emilia's self-sacrificing truth-telling could have a special force within this context. (The irony that Roderigo's letters would have incriminated Iago anyway would not be stressed.)

To fit Othello One with the rest of the play, care would need to be taken that Iago's powers of deception and Othello's susceptibility to them are focused on Desdemona. Iago is not able to cause others to think ill of Desdemona; both Cassio and Roderigo are proof against his insinuations. Only with Othello does he succeed. Othello is not generally so credulous or finally so rash; even the on-the-spot demotion of Cassio proves to be merely temporary. It is only concerning Desdemona that he behaves as he does in this scene.

Because Othello One so quickly accepts Iago's insinuations as true, this conception of the role makes especially heavy demands on its actor. If he is not to seem merely weak and gullible (another Roderigo), he must be able to summon compelling emotional force on short order and be able to show his key moment of acceptance through cryptic half-lines and body-language. Yet he must not allow himself to be too strong. If, for example, he stresses his self-delusions (as Olivier did), he must not go too far in this direction or Iago will tend to become 'merely ancillary' (as F. R. Leavis put it); and this would harm the whole play since Iago has more lines than Othello does. The actor will need to beware of anticlimax. If he reaches too high an intensity at the outset, he will have difficulty sustaining dramatic interest through his waverings in the subsequent phases of the scene.

Othello Two is not so free and open a nature as Iago takes him to be. He shows an ability to conceal his feelings from others (at least partially) until they are revealed in soliloquy that fits in with his frequent tendency elsewhere to play self-assigned roles that suit his purposes. This kind of instrumental self-dramatization could readily be emphasized in the hearing with the Duke and Senators, for example, where his account of his feeling for Desdemona would be chiefly concerned with assuring his superiors that their general was not so infatuated with his bride as to neglect his duty. In his handling of the brawl, he could be shown to be very concerned with reassuring Montano (the fact that he offers to be his surgeon would be emphasized) while his plan, in due course, to restore Cassio in his favour would show his politic sense of timing. Later, his impulses towards self-dramatization could be shown to have gone out of control, to the point of madness, as when he casts himself as a 'sacrificer' when he murders his wife. His final 'Soft you, a word or two before you go' might also be played as a piece of instrumental self-justification.

Othello Two can draw support for other features from elsewhere in the play. His sense that Iago knows more than—out of affection—he chooses to tell, echoes his thought at the trial of Cassio:

> I know, Iago,
> Thy honesty and love doth mince this matter,
> Making it light to Cassio.   (2. 3. 239–41)

There is considerable context elsewhere for the sense of inferiority he expresses in his soliloquy. Going along with the frequent mention of his blackness in the dialogue, he might be portrayed as very black of skin and Desdemona very 'fair'. As with Othello One, the difference between Venetian manners and those of the Moor could readily be emphasized, as in the gallant courtesies of Cassio with Desdemona that first spark Iago's plot.

This heightened sense of being an alien gives Othello Two more grounds for suspicion than has Othello One. He also makes a higher estimate of Iago's knowingness than does Othello One, and thus makes more credible the credit he gives his insinuations. But the chief strength that Othello Two has over all of the other options is that his moment of acceptance comes in the course of a soliloquy, and thus has the full reliability that by stage convention attaches to such disclosure. Earlier, the actor will want to have revealed from behind his mask just enough of his inner turmoil to build a progression toward the revelations in the soliloquy.

For the actor of Othello Three, the chief problem is that his moment of acceptance comes off-stage, a problem that Shakespeare seems to have tried to ease with the lines with which Iago introduces his re-entrance:

> Look where he comes. Not poppy nor mandragora
> Nor all the drowsy syrups of the world
> Shall ever medicine thee to that sweet sleep
> Which thou owedst yesterday.

Only here in this scene does Iago express to the audience his confidence that his slander has achieved its intended effect.

For Othello Three the exchange with Desdemona will need to be given the fullest possible weight. Again as in Phase One, Othello will need to communicate his feelings through a series of half-lines. In its constraint, this exchange should contrast with the playfulness of their exchange at the beginning of this episode. Desdemona Three should be particularly attractive. Her physical appeal for Othello at this point can draw on the fact that he has been more and more demonstrative towards her. At their reunion in Cyprus, he told Desdemona:

> Honey, you shall be well desired in Cyprus,
> I have found great love amongst them. O my sweet,
> I prattle out of fashion, and I dote
> In mine own comforts.
>
> (2. 1. 205–8)

After the brawl, he was no longer self-conscious about his endearments; he called her 'sweeting'. At the beginning of this scene she was 'sweet Desdemona', to whom he twice promised: 'I will deny thee nothing.'

Later of course, he will expatiate to Iago about her qualities: 'the world hath not a sweeter creature! She might lie by an emperor's side, and command him tasks' (4. 1. 179–81) only to conclude: 'I will chop her into messes.' It is the same mixture of attraction and loathing that in 3. 3 led him to call his love a whore, and it will be acted out in the 'brothel scene' (4. 2) in which he visits 'that cunning whore of Venice / That married with Othello' (ll. 92–3).

In preparation for the 'Othello's occupation's gone' speech, Othello Three can make much of his generalship and its importance to him. Both before and after this scene, there are also abundant opportunities to prepare for the self-centredness and self-pity that are emphasized in the third phase. In his long speech to the Senators, for a small example, the Moor seems to end his survey of his adventures only then to add:

> And of the cannibals that each other eat,
> The Anthropophagi, and men whose heads
> Do grow beneath their shoulders.
>
> (1. 3. 142–4)

Othello Two may well make the addition because he observes the strong interest of his listeners and it suits his purposes to enhance his image in their eyes as a widely experienced soldier. Othello Three may simply be warming to his subject, as a spell-binding—and somewhat self-indulgent—talker; he thus suddenly recalls and throws in still more remarkable wonders of the world he has seen.

The fact that Othello Four does not accept Iago's insinuations as true until the end of the scene gives this option the strongest claim to credibility. It also presents its actor with a number of challenges. To avoid anticlimax (and not seem merely obtuse), his 'Now do I see 'tis true' must come at the end of a mounting process of acceptance through the preceding phases, punctuated by swings of resistance that are, however, of a descending degree of strength. These waverings may make it difficult for Othello Four to establish his final acceptance as conclusive.

The decisive importance of Othello Four's passionate nature can be prepared for in earlier scenes. His initial self-control under stress can be played not as simple self-confidence but as deliberate dispassionateness, in which his feelings are being held tightly in check. When the Moor encounters difficulty in getting to the bottom of the brawl's cause, he declares:

> Now, by heaven,
> My blood begins my safer guides to rule,
> And passion, having my best judgement collied,
> Essays to lead the way. (2. 3. 197–200)

For Othello Two, this passage may aim at rhetorical effect, leading up to the threat: "Swounds, if I stir, / Or do but lift this arm, the best of you / Shall sink in my rebuke' (ll. 200–2). Othello Four, though, should probably be here acknowledging a genuine stirring of passion, in a way that anticipates his irritation in 3. 3 with Iago's pretended evasiveness: 'What dost thou mean? . . . By heaven, I'll know thy thoughts.'

As he moves through the successive phases, Othello Four has the opportunity to play a more and more active role in his own torments. In Phase Four he may even genuinely take the initiative from Iago. Often before, Iago ostensibly holds back. Now Iago might find himself truly struggling to keep up with Othello's violent reactions. In none of his soliloquies, for instance, does Iago contemplate murder as part of his revenge; it is Othello who introduces the idea. At the least, Othello Four is a full partner in his own torment and takes a kind of satisfaction in it, as may be seen in the passage following Iago's account of Cassio's 'dream':

OTHELLO   O, monstrous, monstrous!
IAGO   Nay, this was but his dream.
OTHELLO
But this denoted a foregone conclusion.
IAGO
'Tis a shrewd doubt, though it be but a dream,
And this may help to thicken other proofs
That do demonstrate thinly.
OTHELLO   I'll tear her all to pieces.

Later, the effect will be even clearer, when Iago mock-reluctantly tells Othello that Cassio did:

IAGO   Lie—
OTHELLO   With her?
IAGO   With her, on her, what you will.
OTHELLO   Lie with her? Lie on her? We say 'lie on her' when they belie her.
Lie with her? 'Swounds, that's fulsome! . . .

(4. 1. 33–6)

The Moor's 'shadowing passion' that throws him into a trance is as much his own doing as Iago's.

The playwright John Whiting has written:

The basic, the unalterable factor of drama is the moment 'when'; the moment of happening which is contained in the action. The dramatist must concern himself with this moment of action and not leave it, as so often happens, to be imposed by the director or players. In other words, the dramatist must create what is done and *when*, and not only the words to be spoken.[1]

In a general way, Shakespeare does indicate *when* Othello accepts Iago's insinuations as true. It comes sometime in 3. 3 and neither before the first option nor after the last. Within these limits of interpretation, however, each of the four possibilities has validity. Shakespeare does not specify for the actor a single 'moment "when" '. Although each of the four options has its strengths and weaknesses, none is so strong as to preclude the others or so weak as to be itself excluded. As such they represent a rich resource from which the actor of Othello may choose the version best suited to his own capacities and the needs of the production as a whole. Having made this choice he may further, to taste, shade and highlight features in the other phases.

As different as these options are, they together provide some general guidelines for the portrayal of Othello, whatever choice is made. In the course of the scene Othello suffers a metamorphosis. By the end of it he is no longer 'all in all sufficient' but dependent on an underling, no longer free and uncircumscribed but led by the nose, no longer open but devious and seeking concealment, no longer unshakeable and constant but wavering and wild. As Iago drily tells Lodovico, 'He is much changed' (4. 1. 270). In the silent film *Othello*, Emil Jannings makes his transformation before our eyes in a single sequence; like Dr Jekyll drinking a potion and turning into Mr Hyde, he turns from a

---

[1] John Whiting, 'Writing for Actors', in *The Making of Theatre: From Drama to Performance*, ed. R. Corrigan (Glenview, Ill., 1981), 178.

noble man into a brute. Yet the theatre-poet seems to be cautioning the actor of Othello against so simple and one-directional a change. His voice invites an ebb and flow of feeling in which Othello's better nature can reassert itself, only again to be overcome. Through the gradations of intensity built into the four phases, Shakespeare also seems to bespeak a degree of restraint, even though the scene rises to a powerful climax, with many explosive moments along the way. For Othello must be able to go still further in 4. 1, a similar scene in which he will be brought to the point of striking Desdemona. The great danger for Othello is to become a mere 'roarer', monotonously bellowing his pain.

If in these ways Shakespeare provides direction for the actor of Othello, he also allows a large degree of freedom. He might easily have indicated a single, clear-cut point of no return as in *Otello*, where Verdi and Boito have Desdemona incriminate herself in Otello's eyes by placing her plea for Cassio shortly after rather than immediately before Iago's first insinuations. Instead, Shakespeare's four options leave it to the actor to choose the moment of decision that best suits what he can bring to the role, a moment that may well serve as the pivot or fulcrum for his whole portrayal. The multiple phases also afford bounteous opportunities for varying Othello's agony, as each one spotlights a different set of facets in his nature. Here as always, Shakespeare is more than anything else a rich resource of stimulus and suggestion.

John Russell Brown has observed that we should keep Shakespeare's plays 'in constant rehearsal in the theatre of our minds'.[2] There is a sense in which this is true. One should always be mindful of the whole deck of cards from which a given production may deal a certain hand. Still, the theatre of our mind should have not only a rehearsal hall but a main stage, on which a production goes beyond the exploration of possibilities to the final choices of a public presentation. For these choices have a logic of their own—as was just demonstrated in *Othello*—and they can either enhance one another if the logic is followed or detract from one another if it is not. I thus part company with Brown in his manifesto, *Free Shakespeare* (1974). Although I share his desire to liberate actors and spectators from the overweening dominance of directors who seek to impose a tight interpretation on the text, the virtual autonomy Brown would confer on the individual actors seems to me an attempt to prolong the exploratory rehearsal

[2] John Russell Brown, *Shakespeare's Plays in Performance* (New York, 1967), 70.

phase, with its private discoveries of illuminating moments, into the phase of public performance, in which these moments have been sorted out and integrated into a coherent whole. A play does not become fully a play until it gathers itself together, steps on to the stage, and meets its public. What happens when that step is taken on film and television will be studied in Chapter 9.

9

The Latitudes and Limits of Performance: The BBC Television *Measure for Measure* and Zeffirelli's *The Taming of the Shrew*

UNTIL recently, the analysis of Shakespearian performance has been extremely difficult. The would-be analyst has had to depend upon a given live production or the commercial presentations of a film or television show. Only under special circumstances were the necessary repeated viewings possible. With the advent of videotape and the greater availability of films for non-commercial use, these difficulties have largely been removed. The tapes and films can be run and rerun at will. Of course, the complete rapport of a live performance-ensemble is not possible because there is no chance for the players to respond to the audience's responses. That is a limitation to be kept in mind in what follows.

A further difficulty has been that an analyst could not depend upon a reader's having seen the performance under consideration, and the reader in turn has often had to rely on the analyst's verbal re-creation of the performance event. Once tapes and films become as readily available as books, this difficulty also will be a thing of the past. That day, however, has still to arrive. Although ideally the reader of this chapter would have available the BBC television production of *Measure for Measure* on tape and Zeffirelli's *Taming of the Shrew* on film or tape, I will not assume that such is the case but rather make my analysis as self-explanatory as I can.

I have chosen these two productions in order to illustrate progressively greater degrees of interpretative freedom. BBC television gives *Measure for Measure* a 'reading'. Only a few of Shakespeare's lines are cut; the performers' choices are drawn from within the limits of Shakespeare's apparent intentions. Costumes, settings, props, and camera shots are boldly interpretative, but they serve to highlight features in the text. Zeffirelli's *Taming of the Shrew* might be called a 'free translation'. He does not hesitate to cut and rearrange the dialogue, even add a bit. To reach a modern film audience, Zeffirelli exaggerates attractive features in the text, clarifies its points of difficulty, strengthens its weak points. It borders on adaptation. But Zeffirelli's concern is to enhance Shakespeare's work rather than to adapt it to his own purposes. Most productions of Shakespeare fall into these two categories or somewhere between them.

THE BBC TELEVISION *MEASURE FOR MEASURE,* 2. 2 AND 2. 4

The two interviews between Angelo and Isabella are very much a pair. They raise some general interpretative questions:

1. *How far along the path of villainy has Angelo come by the beginning of the sequence, and how much further does he move in the course of it?* Later in the play, having had his way (he thinks) with Isabella, Angelo must be so villainous as to go back on his supposed bargain and order Claudio's execution. In the last act, he must be capable of bare-faced hypocrisy in the face of public accusation. Before 2. 2 his severity and self-righteousness have been brought out. 2. 1 emphasizes the doctrinaire quality of his sense of justice. Elbow's incompetence reminds us of how far from the actual administration of justice is Angelo's purist zeal, especially when he walks off from the problem in mid-course, leaving Escalus to cope with it. Angelo's exchanges with Escalus and the Provost suggest responsible yet more charitable attitudes than his towards Claudio's offence and punishment. In his second soliloquy within the sequence, Angelo speaks of 'my gravity, / Wherein—let no man hear me—I take pride', thus acknowledging not only his 'pride' but also, apologetically, his conscious concealment of it. Clearly Angelo is less than 'angelic' before he becomes infatuated with Isabella; the question for interpretation is how much less. As Isabella later puts it, 'I partly think / A due sincerity governed his deeds, / Till he did look on me' (5. 1. 442–4). In this sequence, the actor of Angelo will need to judge both the degree of his prior 'sincerity' and the degree to which his desire for Isabella and his other faults corrupt it.

He will also need to decide how corrupt Angelo becomes in the course of the sequence. Angelo himself is engaged in this same activity. His first soliloquy is dominated by expressions of amazement and disgust at the perversity of his desire for Isabella. He puts strings of questions to himself, punctuated by a few lines of honest self-condemnation. He is not so much struggling against temptation as—with loathing wonderment—defining its nature.

Prudential considerations are notably absent from his mind. In his situation, marriage is out of the question since public scandal would forbid his marrying Isabella and pardoning his brother-in-law. On the other hand, as her brother's executioner, he could scarcely hope to woo and seduce Isabella. If he is to possess her, circumstances thus virtually dictate the extortion plot he will hatch. But to Angelo (unlike his counterparts in Shakespeare's sources) such considerations are beside the point. It is her virtue that chiefly attracts him (although he does acknowledge his yearning to hear her speak again and feast upon her eyes), and his desire to foul it. It is very like Angelo to think of himself as a saint, whom the devil is tempting with another saint, and he defines the temptation precisely in his rhetorical question: 'Dost thou desire her foully for those things / That make her good?' If he possessed her through marriage, his desire would not be foul; if through seduction, she would foul herself and thus not be attractively good. This is the perverse logic of his conduct.

Between this soliloquy and his next one, Angelo has presumably attempted to resist his temptation. Shakespeare chooses not to show us this struggle (as he did with Claudius's attempt to pray in *Hamlet*) but its aftermath (as did one of his sources, *I Promos and Cassandra*). Angelo begins

> Why does my blood thus muster to my heart,
> Making both it unable for itself,
> And dispossessing all my other parts
> Of necessary fitness?

Does he feel faint or gasp for air?

> So play the foolish throngs with one that swoons—
> Come all to help him, and to stop the air
> By which he should revive . . .

Although one would think better of Angelo if he struggled harder against his foul desire, the soliloquies do show him suffering terribly from it—in soul, mind, and body.

2. *Should the points of resemblance between Isabella and Angelo be emphasized, or their differences?* In some obvious ways, Isabella and Angelo are diametrically opposed. In their first interview, his is the voice of stern justice, hers of compassion. In the second interview, she defends her chastity against his attempts at extortion. Temperamentally, however, the two are remarkably alike in their intellectuality and self-righteousness. Both are obliged to recognize sexual appetite as a fact of life (her brother's, his own) and come to terms with it,

however much they may at heart despise it. Neither is forthright. In 3. 1 she will lead calculatingly up to revealing Angelo's proposition to her brother, even as Angelo leads calculatingly up to propositioning her.

Angelo is a despicable sinner, Isabella the innocent object of his sinful desires and schemes. Yet she is not without fault. Both with Claudio and Angelo, she shows herself at moments of stress to be subject to fierce outbursts. When in 3. 1 Claudio pleads 'let me live', she—for fifteen lines—calls him a 'beast' and a disgrace to their father, declares his sin 'not accidental, but a trade', twice refuses to listen to him, and wishes him dead, quickly. With Angelo, she not only repudiates his 'seeming, seeming', but then descends to making a threat that is nothing short of blackmail:

> Sign me a present pardon for my brother,
> Or with an outstretched throat I'll tell the world aloud
> What man thou art.

Not at all taken aback, Angelo immediately faces down her threat ('Who will believe thee, Isabel?') and goes on to raise the stakes of his extortion:

> Redeem thy brother
> By yielding up thy body to my will,
> Or else he must not only die the death,
> But thy unkindness shall his death draw out
> To ling'ring sufferance.

How far they have sunk from their high-minded debates about justice and mercy!

Their interpreters will need to decide the extent to which they are poles apart or two of a kind.

3. *To what extent can the audience be confident of understanding the 'speechless dialect' by which—beneath their abstract 'debater's points'—Angelo and Isabella communicate?* The breakdown of verbal communication in 2. 1 (deliberate on Pompey's part, unintentional on Elbow's) may well have left the audience in a muddle as to just what happened between Froth and Elbow's wife in Mistress Overdone's taphouse. But it will also have alerted us to the need for the sort of acute and intuitive ability to read between the lines that Escalus shows in dealing with the muddle. In the first interview between Angelo and Isabella, Shakespeare takes pains to put us on the look-out for a softening of Angelo's rigour, using Lucio and the Provost as indicators. The parameters of Angelo's change are clearly marked. It occurs sometime after his lines, 'Be satisfied. / Your

brother dies tomorrow. Be content' (ll. 106–7). After this statement, instead of continuing the earlier back-and-forth exchanges with Isabella, Angelo has nothing to say until his line, 'Why do you put these sayings upon me?' (l. 137). It is during this passage, too, that Lucio not only encourages Isabella but for the first and only time sees signs of impact on Angelo: 'O, to him, to him, wench! He will relent. / He's coming; I perceive't' (ll. 127–8). The Provost also puts in 'Pray heaven she win him!'

But we are in for a surprise if, like the others, we have thought that Angelo is simply relenting. At what point do we realize that the cause of Angelo's change is his desire for Isabella? We can't be sure of it until his confessional soliloquy at the end of the scene. In retrospect, one may note that as early as line 82, he called her 'fair maid'. One can see that her later appeal is innocently apt:

> Go to your bosom;
> Knock there, and ask your heart what it doth know
> That's like my brother's fault. If it confess
> A natural guiltiness, such as is his,
> Let it not sound a thought upon your tongue
> Against my brother's life.   (140–5)

The clearest clue is his aside in response: 'She speaks, and 'tis such sense / That my sense breeds with it' (ll. 145–6). At the time, his play on 'sense' may not be altogether clear, although 'breeds' gives a strong sexual colouring to it. With hindsight, however, one can be sure that this line marks the latest limits for the awakening of his desire. Its wording, moreover, suggests that he has already been feeling her attraction.

Just where within these limits, and how overtly, the actor shows the change, is a matter of interpretation. This is one of those fine-tuning passages in which Shakespeare provides options for both enactment and response. But the audience will almost certainly to some degree be surprised when it recognizes the onset of Angelo's desire for what it is—even as Angelo himself is.

We are less subject to surprise in their second interview since we have the advantage of Angelo's two intervening soliloquies. Even so, unlike Richard III with Lady Anne, Angelo does not disclose in advance his purposes or methods. Like Isabella, we must discern his meaning as he speaks.

Angelo makes his proposition to her three times, becoming more and more overt about his own involvement in it. At first he does not say to whom she should give up her body to 'sweet uncleanness'. She never responds to the first proposition. When he asks, 'Might there not be a charity in sin / To save this brother's life?' she takes him to mean his own sin if he pardons Claudio and offers to take that sin on her own head. Angelo rightly observes, 'Your sense pursues not mine'. With astonishing (and delicious) self-righteousness he adds: 'Either you are ignorant, / Or seem so craftily, and that's not good.' Look who's talking! He then declares, 'To be receivèd plain, I'll speak more gross' and makes his proposition a second time. It is still hypothetical, but he now identifies Isabella's partner as 'a person / Whose credit with the judge, or own great place, / Could fetch your brother from the manacles'. Isabella's response is unequivocal: 'Better it were a brother died at once, / Than that a sister, by redeeming him, / Should die for ever.' Angelo is not deterred, however; and after further argumentation, he takes encouragement from Isabella's agreement that 'women are frail' and makes his final disclosure that it is he himself who desires her. Even after his declaration of love at line 141, however, she says that he may be only pretending to make such a proposition.

Why doesn't Isabella catch his drift earlier? We need to remember that she has not had our advantage of hearing his soliloquies. Her innocence and respect for his office are enough to account for her failing to respond directly to his first proposition. She seems genuinely bewildered ('How say you?' l. 58). It is hard to believe that she doesn't have some notion that Angelo might have himself in mind in his second proposition. An unwillingness on her part to face that truth may at this point become a factor. Also, with a brother's life at stake, no one would want to jump to a hasty conclusion about what is after all still a hypothetical case. The point at which Isabella essentially realizes Angelo's desire for her is a key point of interpretation. If it comes relatively late, for example, her strong repudiation of 'foul redemption' (ll. 105–13) may be seen as a spontaneous revulsion towards the idea. If her realization comes before that passage, then its strength may be seen as a subtextual attempt to rebuff Angelo's exploratory feeler and thus prevent his open declaration of love.

In any case, the audience's realization of Angelo's intention will precede Isabella's. Thanks to having heard his soliloquies, many of the audience will feel sure about it after his first proposition. Even the most cautious should be confident about his meaning after his second proposition. The audience is then in suspense not about what Angelo would like to do but whether he will go ahead with it and how. We are then in a position to see how Isabella's answer to Angelo's 'Women are frail, too', says just the wrong thing. In her self-righteousness, she cannot resist deploring the vanity and credulousness of her sex, regrettably shifting from talking of women as 'they' and 'them' to including herself: 'for we are soft as our complexions are' (l. 128). In *I Promos and Cassandra*, Angelo's counterpart was persuaded to solicit Isabella on the supposition that 'frailty' must run in her family and she be as susceptible to it as her brother. Angelo takes his cue from her admission to the frailty of all women. Does he mistakenly assume that she is thus indicating a softening of her earlier repudiation? However that may be, he is emboldened by it and proceeds.

By this time, the audience has been initiated by stages into a knowing awareness of the unspoken meaning beneath the dialogue. With Elbow and Pompey, we may have been simply muddled; in the first interview between Isabella and Angelo we will have intuited his change of heart but probably at first have mistaken its real nature; in this scene we will have had at first to do some surmising but this time will have had our surmises fully confirmed. In the scene that follows, we know from the beginning that Isabella is slowly leading up to telling her brother.

The main outlines of the BBC television version are boldly drawn. Its emphasis is on the contrasts between Angelo and Isabella, not their resemblances. His voice is loud and usually harsh; hers is usually soft. Visually, her habit is all white; Angelo's attire is mostly black; his black hair and pointed beard have a devil-like look. For the first interview he wears a white collar; for the second, he wears a dark robe over a white shirt, with his hairy chest exposed.

The properties are few but frankly symbolic. During his second soliloquy Angelo looks at himself in large mirrors. As Angelo's desire for Isabella develops, a nude male statue becomes more and more prominent in the background. Both Angelo and Isabella in soliloquy address a large 'chair of state' as if they were in the presence of a moral eminence.

The choreography of their first scene is simple. At first he sits (at a desk writing with a quill), she stands (near the entry, hands folded). At 'Tomorrow?' (l. 85) she comes to his table. When she tells him to ask his heart 'what it doth know / That's like my brother's fault' (ll. 141–2), he rises; he turns away from her for his aside, 'She speaks, and 'tis such sense / That my sense breeds with it' (ll. 145–6) and he starts out at 'Fare you well' (l. 146). When she calls to him 'turn back', he pauses, and after her 'I'll bribe you' (l. 149) he starts back towards her, furious. Her explanation mollifies him, he stops at his desk, and she departs.

In their second scene it is he who comes to her at 'for I can speak /

Against the thing I say' (ll. 59–60). He starts a slow half-circle around her at 'Admit no other way to save his life' (l. 87) and completes the circle by 'We are all frail' (l. 122). At 'I think it well', he comes closer, his voice softer, while she ever so slightly shakes her head. With 'My words express my purpose' (l. 148), he starts to kiss her, at which she pulls back for her denunciation of his *'seeming!'* (l. 150). Her voice has become loud, 'I'll tell the world aloud / What man thou art' (ll. 153–4). It is his voice that is now quiet: 'Who will believe thee, Isabel?' (l. 154). He starts circling her again. At 'Redeem thy brother' (l. 163) he seizes her and utters his threats in her ear, then leaves.

The director's use of the cameras is intriguing. For the most part, he shows the face of the speaker. But in both scenes, we at first see Isabella, when she speaks, from a distance and over Angelo's shoulder, whereas when Angelo speaks we see his face direct and close-up. She comes fully into the picture only after she approaches him or he approaches her. Thus the viewer at first sees the scenes from Angelo's vantage. In the first scene, Isabella only gradually comes into importance to the camera, and to Angelo. In the second scene, she is again seen at first from Angelo's vantage but the effect is much different. When she appears, before Angelo has quite finished his guilty soliloquy, she looms—in her white habit—as a vision of feminine purity, with which the all-too-faulty male must deal. This same effect will be even more pronounced when she first appears to Claudio. Lines are cut so that she is silent, and a close-up of her is prolonged. To Claudio she must seem the very embodiment of hope. We, however, know that she is soon going to represent to her unshaven, dishevelled brother the unblinking challenge of pure honour.

Direct close-ups of Isabella are sparingly used, they are saved for key speeches. In the first scene the chief such passage begins with her 'So you must be the first that gives this sentence' (l. 108). This passage also includes the scene's first 'reaction shots', in which Angelo's change of heart is suggested while Isabella speaks. The first of these shows Angelo leaning back in his chair after 'Nothing but thunder', obviously impressed. The second comes after Lucio's 'he will relent' (l. 126). Angelo's gaze seems softer here than before, but I see no clear indications of stirring desire in him until his 'my sense breeds with it' aside.

The handling of Lucio raises interesting critical questions. In the text there is no doubt that he serves essential functions in the first part of the scene. He stops Isabella from giving up after only one plea, coaches her in particularized ways that she seems to heed ('You are too cold'; 'touch him'). But thereafter his comments are mostly generalized encouragement. After line 73 it is a matter of interpretation whether Lucio's support to Isabella is necessary or merely officious. One suspects that his key comment on Angelo's 'relenting' is there partly to make sure that the Elizabethan audience, some of whom may not have had good sight-lines on Angelo's face, was alerted to his change.

On the tape, Lucio seems so officious as to be intrusive. For one thing, except for her first feeble effort, Kate Nelligan's Isabella is so fervent that she is far from being 'too cold'. For another, thanks to close-ups, there is no need for verbal underlining of Angelo's responses. Lucio, in fact, seems a distraction, getting in the way of the absorbing interaction of the two principals. Arguably—given the television rather than theatrical medium and an especially heartfelt Isabella—a less literal rendering would have been truer to Shakespeare's evident intentions. As it was, the director cut altogether the kibitzing of the Provost. Perhaps more of Lucio's lines should have been cut as well.

In general, the BBC television reading of the text is straightforwardly responsive to Shakespeare's evident intentions. As the lines in the second soliloquy suggest, Tim Pigott-Smith's Angelo is physically affected by the coursing of his blood. As with his change of heart in the first scene, the timing of Angelo's overt advance on Isabella in the second scene is well within Shakespeare's guide-lines. Pigott-Smith is especially sensitive to Angelo's egotism. He emphasizes 'me' in 'Why do you put these sayings upon me?' and 'How, bribe me?' and actually points to himself at 'Plainly conceive, I love you'. His Angelo may be thought untender for a man so irresistibly overcome with desire. Only in localized places does he soften his brusquely challenging manner. In the first scene during his soliloquy he looks fondly to where Isabella had stood:

> What, do I love her,
> That I desire to hear her speak again,
> And feast upon her eyes?

In the second scene he becomes more seductive shortly before he tries to kiss her. It should be remembered, however, that by the perverse logic of his desire to foul her virtue, he does not really wish to seduce her—that would take away her virtue. He is attempting a kind of rape, and the general harshness of his manner—when refused he becomes downright vicious—makes that clear.

A desire to clarify and simplify characterizes every aspect of this

production. Kate Nelligan sees no basis for the doubts that commentators have expressed about the rightness of Isabella's determination
to put her chastity above her brother's life: 'There's a completely
forceful text argument that she's an incredibly strong-minded,
eloquent, genuine, feeling, warm, good woman who's caught in an
intolerable position.'[1] She plays the role accordingly, making an
unqualified claim on our sympathies that the production furthers by
contrasting her with a thoroughly unsympathetic—though strongly
rendered—Angelo. In personality as in costume, they are as different
as white and black. Ironic resemblances between the two are ignored.
The tape, thus, heightens the text's tendency towards melodrama,
lessens its qualities of problematic comedy. What it loses in subtlety
it gains in stark strength, however; and the conviction of the acting is
so persuasive that it is only after the fact that one reflects on its over-
simplifications.

ZEFFIRELLI'S *TAMING OF THE SHREW*, 2. I

Any version of the first encounter between Petruccio and Katherine
will need to answer the following key questions: How evenly
matched are the two in their conflict? How physical is it? Do they
show any tenderness towards each other? Why does she silently
accede to his announcement of their marriage?

Shakespeare's text indicates a contest that is primarily a matching
of wits. There is one positive indication of physical violence, the stage
direction 'She strikes him' (l. 217). Two lines strongly suggest
physical actions: his 'Come, sit on me' (l. 198) and her 'Let me go'
(l. 236). He three times refers to her limping (ll. 247, 251, 254) in a way
that suggests that she is actually doing so. Otherwise, their give and
take in the text is verbal. As I read it, Kate gives about as well as she
takes. He has the big laugh-line in the exchange: 'What, with my
tongue in your tail?' But elsewhere she holds her own in their
insulting word-play.

Not all of Petruccio's speech, of course, is insulting. His two longest
speeches are in praise of Kate. Their length stands out amid their one-
line exchanges and may be no accident. Does she like the flattery? She
isn't likely to have heard much flattery previously! Certainly she does
not interrupt. When he starts a third speech, comparing her to Diana,
she wants to know: 'Where did you study all this goodly speech?' The
implication that his eloquence must be second-hand is less than

---

[1] BBC TV Shakespeare, *Measure for Measure* (London, 1979), 23.

flattering, but the admission that his speech is 'goodly' is the nearest thing to a compliment she says to him during the episode.

When he announces their wedding-day, her immediate reply is 'I'll see thee hanged on Sunday first' (l. 294). Why does she say no more for the rest of the episode? Was her last speech merely a token of protest? Or is she outwitted and nonplussed by his going on to claim a bargain between them, 'That she shall still be curst in company' while loving in private? The more she protested now, the more she would confirm the 'bargain!'

Zeffirelli gives clear-cut answers to all of the key questions. Stage Petruccios often dominate their Kates from the outset. Zeffirelli is careful to avoid this by strengthening Elizabeth Taylor's hand. Before their first interview, he allows Richard Burton to see her in action from a distance and to hear her in full (non-Shakespearian) cry: 'fat-fingered gut-slugger!' Not a little daunted, Petruccio's soliloquy immediately before their encounter is not simply an exposition of his plans. To martial music, which mingles with sounds of Kate smashing furniture, he shakes hands in formal farewell to his servant and proceeds to think through his strategy. He is verbally girding his loins. Before entering the fray, he curls his moustache, bares his lower teeth, rolls up his sleeves, and rumples his hair. Clearly, he sees Kate as a worthy opponent.

He is right. He takes a great deal of physical punishment from her. Before they are through, she will hit him with her fists, throw barrels at him and a stair-railing. Zeffirelli cuts much of the repartee in the text and often makes substitutions to clarify what remains. Her 'No such jade as you' (l. 201) becomes 'No such load as you'; her 'A witty mother, witless else her son' (l. 258) becomes 'A witty mother, with a witless son'. Zeffirelli's emphasis is on rough-and-tumble high jinks. He not only adds a great deal of it but heightens what was there in the text. Instead of striking him once, she kicks him repeatedly in the face.

The scene is structured as a love-chase. After 'Too light for such a swain as you to catch' (l. 204), she gives a non-Shakespearian call: 'Father, this man . . .' and when he turns, she slips away. They then play hide-and-seek through interpolated incidents in the Bianca story. Thinking she has given him the slip, she flops down on the fleece in the wool-loft, whooping with glee, only to see him start to hoist open the trap-door in the loft with his head, which he succeeds in doing, even after she has piled three sacks on it. She escapes and in her pursuit he must swing precariously across a courtyard, crashing through a balustrade, break through a wall, and chase her across a tile

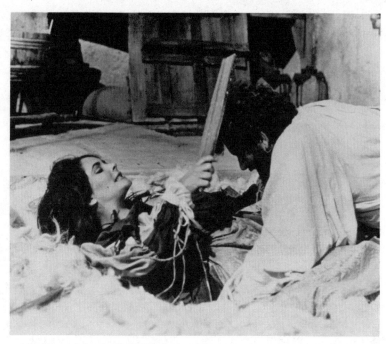

5. Katherine (Elizabeth Taylor) and Petruccio (Richard Burton) struggle in the wool-loft in Zeffirelli's film *The Taming of the Shrew* (1966).

rooftop, through which they both fall into the wool-loft. The sequence is full of analogues to sexual penetration.

This is not mere slapstick. It exaggerates the physical violence, but the exaggeration is to scale and rises in climactic sequence. Also, the physical action is aptly integrated with the dialogue, much of which has been rearranged to that end. It is after Petruccio has succeeded in thrusting his head through the trap-door that he says, 'What, with my tongue in your tail?' It is while he is chasing Kate across the roof that Baptista asks, 'how speed you with my daughter?' (l. 275) to which Petruccio replies, balancing on one foot, 'How but well, sir? How but well?' It is while he declares to her, 'I find you passing gentle' (l. 237) that she bangs him on the head with a board.

Furthermore, the apache-dance violence is counterpointed with moments in which both Petruccio and Kate show strong attraction to one another. It is love at first sight. After 'Good morrow, Kate' Petruccio pauses, looks her up and down appreciatively, background music sounds. They each hugely enjoy the love-chase. When she bolts a door to keep him out, she still puts her ear to it in order to hear what he's saying on the other side. When she has hurt her foot in the fall through the roof and so limps (ll. 247–51) and begins to weep, he shows real concern, again to background music, and helps her to get up and to walk. His motives, it is true, are less than pure: when she starts across the roof he thinks first of her dowry and interpolates in alarm: 'My twenty thousand crowns!'

After another Bianca insert, we see him escorting her to meet the others, with her arm twisted behind her back. When he announces their wedding-day, she, as in the original, says that she will see him hanged first, at which he locks her in a room. His subsequent speech (ll. 297 ff.) is punctuated by her exclamations. After the much altered lines ''Tis a world to see / How tame, when she and I are alone, / A milksop wretch can make the curstest shrew' (ll. 307–9), he listens for another of her explosions. He hears none. Behind the locked door, Kate has climbed up to watch through a small window. She looks very beautiful though sad. He blows her a kiss, 'kiss me Kate'. Then as she seems to recall the love-chase, a little smile forms, even while she reflectively bites a fingernail.

Although Zeffirelli takes many liberties with the text, he is still working within its spirit, if not always according to its letter. That is what distinguishes 'free translation' from adaptation, in which the adapter is serving his own purposes rather than Shakespeare's. Zeffirelli's film addresses directly and imaginatively each of the scene's key interpretative questions, finding answers that suit its two stars, its film medium, and its popular audience. In it the matching of wits between Petruccio and Kate is much less verbal than in the original, much more a matter of rough-and-tumble derring-do. At the same time, Zeffirelli softens the feelings of hostility between the two. Taylor is much more a 'lusty wench' than a sharp-edged shrew in need of taming. Nervously chuckling, Burton gains the upper hand not by being 'more shrew than she' (4. 1. 76), but by high-spirited, hard-bitten, and wily gamesmanship, breaking through or getting around each of her lines of resistance. Their mutual attraction is so overt as to make of their first encounter a lovers' quarrel. If Zeffirelli thus takes a step further the play's tendencies towards knock-about farce, his approach none the less partakes of Shakespeare's theatre-poetry. Just as the impetuous pace of his *Romeo and Juliet* film caught the youthfulness of the original, so the delight he takes in *The Taming of the Shrew* in subverting social conventions is in tune with Shake-speare's own. As a consequence, his 'free translation' version of this scene succeeds in drawing hearty laughter from the audience, something that 'readings' of Shakespearian comedy on film or television have rarely achieved.

Even so, it is true that Zeffirelli's *Taming of the Shrew* seems somehow less than its original, as does the BBC television *Measure for Measure*. Both versions are less distinctive than Shakespeare, easier for an audience to appreciate but less challenging, more theatrically conventional, tending more than he does towards generic farce or melodrama. They deal in bold outlines, verging on caricature, to the neglect of Shakespeare's fine shadings. Partly, of course, this discrepancy comes about because the creator's genius exceeds his interpreters' talents. In addition, the interpreters are engaged in an act of translation, whether free or literal, into a film or television medium and for a modern audience. An element of popularization enters into their urges to magnify or simplify. Yet in a deeper way any production of Shakespeare will necessarily seem less than its text. A play may have greater immediacy and impact when performed than when read, but at the expense of fullness and subtlety. Still more deeply, any interpretation, whether on-stage or off, is bound to seem reductive because it is selective; it is obliged to make choices from the wealth of alternatives the text suggests. In this respect, it not only seems but inevitably is, less than the original.

On the other hand, the theatre-event that occurs when a text is performed has something that the original—when read—cannot; for it includes a relation between players and playgoers that goes on to some degree outside or beyond the text. We in the audience respond not only to Shakespeare's characters but to Kate Nelligan as Isabella and Tim Pigott-Smith as Angelo. This awareness of the players is still more pronounced at Zeffirelli's *Taming of the Shrew*, where we are very much aware of Taylor and Burton as a pair who were as tumultuous in their private lives as Shakespeare's Kate and Petruccio. In turn, the players at a live performance respond immediately to the receptivity or obduracy of a particular audience. This is most evident in comedies, where the actors must include the audience's laughter, or lack of it, in their timing. Since Shakespeare's art does not extend into such extra-textual factors, they receive little comment in this study.

In many respects, however, Shakespeare's texts do provide guidance as to their reception in performance. They can usefully be regarded not only as guides to enactment but as scenarios for audience-response, as will be set forth in the next two chapters.

IO

Audience-Response: *Macbeth*

WHAT is the role of the audience within the performance-ensemble? The subject has received little attention. Most previous comment has focused on reader-response. Audience-response is more complicated because in performance the audience's relation with the author's work is not direct but necessarily mediated by performers and because a member of the audience responds not only as an individual but as part of a group. These complications need to be kept in mind and deserve future study. None the less, a start can be made now towards understanding the relation between Shakespeare and his audience. For he does have a distinguishable though indirect share in the impact of one of his plays when it is performed. With the aid of the printed text and by making due allowance for the latitudes Shakespeare grants his interpreters, one can say roughly what the playwright's share is for a given play and discuss the responses it is likely to produce in an audience.

Here current thinking about reader-response can provide a useful context.[1] Traditionally, commentators have seen readers as slavishly responding to the writer's manipulations. In recent years, many commentators have shifted to the other extreme and declared the independence of readers to respond as it suits them, whether individually and subjectively or collectively in 'interpretive communities'. The shift is analogous to the revolt of performers that Artaud led against the presumed tyranny of the dramatist. Each extreme has a measure of truth and fits certain works especially well, but between these two extremes there is a whole spectrum of other possibilities. Is it not part of the creativity of a writer to define a relation between his or her work and its audience?

Shakespeare's approach to his playgoers is very much the same as that to his players. His texts provide broad outlines within which a range of options are left open.

[1] Norman H. Holland, *The Dynamics of Literary Response* (Oxford, 1968); Wolfgang Iser, *The Implied Reader* (Baltimore, 1974); David Bleich, *Subjective Criticism* (Baltimore, 1978); Stanley Fish, *Is There a Text in This Class? The Authority of Interpretive Communities* (Harvard, 1980); Robert C. Holub, *Reception Theory* (London and New York, 1984).

Take *Richard II*, for example. It is commonly agreed that in the
course of the play Shakespeare engineers a remarkable change in the
audience's feeling about the deposition of the King. In prospect, it
seems a good if painful thing, replacing an incompetent though
legitimate ruler with a capable one. In fact, it comes to seem a
disastrous mistake. Such a change seems to me clearly built into the
text. But when exactly does it occur? Here Shakespeare provides
options for the spectator, just as he did for the actor of *Othello*. The
earliest turning-point would be the long denunciation of the deposition
by the Bishop of Carlisle immediately before the deposition occurs
(4. 1. 105–40). The latest would be Henry's repudiation of Exton and
his assassination of Richard (5. 6. 38–52). Between, the turning-point
for the audience might coincide with Richard's own (4. 1. 234–42),
with the counterplotting of the churchmen who support him
(4. 1. 311–23), with the grieving protests of his queen (5. 1), with
York's account of his humiliation (5. 2), or with Exton's own change
of heart (5. 5. 113–18). These options not only allow the performers to
make certain interpretative emphases but also allow for individual
differences among the spectators. Someone inclined to identify with
Richard might change when he does:

> I find myself a traitor with the rest,
> For I have given here my soul's consent
> T'undeck the pompous body of a king . . .   (4. 1. 238–40)

or someone inclined to identify with Bolingbroke might change when
he does:

> Though I did wish him dead,
> I hate the murderer, love him murderèd.   (5. 6. 39–40)

In these last instances, the spectator's responses parallel those of a
character. Of course, this is not always the case. In melodrama, the
audience's response may be simply the reverse of a character's: the
more the villain gloats, the more we hiss; when he is foiled, the more
he curses, the more we cheer. In Shakespeare, contrary responses are
characteristically more complex. Consider our responses to Graziano
in the trial scene of *The Merchant of Venice*. At first our reactions
parallel his. When Portia turns the tables on Shylock, most audiences
laugh jubilantly at Graziano's mocking: 'O upright judge! / Mark, Jew!
O learnèd judge!' (4. 1. 309–10). At that moment Graziano is
completely in accord with the unfolding of the play. This is one of
those key moments for which Shakespeare seeks a single audience-
response. In unison with him, and one another, the members of the

audience all join in the jubilation. There is something especially gratifying about such moments. (Isn't it one of the great dramatic pleasures that at a play—as at a political rally or church service or sports event—large numbers of people can share the same feeling in the same place and at the same time?) Thanks to Portia, Shylock's legalism boomerangs and, thanks to Graziano, so does his exact language. Graziano's mimicry articulates the audience's realization of this turn-about and gives an outlet for our relief and joy in it.

Thereafter, however, the unanimity begins to dissolve and audience-responses contrary to Graziano's begin to set in. Some laughter usually accompanies his next four sallies (each containing the word 'Jew'), as he crows over each further stage of Shylock's downfall. But the laughter begins to fade—partly because through repetition his mimicry has worn thin (as with the repeated use of the 'second Daniel' echo) and partly because the Christians seem bent not only on humbling Shylock but on humiliating him. There is little or no laughter at Graziano's three final speeches in this episode, and what there is, if any, is uneasy. When Portia directs: 'Down, therefore, and beg mercy of the Duke', Graziano adds:

> Beg that thou mayst have leave to hang thyself—
> And yet, thy wealth being forfeit to the state,
> Thou hast not left the value of a cord.
> Therefore thou must be hanged at the state's charge.
>
> (4. 1. 361–4)

When Portia asks: 'What mercy can you render him, Antonio?' Graziano interposes: 'A halter, gratis. Nothing else, for God's sake.' As Shylock leaves, Graziano's parting shot is:

> In christ'ning shalt thou have two godfathers.
> Had I been judge thou shouldst have had ten more,
> To bring thee to the gallows, not the font. (395–7)

The turn-about that had seemed fair play has now gone too far and become vindictive. Graziano's successive sallies (and especially his intonations when he calls Shylock 'Jew') provide the performers with a ready way to mark the graduated phases in this process. As well, they can provide a chart for audience-response. Shakespeare seems to expect that at Graziano's first sally, everyone in the audience will be with him and that at his last, no one will be. Individual members of the audience are left free to differ, however, about where along the way they part company with him.

Elsewhere too, Shakespeare takes pains to define for the audience the borderline that separates just severity from cruelty by showing us

a character who oversteps it. At the deposition of Richard II,
Northumberland harshly demands that Richard read a list of 'grievous
crimes / Committed by your person and your followers' (*Richard II*,
4. 1. 213–14), thereby precipitating Richard's change of heart towards
his 'resignation'. Northumberland persists in his demands ('My lord,
dispatch. Read o'er these articles') until Henry IV directs, 'Urge it no
more, my Lord Northumberland'. It is a measure of Henry's political
skill that we cannot be sure whether or not Northumberland has
exceeded his new king's brief. With similar ambiguity, the Lord Chief
Justice's imprisonment of Falstaff ('Go carry Sir John Falstaff to the
Fleet'—*2 Henry IV*, 5. 5. 89) exceeds the new King Henry V's already
severe rejection.

In *Twelfth Night* the practical joke at Malvolio's expense gets out of
hand, to become a kind of mental cruelty. It is Feste who doesn't
know when to stop. At the end of Feste's prolonged impersonation of
Sir Topas, even Sir Toby realizes on prudential grounds that they have
gone far enough: 'I would we were well rid of this knavery. If he may
be conveniently delivered, I would he were, for I am now so far in
offence with my niece that I cannot pursue with any safety this sport
to the upshot' (4. 2. 67–71). Some members of the audience may feel
that the joke has already gone too far, or at least lasted too long. The
last scene leaves no doubt about Feste's overreaching. In it, without
implicating Feste, Fabian confesses to his involvement with Sir Toby
and Maria in the 'device'. He calls it 'sportful malice' but equably
maintains 'If that the injuries be justly weighed / That have on both
sides passed,' the device 'May rather pluck on laughter than revenge'.
Feste, however, cannot leave it at that. He must claim his part in 'this
interlude' and give a few last mocking twists of the knife in
Malvolio's humiliation, concluding 'and thus the whirligig of time
brings in his revenges'. Malvolio characteristically over-reacts: 'I'll be
revenged on the whole pack of you.' Still, Olivia is persuasive in
judging that 'He hath been most notoriously abused', for Shakespeare
has taken care to define for the audience precisely the degree to which
this is true.

So far I have considered cases in which the audience's responses are
moving in the same direction, although perhaps at different paces.
Sometimes Shakespeare seeks a divided response. After Cleopatra's
eloquent account of her dream of Antony ('His legs bestrid the ocean;
his reared arm / Crested the world . . .', 5. 2. 81–91), she asks
Dolabella: 'Think you there was, or might be, such a man / As this I
dreamt of?' He politely but succinctly contradicts: 'Gentle madam,
no.' To which she retorts: 'You lie, up to the hearing of the gods.'

Which of the two are we to credit? The choice is important, having to do with such central issues in the play as the characterization of Antony and the value of the imagination, and Shakespeare puts the choice so starkly that we can hardly avoid making it. Yet he indicates no single approved answer. The Cleopatras in the audience are thus left free to agree with her, and the Dolabellas with him. Others in the audience may internalize the conflict.

Shakespeare often encourages conflict in his spectators, especially at the finales of his tragedies. We have already seen in Chapter 6 how the ethics of many of Hamlet's actions and inactions are so complicated as to defeat clear-cut resolution. Similarly, Othello's appraisal of himself at the end as an 'honourable murderer' (5. 2. 300) focuses in an oxymoron the confusing paradoxes with which the audience must cope. For he is both honourable and a murderer yet neither simply honourable nor simply a murderer. Such confusions serve to turn against themselves any expectations the audience may have that the catastrophe will follow formulas of poetic justice. Our feelings are thus freed for a more direct and particular response to the tragedy.

Shakespeare is not always successful in his invitations to audience-response. In the first acts of *Richard III* he in a way succeeds too well. He not only seduces the audience into enjoying the perverse pleasures of 'playing the devil' but also himself bustles about, intrusively helping Richard with opportune situations at every turn (as he does also with Iago and Edmond). He does so with zest. So carried away are we and he by the exhilaration of the experience that his finale falls short of its intended effects. Neither we nor he, it seems, can welcome with more than piety the replacement of Richard by Richmond. He improves his approach in *Macbeth*. Its initial engagement with evil is anything but pleasurable either to the evil-doers or ourselves, and our disengagement from the evil-doers is graduated over an extended period; while on the other hand Malcolm is being more fully delineated than was Richmond. Shakespeare has also learned to avoid the impression of arbitrariness, whether in the characters or the gods or himself. Largely involuntary actions seem to be much more acceptable to an audience than altogether voluntary ones. In one sense, the action of *Richard III* is the product of Richard's will; in another it is the product of the iron will of nemesis, which (because of Queen Margaret's foretelling) we can see to work with mechanical precision. In either case, its unfolding is much less persuasive than in *Macbeth*, where the action seems outside the control of any one person or power, except possibly Hecate, who is mysterious. The play is full of semi-voluntary and involuntary actions, and as it progresses the images of human involuntariness increase: a human being is seen as a creature who walks in his or her sleep, who is 'but a walking shadow, a poor player', an animal tied to a stake.

The same distinction explains why the inaction of *Hamlet* is less distressing to an audience than that of *Troilus and Cressida*. Both plays show worlds in which a slowness to act is a general malaise verging on paralysis. Chapter 6 examined this malaise in detail as it appears in *Hamlet*; in *Troilus and Cressida* the atmosphere of a long siege in stalemate is pervasive. But where the delays in Hamlet are largely involuntary—the result of deadlocked inner and outer forces— the holdings back from action in *Troilus and Cressida* are largely deliberate, often wilful, even spiteful.

As a case in point, consider the battle between Achilles and Hector which promises a resolution of the stand-off. It is long deferred. Achilles refuses to fight but instead 'in his tent / Lies', 'on his pressed bed lolling'. Not only will he not go forth to battle, he declines to come to the opening of his tent at the summons of his commander, Agamemnon; as Ulysses concludes, 'the hart Achilles / Keeps thicket' (2. 3. 253–4). When Hector offers a challenge to 'sportful combat', Ulysses plots to keep Achilles from taking it up, substituting Ajax. It is in the balky rhythm of this play that Thersites should spend most of 2. 1 refusing to obey Ajax's command to bring him news about Hector's challenge. When at last Achilles does agree to fight, his intention is halted by the letter from Hecuba and token from Polyxena. It takes Patroclus' death to bring him forth:

> weeping, cursing, vowing vengeance.
> Patroclus' wounds have roused his drowsy blood . . .(5. 5. 31–2)

When at long last Achilles and Hector fight, Hector evidently gains the upper hand. Yet, going against Troilus' advice that sparing his foes is not 'fair play' but 'fool's play', he courteously holds back from following through on his advantage: 'Pause, if thou wilt.' Yet again, the resolution of their conflict is deferred.

Hector then seems almost to invite his own undoing. His fancy for a suit of armour causes him to abandon his past practice and pursue a fleeing Trojan, an exertion that leaves him feeling: 'Now is my day's work done. I'll take good breath. / Rest, sword: thou hast thy fill of blood and death' (5. 9. 3–4).

In a sense the long awaited, hand-to-hand fight to the finish between Hector and Achilles never does occur. Certainly, it is not a fair fight. Hector's last words to Achilles are, 'I am unarmed. Forego

this vantage, Greek.' Although Achilles will proclaim that he 'hath
the mighty Hector slain!' one cannot even be sure that he does more
than give the order to his Myrmidons to do so: 'Strike, fellows, strike!
This is the man I seek.' The play's denial of satisfying action reaches
an ultimate at the end when Troilus forecasts images of utter stasis:

> Hector's dead.
> There is a word will Priam turn to stone . . .
> Cold statues of the youth . . .   (5. 11. 17–20)

Audiences come to plays expecting to see something happen. When
they see inaction instead, they feel frustrated; yet when the inaction
is involuntary, as it largely is in *Hamlet*, there is no one to blame.
When 'things just happen' or 'just don't happen' in Shakespeare is
when they seem the most natural and persuasive, perhaps because an
audience is most comfortable with a condition on-stage that reflects
its own passivity. But when as in *Troilus and Cressida* deliberate
inaction is dwelt upon, and elaborated, an audience may well feel that
the source of the frustration is to be found in the playwright as well as
in his characters. Is this yet another instance of Shakespeare's
immersion in the imagined world of his play?—so much so that his
conduct is as perversely contrary as that of Achilles? However that
may be, it is to his overall purpose as theatre-poet for the audience to
be put out with such perversity on his part as playwright. Why should
we not bear witness to a playwright's dereliction of his traditional role
as a maker of actions when we have in this play witnessed the
violation of so many other traditional roles?

As here, the rapport that Shakespeare's theatre-poetry creates
among the members of the performance-ensemble is certainly not all
sweetness and light. Within it, the members of the audience will
almost always be challenged in some way, whether we are tempted,
dared, perplexed, frustrated, inspired, enchanted, or disenchanted.
The role Shakespeare assigns the audience is very much like his major
roles for actors. Like them, it is rounded, multifaceted, dynamic, full
of life. Its charge of vitality can be so intense as to be overwhelming
(Milton felt turned to marble 'with too much conceiving'; Keats
'burned' like a phoenix).

Above all, responsive members of Shakespeare's audience, like his
major characters, will *develop* in the course of the play. As we come
to know the prevailing way of life in Elsinore or Vienna and are
attracted towards certain characters and repelled by others, our own
values as witnesses are conditioned. When in Shakespeare's Rome, we
tend to do as his Romans do. However we may feel about suicide in

general, we can scarcely enter into the imagined worlds of *Julius Caesar* or *Antony and Cleopatra* without accepting that it can be honourable there. Yet in *King Lear* we are conditioned to reject suicide as a desirable course for Gloucester. Such conditioning is not complete or dictatorial on Shakespeare's part. On the contrary, he characteristically gives his spectators the freedom to play Adam to his God. Indeed, he depends upon the humanity of our individual responses for the full realization of his plays, as will now be shown in *Macbeth*.

So far I have had little to say about the aspect of audience-response that has received the most previous critical attention: our relative identification or sympathy with a given character. That will be the central concern of this section, which will focus on the relationship that Shakespeare develops between Macbeth and the audience.

Does Shakespeare invite the audience to identify with Macbeth? Certainly he keeps Macbeth at the centre of our attention. Every scene in the play relates directly to him in one way or another. He has an unusual number of soliloquies and asides, which let us know how he sees things. We are taken into his most secret conversations. Shakespeare repeatedly uses a device where Macbeth is concerned that to my knowledge does not occur to anything like the same degree elsewhere: he places us in the position of experiencing, from a safe distance, Macbeth's traumas before he does. So, just before Macbeth does, we encounter the witches; his altered wife (who has unsexed herself in his absence but our presence); his friend's ghost; his fatal enemy (Macduff) on his trail. Banquo reveals himself to us as a threat to Macbeth immediately before Macbeth tells us that he sees him as such. Perhaps the time we most share Macbeth's point of view is when we—alone with him—see Banquo's ghost.

Una Ellis-Fermor has claimed that 'We remain continuously immersed in the character's experience; we never cease to be Macbeth; we are never invited to observe him.'[2] This is a distortion, I believe, more expressive of the kind of experience of Macbeth that we would like to have than of what Shakespeare in fact permits. As discussed in Chapter 3, the mystery of Macbeth's ultimate motivations and his way of reaching decisions in tandem with partners keep us from enjoying a direct and clear apprehension of his inner experience. And it is simply untrue that 'we are never invited to observe him'. One of

---

[2] Una Ellis-Fermor, *Shakespeare the Dramatist* (New York, 1961), 37.

the play's main governing rhythms is the movement from inside Macbeth to outside and back again. It is worth following in detail.

In the first scene in which Macbeth appears, Shakespeare repeatedly shows him moving back and forth between his public self and his private self. After his private raptness on hearing the first prophecies, Macbeth at long last gives voice to his questions and again charges the Sisters to speak, but to no avail. The confirmation of the prophecy about his elevation to Thane of Cawdor occasions a series of withdrawals into privacy. The first is short ('Glamis, and Thane of Cawdor. The greatest is behind.'), followed immediately by a return to his altogether public self ('Thanks for your pains') and an extended confidential exchange with Banquo, this last an intermediate point between his public and private disclosures. The next aside is somewhat longer:

> Two truths are told
> As happy prologues to the swelling act
> Of the imperial theme.

This is interrupted by the brief 'I thank you, gentlemen' before Macbeth gives himself over to the prolonged 'raptness' of his soliloquy, 'This supernatural soliciting / Cannot be ill, cannot be good . . .'.

The same gradualness and subtlety mark Shakespeare's handling of Macbeth's return to his public self. At first Banquo remarks to the others, 'Look how our partner's rapt' and 'New honours come upon him . . .', but Macbeth continues his private train of thought. Only when Banquo directly addresses him does Macbeth return to the public situation: 'Give me your favour . . .' This is interrupted by another confidential exchange with Banquo before Macbeth concludes the scene with 'Come, friends'.

Thus Shakespeare, in the interests of convincing psychology, softens the conventions of soliloquy. When it suits his purposes of heavy irony in the very next scene, he can be much more abrupt. Without transition he gives Macbeth a six-line aside as he exits, stressing in no uncertain terms that the obstacle presented by the newly named heir to the throne has not lessened his wavering determination but rather hardened it.

The next episodes take us alternately inside and outside the conspiracy, entering inside it at greatest length and depth immediately before and after the assassination. The Porter takes us outside Macbeth again, where we remain for the rest of the scene, even though there are important inner developments we would very much like to have revealed. Is Lady Macbeth's fainting genuine? What are the long-term after-effects of his crime on Macbeth? Has his first taste of killing off the battlefield released impulses that led to his unplanned killing of the grooms? Has Macbeth already begun to leave Lady Macbeth behind? Shakespeare chooses to leave us wondering about these matters.

The next scene and nearly fifty lines of the one following are also external. We are not again taken into Macbeth's confidence until his 'To be thus is nothing / But to be safely thus' soliloquy, which reveals a very different Macbeth from our last previous inside look at him: 'Wake Duncan with thy knocking. I would thou couldst' (2. 2. 72).

The first four scenes of Act 3 provide an insight into Macbeth's inner life preceding and following the killing of Banquo that is comparable in length to that surrounding the killing of Duncan. They accomplish an interesting changing of partners in Macbeth's secret life. After having heard Banquo's opening confession of his hopes that the oracles will prove as true for him as for Macbeth, we may feel at first that Macbeth's honouring of him as his 'chief guest' is like Duncan's blind trust of himself. Yet something about the abruptness of his assumption of the royal manner (the stage direction states that he enters '*as King*', in his very first line he uses the royal we) and Banquo's exaggerated (and false) declaration of 'indissoluble' duty seem to hint at inner changes in Macbeth's attitudes as well as Banquo's. Is he irritated that Banquo will be missing the day's council to go riding? Why does he enquire so insistently into details of the ride? If we have sensed any such hints, they are immediately confirmed in Macbeth's declaration, in soliloquy, that 'Our fears in Banquo / Stick deep'. So much for Banquo as a partner.

His separation from his wife is more gradual. The public indications of a change are clearer than with Banquo, both in his manner ('we will keep ourself / Till supper-time alone') and hers ('Say to the King I would attend his leisure / For a few words'). These are confirmed during their private conversation, not only because Macbeth has converted his former partner into a mere spectator of his exploits ('Be innocent of the knowledge, dearest chuck, / Till thou applaud the deed', 3. 2. 46–7), but because she has mistaken his brooding about Banquo for remorse for Duncan (ll. 8–12). His new partners are the Murderers, whose resolution—along with his own—Macbeth then proceeds to harden. The confederacy, however, extends only to their report of the killing of Banquo but escape of Fleance. In the public situation of the banquet scene, Lady Macbeth at first 'keeps her state' but in the crisis of Macbeth's seeing Banquo's ghost, she returns briefly to her earlier partnership with him, chastizing Macbeth's conduct with her tongue ('Are you a man?') By the end of the scene, however, he has again left her behind. She is left exhausted, he exhilarated and determined to know by the worst means the worst.

The banquet scene marks the beginning of Macbeth's inability to keep his secrets. Despite Lady Macbeth's best efforts, his talk of 'sights' spills out, to be overheard by Ross. He questions Lennox with surprising openness, 'Saw you the weird sisters?' (4. 1. 152), and in the last act he is utterly public in his ravings about the prophecies. At last his private and public selves are one.

In addition to shifting his focus back and forth between Macbeth's public and private selves, Shakespeare also invites us to observe his hero from a variety of external perspectives. In the second scene the bleeding Captain glorifies the exploits of 'brave Macbeth'. Yet the Captain's style is so epic and his zest for violence so extreme (he exults in the way Macbeth 'unseamed' an enemy 'from the nave to th' chops', how he bathed 'in reeking wounds') that his account is clearly not choric, not the 'voice of the event' but rather a single perspective on it. The mirror that Banquo holds up to Macbeth is also sharply angled. Of course his main function in this respect is to show more resistance to the prophecies than does Macbeth. Close attention to his words also shows that Shakespeare is focusing Banquo's comments on two aspects: the crown and the theological dangers of trafficking with the supernatural.

Such abstract focusing also goes on in 1. 4, which might have been entitled 'Cawdorism' or 'Treachery'; and in 1. 6, which might have been entitled 'The False Welcome'. As with the dead Cawdor, Shakespeare begins the latter with a definite instance—in this case, the castle—and then widens its implications. It seems an emblem of Lady Macbeth's advice to Macbeth in the scene just before to 'look like the innocent flower, / But be the serpent under't'. No sooner have the King and then Banquo commented on the sweetness of the air surrounding the castle than the serpent appears: '*Enter Lady Macbeth.*' Her expression 'our house' helps to extend the implications of the castle to include 'our family' and Duncan's repeated references to 'our hostess' and the absence of 'mine host' emphasize the violation of hospitality that the Macbeths are contemplating. Macbeth himself will make the point explicit in his soliloquy, which immediately follows: as the king's host, he 'should against his murderer shut the door, / Not bear the knife myself'.

After the murder of Duncan there is a pattern of growing hostility in the external comments on Macbeth. There is the initial questioning of the crime by Banquo and Macduff, until the flight of Malcolm and Donalbain fixes the blame on them. In 2. 4 there is a note of troubled acquiescence in the new regime, as we note Macduff's decision to go to his home rather than to Scone for the coronation and sense his dark but masked misgivings: 'Well, may you see things well done there. Adieu, / Lest our old robes sit easier than our new.' After the killing of Banquo and the appearance of his ghost, the banquet scene breaks up in disorder, with Ross asking 'what sights' Macbeth has been raving about and Lennox wishing him 'better health'. In 3. 6 Lennox at first talks with a lord out of both sides of his mouth about recent events (perhaps because they are being spied upon) before the lord to whom he is speaking makes an open, straightforward denunciation of the 'tyrant' and Lennox responds in kind with hopes for immediate relief from 'a hand accursed!' To Macduff's wife, Ross speaks of the times as 'cruel' and wildly fear-ridden. Malcolm's stratagem of making himself out to Macduff to be worse than Macbeth causes Macbeth to be charged with a host of sins, some of them unexpected, such as lechery. In the last act, Macbeth is freely called a 'tyrant'. Caithness allows for a difference of opinion about him: 'Some say he's mad, others that lesser hate him / Do call it valiant fury.' But he goes on to conclude that 'for certain / He cannot buckle his distempered cause / Within the belt of rule'. And he leaves no doubt that all of Macbeth's subjects hate him, in one degree or another.

In sum, does Shakespeare invite his audience to identify with Macbeth? Spectators will of course differ, and by at first changing so frequently between Macbeth's public and private selves Shakespeare allows for such differences. These changes also tend to moderate both extremes. Even those most inclined to identify with him will not—if they are responsive to Shakespeare's pointers—be able to do so altogether. Shakespeare's method of showing us Macbeth's public as well as his private self and of observing him from a variety of external perspectives tends to discourage our total immersion in Macbeth's point of view. On the other hand, Macbeth's unusually frequent asides and soliloquies oblige even those least inclined to identify with him to realize how he himself sees his situation.

It might be thought that Shakespeare most seeks our identification with Macbeth in the last act of the play since it is there that he is most overt about his thoughts and feelings. But that is not my own view. For one thing, he is there making his disclosures to the world at large, not confiding his secrets to us alone. For another, he has less to disclose. In order to bring himself to commit his crimes, he has had to kill more and more of himself. He has now become a hardened criminal, burnt out, and so desperate at the end as to seem mad. For these reasons I conclude that whatever degree of identification with Macbeth we may have felt at the beginning has lessened by the end.

Is the audience invited to sympathise with Macbeth? Noted critics have disagreed; yet on close inspection their disagreement may be seen to derive from a vagueness in the meaning of 'sympathy'. To Wayne Booth, for example, it means 'moral approval'. To Robert Heilman it means 'human understanding'.[3] I propose therefore to appraise Macbeth's career through a mix of somewhat more precise terms—such as admiration, respect, approval, wonderment, understanding, disapproval, condemnation, pity, and the like.

As already discussed, in his exchanges with the Weird Sisters he excites our fellow-feeling as one human being to another in the face of the supernatural, especially because he has apparently been singled out by supernatural agencies unbeknownst to himself. We do not, however, approve of the rapidity with which his thoughts after the first prophecies turn to 'murder' and wish that he had shown the kind of resistance exemplified by Banquo. The fact that Macbeth should feel such temptation is certainly understandable, nevertheless, and the fact that he shows some resistance to it helps to retain our sympathies. His mental anguish over his inner conflict awakens our pity: we feel sorry for him in his suffering, even though his suffering comes ultimately from his own guilty desires.

From the time Macbeth decides to kill Duncan, he no longer has our approval for his conduct. We recognize, however, mitigating circumstances—that a number of factors have conspired to reinforce his own worst inclinations and bring him to this decision: his recent taste of glory, the encouraging prophecies, the influence of his wife, the all-too-convenient opportunity. Furthermore, Macbeth and Lady Macbeth arouse a kind of wonderment at their adventuring into new realms of forbidden experience, outdaring the world. It takes a certain courage to kill a king.

Again, Macbeth's sufferings—guilty as they are—are still more intense after he has done the deed than before, and they make us feel sorry for him. By and large he and his wife experience a joyless triumph. Shakespeare allows one possible moment of exultation. When Macbeth first returns after killing Duncan, Lady Macbeth

---

[3] Wayne Booth, 'Shakespeare's Tragic Villain', in *Shakespeare's Tragedies*, ed. L. Lerner (Harmondsworth, 1964), 180–90; R. B. Heilman, 'The Criminal as Tragic Hero', *Shakespeare Survey*, 19 (1966), 12–24.

greets him with 'My husband!' (We may recall her earlier scorn when
he was backing away from the assassination: 'Such I account thy
love.') Otherwise, Shakespeare's emphasis is on their miseries; he
chooses not to show Macbeth's elevation to the throne.

At what point do we turn decisively against Macbeth? Shakespeare
allows the spectator a range of choices. It seems safe to say that for
most the turning-point does not occur before the decision to kill
Duncan and that for very few does it occur after the killing of the
Macduff family.

Nature's revulsion is immediate and extreme. On the 'rough' night
of the assassination, horses ate one another. Society's adverse reaction
takes longer, but as we have just seen it is no less complete. For those
who like myself accept the authenticity of Hecate's speech in 3. 5, the
overt hostility towards Macbeth also includes the other world. He is
there seen as a 'wayward son' and condemned to confusion.

Even amid this mounting and eventually total disapproval, Macbeth's
actions remain understandable. Ruthless as it is, his decision to kill
Banquo and Fleance makes sense for a king determined to retain the
throne and pass it on to his line of descendants. One must indeed
admire the audacity he shows in daring fate, to try to alter the
prophecy that Banquo shall 'get kings'. He shows strength of mind,
too, when he finally faces down Banquo's ghost. Again we cannot but
pity anyone who is condemned to suffer such 'sights', however much
they are consequences of his own doing—as we pity the victim of
delirium tremens or drug nightmares.

Our realization of his suffering helps to make understandable his
determination to 'know by the worst means the worst'. Even the
atrocity of the slaughter of the innocent Lady Macduff and her
children has a kind of logic in it. It is made understandable by the
prophesied threat to Macbeth's line posed by Macduff and all future
'thanes of Fife' and (as Macbeth now sees it) to his very life.

Shakespeare wisely breaks his previous pattern and chooses not to
seek any pity for Macbeth because of the suffering he might have felt
for his last 'unfortunate' victims. Our revulsion against this deed, and
our cumulative feelings against his previous murders, find satisfying
expression in the counter-forces we see gathering against Macbeth.
Our condemnation of him, however, certainly does not preclude pity
for his plight. For one thing, it is clear that Macbeth is far
outnumbered and that his own men won't fight on his behalf. He is
thus extended the pity we give to losers, and his resistance is not a
threat that we feel needs to be strenuously overcome but rather the
game efforts of an essentially beaten fighter. Furthermore, oddly

enough, the flood of pity we feel for Lady Macduff and her children seems to me to carry over to those who have brought their sufferings on themselves: to Macduff, then Lady Macbeth in her sleep-walking scene, then Macbeth at the loss of his wife and everything that mattered to him.

At the end, Macbeth makes a 'last stand' that commands a kind of admiration. He has at last been stripped of all the partners on whom he has leaned, including the Weird Sisters and their prophecies. For the first time we see him standing on his own two feet and finding in himself the courage to cry: 'Lay on, Macduff, / And damned be him that first cries "Hold, enough!" '

What can be observed in general about our sympathies? For one thing, Shakespeare seems to be taking care not to make his hero too attractive a figure at first. Perhaps he had learned his lesson with Richard III, whom he made too devilishly appealing. On the other hand, Shakespeare does not ask us to turn altogether against Macbeth either. He makes us see the logic in his enormities, the courage with which he meets his numerous traumas, the pitifulness of his sufferings. At the very least, Macbeth's own revulsion towards his acts maintains a bond of understanding with our own revulsion towards them.

Our sympathies and antipathies towards Macbeth are thus subtly modulated from phase to phase of his career. That is why we cannot accept as sufficient Malcolm's bold dismissal of 'the dead butcher and his fiend-like queen'. We know that there was much more to them than that.

Thus far I have addressed the questions of identification and sympathy from the customary vantage of a viewer who remains consistent in his attitudes throughout. The fact is, however, that we as viewers of *Macbeth* change as the result of our experiences in transit and that these changes influence our judgements and sympathies. The play confronts us, like Macbeth, with the unknown and the unthinkable and dares and lures us to venture into them. It is no play for saints, or for hardened criminals. For full effect, its participants, off-stage as well as on, must to some degree be caught up in its tug of war, both towards and away from things evil. As spectators we must—like Macduff with Malcolm—have an initial tolerance for the wrongdoing of others, a tolerance that can be stretched, again and again. And for most spectators, Shakespeare invites a good deal more complicity than that. Take, for example, his handling of the murder of Duncan. By not showing the deed,

Shakespeare obliges the spectator to join in the act, at least to the extent of imagining its accomplishment. Without realizing it we may even be wishing Macbeth on. For how many in the audience would not feel disappointment if Macbeth emerged from Duncan's chamber to announce that he had decided not to commit the crime? Having thus drawn us into complicity, Shakespeare then reinforces our sense of guilt by again and again causing us to return, in our imaginations, to the scene of our crime—first with Lady Macbeth with the daggers, then at its discovery by others, then at Macbeth's own return when he kills the grooms.

It is as if something wild and demonic has been released that takes possession of all concerned (back-stage superstitions about the Scottish play are well placed). It is as if, in the process of deciding to kill Duncan, Macbeth and Lady Macbeth not only 'dash'd out the brains' of any human child they might have conceived in their imaginations but brought forth a vicious brain-child. Their psychic coupling at this point is not of man with woman but of normal masculinity with super-masculinity ('bring forth men children only' rightly marvels Macbeth of his wife, who has achieved the demonic possession and sex-change for which she had prayed). The result is a strange being—at once beyond human in its daring and less than human in its lack of feeling—who takes over the inner life of the play. It works through Macbeth himself but is both more and less than he. This child of evil cannot bear to look at its first crime (the play seems to hide its eyes as well as ours from the killing of Duncan), but once having developed a taste for blood, it runs amok. Its deepest craving— as gradually comes clear—is to kill children, and the possibility of children. Having killed an old man and driven away his sons, it kills a middle-aged man and tries, though unsuccessfully, to kill his young son. It then succeeds in killing all of Macduff's 'pretty chickens and their dam'. Its crimes are thus ultimate ones—against life and fertility. Like lust in action, it at last turns in revulsion on itself, allows itself to be trapped, alone, before offering suicidal resistance.

Thus sketched, the course of the play may sound like the career of a tabloid psychopath. Shakespeare has made it into the stuff of art by disclosing the understandable humanity of the obsessions involved, and by obliging us in the audience to admit, in some degree, our susceptibility to them and our complicity in the enormities they cause.

Strictly speaking, the moral tug of war in *Macbeth* is not between positive good and evil. Malcolm's virtues are chiefly defined by his denial of vices. Even the grace of Edward the Confessor is chiefly manifested in its ability to counteract the king's evil. It is the power of evil that is central, and human resistance or susceptibility to it. The play's characters provide a spectrum of susceptibilities to evil that extends from Macduff's initial tolerance to Hecate's utter dedication. Lady Macbeth's commitment is immediate and total, at least where her conscious will is concerned; Banquo's is gradual and partial, providing a measure for Macbeth's more rapid initiation.

Shakespeare has organized his whole play to move towards, then away from evil. Like the merest ghost story or horror movie, it begins with a dare: 'Thunder and lightning. Enter three Witches.' There are to be no primroses on this path to hell—no sensual pleasures, not even the wickedly funny comments of a Richard III; no disguising of crime and sin as anything but what they are. At most, Shakespeare offers fearsome thrills. Throughout, he challenges the will of his spectators to know by the worst means the worst.

Besides throwing down dares, he offers tantalizing glimpses into the seeds of time, lures that lead us, like Macbeth, into complicities that we will regret. Of course, most plays draw much of their dynamism from the audience's desire to know as much as possible as soon as possible, especially as to what is going to happen next. The root meaning of theatre is 'seeing place' and as theatre-lovers we are eager to see the curtain pulled aside, the mask removed, and everything that is secret come into the open. As lovers of drama (root meaning 'thing done'), we are no less hungry for action.

As playgoers we welcome whatever contributes to these satis-factions, however objectionable their agents may be in other respects. Shakespeare draws on both proclivities in the spectators of *Macbeth*. Furthermore, he is careful at the outset not to offer positive alternatives to the path of temptation. Our choice is between decision and action (though destructive) and non-action and tormenting indecision. He sharpens our desire to know by constantly focusing his dialogue on the future and by offering bits of foreknowledge that are as tantalizing to us as to Macbeth.

Besides reinforcing our pulls towards evil, Shakespeare works to overcome our resistances to it. Macbeth and Banquo win our confidence by the initial resistances that they express; their weakenings then give impetus to our own. Like them we feel swept along by the rush of events. The playwright himself seems to be caught up in the early momentum towards the assassination. At times he intrudes to aid and abet the assassins. With a heavy hand he makes Duncan so mistakenly trusting as to seem to 'ask for' what he gets from his hosts. Their plan to blame the sleeping guards being notably implausible, Shakespeare improves upon it. By having the King's sons flee, he effectively turns public suspicion away from the true criminals.

Our vicarious 'identification' and 'sympathy' with Macbeth during his temptations is thus enhanced by our own direct experience of analogous trials. When the play is over, it is easy enough to look back and condemn him as a 'moral defective'. At the time he makes his immoral decisions, however, such detachment and highmindedness is not so easy. We can scarcely condemn him very harshly for succumbing to temptation because we too have, to some degree, felt that same tug and to some degree have given way to it. Indeed his immoral choices may be the very ones we as playgoers secretly hope he will make. Our special feeling for Macbeth is thus not exactly that we 'become' the hero but that—through him—we can have experiences like his. We too are among his 'partners'.

When it comes time for us, like Macbeth's other accomplices, to end our partnership with him, Shakespeare again reinforces our vicarious attitudes with our direct experiences as spectators. The life of crime on which we entered has proved to be anything but pleasant. Our very sense of time suffers a wrench. After the rush to the decision to kill Duncan, time progressively slows down immediately before and after the act. There may indeed be an overlap between the knockings that Macbeth and Lady Macbeth hear at the end of the murder scene and those that the Porter hears at the beginning of the next. Our time, as well as that of imaginary Scotland (where the sun fails to rise), thus stands still, leaving us 'rapt' in the painful moment. Besides the anguished tug of war we have undergone and the torments of half-true foreknowledge, we have had to endure more and more fearsome horrors. We join Macbeth in his cry, 'No more sights!' Perhaps we do not in the process grow as callous and jaded as Macbeth, but Shakespeare seems to suppose that the shocks he gives us will need to be very strong in order to turn us decisively against Macbeth. For there is an element of betrayal on our part in such a turn, Macbeth having served as our agent in the acts for which we then leave him to suffer. Such satisfaction as we take in his downfall and death is thus qualified by our own guilt, a particularly pointed feeling that 'There but for the grace of God, go I'. Yet if there is an overreaching Macbeth in most of us, there is also an inner Macduff who will go along only so far and then says 'No!' Shakespeare built his play on that confidence.

The last part of this discussion has become as much an analysis of audience-response to the playwright as to his hero. The next chapter goes even further in this direction, and is primarily concerned throughout with the relation between the playwright and the audience in *King Lear*.

The Playwright and the Audience: The Outrageousness of *King Lear*

WHY do audiences not walk out on *King Lear?*
They walk out on Edward Bond's adaptation, *Lear* (London, 1972).
They did so both times I have seen it performed, at Yale when it
was new, and at its revival in Stratford-upon-Avon in 1982. Both
productions were good. The audience was simply repelled by what it
was seeing. The first scene includes a rash execution of a worker by
Lear, and the fourth scene, the mutilation of one of Lear's counsellors
by his two rebellious daughters. The mutilation includes cutting his
tongue out (one of the daughters laments, 'O Christ, why did I cut his
tongue out? I want him to scream!'), smashing his hands, and
deafening him (the other daughter interrupts her knitting, and coolly
pokes the knitting needles into the victim's ears: 'I'll just jog these in
and out a little. Doodee, doodee, doodee, doo.') Even so, no one in
either audience left until the first intermission. A good many never
came back. Later, at Yale, people began walking out during the
performance, muttering and hissing. The exodus was especially
pronounced after Lear had his eyes removed by a technician who had
invented an elaborate instrument designed to 'extract the eye
undamaged and then it can be put to good use':

Note how the eye passes into the lower chamber and is received into a
soothing solution of formaldehyde crystals. One more, please (he removes
Lear's other eye and then sprays aerosol in the eye-sockets). That will assist the
formation of scab and discourage flies.

Bond is a serious playwright, and his violence, he explains in his
preface to the play, is not gratuitous but principled:

I write about violence as naturally as Jane Austen wrote about manners.
Violence shapes and obsesses our society, and if we do not stop being violent
we have no future. People who do not want writers to write about violence
want to stop them writing about us and our time. It would be immoral not to
write about violence.

Bond does his moral duty with enthusiasm! He enters immediately
into Shakespeare's way with violence and seems at times to be trying

to go one better. Shakespeare's way is to literalize metaphors (as when Lear's mental blindness becomes Gloucester's physical blindness) and to push what is already horrific one step further (as when Edgar feels that he has known the worst, only then for the first time to see his estranged father enter blind). Bond does the same. In Shakespeare, King Lear, mad, says: 'let them anatomize Regan; see what breeds about her heart. Is there any cause in nature that makes these hard hearts?' In Bond, this imaginary autopsy is made literal—a technician cuts open the body of one of Lear's daughters and shows her inner organs. Lear puts his hands into her body and 'brings them out with organs and viscera'.

How much is too much? At what point will the members of an audience decide that they have had enough and leave? This is not a decision that most spectators take lightly—and not just because of the high cost of theatre tickets. Walking out on a play while it is under way is a drastic act. Rarely an expression of boredom or mere displeasure, it is characteristically, as at the Yale *Lear*, a spontaneous revulsion from the unacceptable. Usually it will include an element of escaping pain; often this will be mixed with protest. It is drastic because it breaches the tacit compact that the members of an audience make when they come to the theatre: that they will sit still until the performance is over. Such considerations are pertinent to *King Lear* because Shakespeare subjects its audience to exceptional sufferings. Why do we endure them?

Of course, all tragedies inflict pain on their audiences. Philosophers have long pondered the nature of the positive features which none the less draw us to attend tragedies and see them through—the beauty of their artistry, for example, and the honesty of their truth to life, however awful it may be. The main reason we do not walk out on them is that these positive features are strong enough to make us want to stay more than we want to leave. Such positive features are important in *King Lear*. In this chapter, however, I will focus on something that has received virtually no critical attention: how the painful features themselves are handled. This is apropos to *King Lear* because there is something distinctively outrageous about much of the suffering in the play, off-stage and on.

The imagined world of *King Lear* is notoriously cruel. The inclination of the characters to compare themselves and one another to ferocious animals (a dragon, a boar, a sea-monster, a wolf, a lion) seems all too apt. Almost everyone is possessed by enormous energies. The King himself is four score and upwards yet driven by passions of tremendous force, so strong as to be quelled only by a terrible storm. This is a 'tough world', as one of the characters puts it. Towards each other, they are all hard-hearts in one sense or another; about themselves they seem thin-skinned (a combination of traits that is not unknown in ordinary life). Hence they are harsh with one another, and themselves suffer deeply from the harshness they receive in return. Hence, by mutual over-reaction, they escalate every situation to drastic extremes. Yet certain of the characters are extraordinarily long-suffering.

In various metaphorical ways, the characters are displaced persons, homeless people; many are literally house-less. They live in a world in which prevailing religious, political, and social systems and codes do not work. The play makes it painfully clear that what we now call feudalism no longer functions as it should, neither does the back-to-nature impulse of Lear and Edgar, nor the modern-style pragmatism of Edmond, Cornwall, Goneril, and Regan.

With traditional identities thus disavowed or disregarded, it is no wonder that individual personal relationships are very intense. A number of critics have pointed out that *King Lear* is pre-eminently a play about human relations, 'concerned', says Winifred Nowottny, 'with what people expect, need, and get from others, and with what they choose to give or to deny'.[1] Arthur Sewell makes the same emphasis ('all the characters are conceived—and this is central to the vision—in their relationships with other people') and goes on to suggest a larger set of relations as well: 'Man is nowhere so certainly exhibited as a member of all organic creation and of the elemental powers. Man's membership of society is more than legal, is more than political, because it is subtended in a wider membership, in which plants and animals, the wind and the thunder, are also included.'[2] Maynard Mack shows how this vision of 'human reality as a web of ties commutual' influences not only characterization and action, but language, theme, and setting. He studies, for example, the language of social status (words like knave and villain) and of social responsibility (such as proper, duty, bond).[3] This language is part of the subtle web of human interrelations that the play's violences tear apart.

Individual personal relationships are especially important in *King Lear* because the play's positive values reside in certain of them. These are love-relationships of a non-romantic sort: of Lear with Kent and the Fool; of Lear with Cordelia; of Gloucester with Edgar. These

---

[1] Winifred Nowottny, 'Some Aspects of the Style of *King Lear*', *Shakespeare Survey*, 13 (1960).

[2] Arthur Sewell, *Character and Society in Shakespeare* (Oxford, 1951), 118.

[3] Maynard Mack, *King Lear in Our Time* (Berkeley, 1965).

two last are the most central. In both, the traditional bonds linking parent and child are violated to the verge of annihilation by the folly of the fathers; yet both are restored, thanks to the humbled recognition of error by the fathers and the enduring love, trust, and faith of the wronged children. Their reconciliations amount to a fresh definition of what it means to be a father and a child.

As usual in Shakespeare, the audience is invited to enter the world of *King Lear*, not only vicariously, because we sympathize or identify with certain of the characters, but directly, because our encounters with the play are like those of the characters. Our minds are stretched as on a rack by the polarities the play encompasses. Like the characters, we often feel bewildered and lost. Like them we suffer— the sight of Gloucester losing his eyes hurts our eyes too. Like them, despite powerful urges to escape the pain, we endure these sufferings and like a few of them, we survive it all and walk away at the end, dazed and sombre, as if in the 'dead march' with which the Folio edition of the play ends.[4]

Subliminally, the audience's attitude towards suffering will be conditioned by those of the characters. If we are inclined to avoid it, we will find ourselves in the company of the very foolish King Lear and Gloucester, who seek to escape their agonies through physically running away and through withdrawal into madness, nihilism, or suicide. The two also show us the consequences of insensitivity to the suffering of others. If we are inclined to harden ourselves towards others' suffering or even take satisfaction in it, we will be in the company of the villains of the piece, an association that—after the initial excitement of their dynamism—becomes less and less attractive. The most sympathetic characters show a capacity to suffer patiently the wrongs done them by loved ones. It is their company that we are encouraged to keep. All of the characters (the Fool excepted) manage to endure their sufferings to the bitter end.

The audience is also like the characters in finding an essential

---

[4] Thanks to recent studies, the Quarto and Folio texts of *King Lear* are now seen to have their own integrities, which are blurred by the conflated versions that modern editors have concocted. In 'Quarto and Folio *King Lear* and the Interpretation of Albany and Edgar', in *Shakespeare*, ed. D. Bevington and J. Halio (Cranbury, NJ, 1978), 95–107, Michael Warren has gone so far as to maintain that the two texts are 'sufficiently different to require that all further work on the play be based on either Q or F, but not the conflation of both' (p. 105). While recognizing the differences, I believe that the two texts are similar enough to permit a discussion which applies to both, the overlap between the two providing—for my purposes—an 'essential *King Lear*'. Where appropriate, variants will be taken into account. Unless otherwise indicated, quotations are from the Folio text, *The Tragedy of King Lear*.

relationship called in question, one that involves our very identities as spectators and our bonds of understanding with the playwright. In general, as discussed in Chapter 4, a playwright, along with his players, is linked with his playgoers in a kind of love-relationship, participating as they all do in mutually imagining the events of the play. This relationship involves mutual vulnerability, a baring of feelings that requires trust, sensitivity, and responsibility on both sides. Even the modern attempts of Brecht and other playwrights to distance, offend, or threaten the spectator seem to me merely sophistications of the basic love-relationship. Most of the time Shakespeare is the most considerate of partners. He often challenges the imagination of his audience; but he characteristically pulls no tricks or surprises, lets us know well in advance what is coming and follows through on it, often flatters us by letting us know more than even the most discerning of his characters.

In *King Lear*, these patterns are violated. Repeatedly, our expectations are raised, only to be disappointed or reversed. Situations are pushed to 'the extreme verge' of acceptability. Again and again, the playwright and his play become so outrageous that the members of its audience may come close to walking out.

'Outrageous' may be too strong a word for the first scene. 'Outlandish' might be better. It bothers almost everyone. As Coleridge remarked, '*Lear* is the only serious performance of Shakespeare . . . derived from the assumption of a gross improbability.'[5] No one has been more perturbed about it than Tolstoy. He in general responded to Shakespeare's plays with 'an irresistible repulsion and tedium' but was particularly incensed by the 'absurdity' and 'unnaturalness' of this scene, all the more because in it Shakespeare was wilfully altering his source-play, the anonymous *King Leir*, which Tolstoy thought 'incomparably and in every respect superior to Shakespeare's adaptation'. Tolstoy especially objected to Shakespeare's weakening or removing the motivations which he found in his source. For instance, in the source the King abdicates because, having become a widower, he wants to devote his life to saving his soul. He puts on the love-game as a kind of trap for Cordelia. When she tells him how much she loves him, he plans to say: if you love me that much, then you should let me choose your husband. Shakespeare's 'adaptation' seems to Tolstoy vastly inferior. The strife among his characters 'does not flow from the natural course of events nor from their own

⁵ *Coleridge on Shakespeare*, ed. T. Hawkes (Harmondsworth, 1969), 201.

characters but is quite arbitrarily established by the author, and therefore cannot produce in the reader the illusion which represents the essential condition of art'.[6]

In his 1681 adaptation, Nahum Tate sought to remedy such shortcomings. In his dedication, he congratulates himself as follows:

'Twas my good fortune to light on one expedient to rectify what was wanting in the regularity and probability of the tale, which was to run through the whole, as love betwixt Edgar and Cordelia; that never changed word with each other in the original. This renders Cordelia's indifference, and her father's passion in the first scene, probable . . .'[7]

Tate's master-stroke was to have Cordelia and Edgar marry at the end.

We may not agree with Tate and Tolstoy that the alternative versions are better than Shakespeare's. But the two are certainly right that the other versions are more clearly motivated than his. In fact, as Tolstoy's analysis shows, Shakespeare appears to have gone out of his way to avoid such motivation, especially in King Lear himself.

Interpreters have differed as to what is most bothersome about his behaviour. They have objected, in various combinations, to Lear's plan to divide his kingdom, to his claim to retain the name but not the power of the king, to his love-contest and blindness to the relative moral worth of his daughters. Others, myself included, agree with Gloucester in regarding the disinheritance of Cordelia and banishment of Kent as the chief enormities; Gloucester expostulates: 'The King falls from bias of nature: there's father against child . . . And the noble and true-hearted Kent banished, his offence honesty! 'Tis strange' (1. 2. 108–15).

Not only the King's conduct is 'strange'; so in these matters is that of the playwright. Maynard Mack has remarked on how Shakespeare's practice here differs from that in *Hamlet*, *Othello*, and *Macbeth*, where he takes great care to show 'the inward origin of acts of will'. In *King Lear*, Mack observes, the violences are thrust upon us 'with the shock that comes from evil which has nowhere been inwardly accounted for' (p. 92). About most of the leading characters in the play, I would differ from Mack. The villainy of Edmond, Goneril, and Cornwall seems to me as well accounted for as that of other Shakespearian ill-doers. Asides and soliloquies make clear the attitudes of Cordelia and Edgar. But where the wrath of the King is concerned, Mack is brilliantly right. To be sure, Lear's explosion is

[6] *Tolstoy on Shakespeare*, trans. V. Tchertkoff (New York and London, 1906), 48.
[7] Nahum Tate, *The History of King Lear* (Lincoln, Nebr., 1975), 1–2.

not a complete surprise. We know that Cordelia is his favourite
daughter, ('our joy'), and can understand his disappointment that she
is so 'untender'. His reaction is not instantaneous. He tries to coach
her to give a response more acceptable to him. His fuse may be short
but he does have one.

Still, when his outburst comes it has for the audience just the kind
of shock that Mack describes. Shakespeare has done nothing to
prepare us for the fury of Lear's words or the completeness of his
repudiation of Cordelia. Shakespeare then, however, regains some of
our confidence by returning to his customary way of dealing with
unusual behaviour. He has it named (in this case by the King himself)
as 'wrath' and made the object of remonstrance (by Kent and then
France).

The King's banishment of Kent is less shocking than his disowning
of Cordelia. It is given a longer build-up, Kent is more bluntly
provocative, and the King's explosiveness has already been shown. At
the end of the scene, Regan labels the banishment an example of her
father's 'unconstant starts'.

When Gloucester disowns Edgar and seeks his life, it is again the
outburst of paternal wrath that is shockingly unaccounted for. In
general, both fathers are at first seen from the outside. Indeed, by a
remarkable use of point of view, Shakespeare in the first three scenes
consistently invites the audience to share the perspectives of their
offspring, who—through soliloquy or aside or private conversation—
take us into their confidence, usually concerning their relationship
with their respective fathers.

In other respects, Shakespeare in the gulling of Gloucester follows
his standard procedure for presenting the successful practices of a
villain on his unsuspecting victims. The procedure is most overt in
Titus Andronicus, when Aaron tricks Titus into allowing his left
hand to be cut off, on the promise of regaining his two imprisoned
sons, only to send Titus their heads instead. The audience is darkly
forewarned that Aaron is going to practise some deceit on Titus soon
(3. 1. 187–90), and immediately after the heads are delivered the
messenger gives names to the ill-doing and extends heartfelt sympathy
to its victim (ll. 233–9). So Edmond in his soliloquy at the beginning
of 1. 2 forewarns us of his animus and plot against Edgar. And in his
soliloquy at the end of the scene he labels the vulnerabilities of his
father and brother:

> A credulous father, and a brother noble,
> Whose nature is so far from doing harms

That he suspects none; on whose foolish honesty
My practices ride easy.   (1. 2. 168–71)

But we are not prepared for the violence of Gloucester's outburst
against Edgar: 'Abhorred villain, unnatural, detested, brutish villain—
worse than brutish! Go, sirrah, seek him. I'll apprehend him.
Abominable villain!' (1. 2. 78–80). For his own purposes, Edmond in
response urges Gloucester to 'suspend your indignation' against Edgar
lest it be premature. Gloucester then momentarily assures himself
'He cannot be such a monster', only in the next speech to revert to
repeatedly calling his son a 'villain'. No one, however, remonstrates at
the rashness of his later call to bring 'the murderous coward to the
stake'. Unlike the King, who has Kent, France, and then the Fool to
point out the error of his ways, Gloucester is instead confirmed in his
conduct by the comments of Regan and Cornwall.

One consequence of these shocks is to make the audience conscious
of the playwright. Ordinarily we are so caught up in the imagined
world of the play that we forget that it is the work of a playwright.
Here, however, the behaviour of the King and Gloucester seems so
uncalled for that we may well feel, with Tolstoy, that Shakespeare's
contrivance is showing through; his arbitrariness may seem as
shocking as theirs. So cavalier is he about showing his hand that when
Edgar appears precisely on cue to be duped, Shakespeare has the
audacity to have Edmond remark, 'Pat he comes like the catastrophe
of the old comedy'.

In the face of such high-handedness why do we not walk out?
Largely, of course, it is because the play has only begun and the
disorders are so immediate and extreme that sheer curiosity makes us
want to see how it all turns out. Also our impulses to stay, despite
provocation to leave, receive positive reinforcement from the example
of Kent. When confronted with what he regards as outrageous
behaviour, the King cannot bear to look upon those who cross him. He
commands Cordelia, 'Hence, and avoid my sight!' and orders Kent to
'turn thy hated back / Upon our kingdom'. At the time, Kent responds
in kind: 'Freedom lives hence, and banishment is here.' (Shortly we
will also hear that France 'in choler parted'). But in fact Kent decides
to stay on, in disguise as Caius. His timing is perfect, if one looks on
his decision as a cue for audience response. It comes (1. 4. 1–7) just
when we are most likely to be concluding that the first scenes are so
implausible as to be unacceptable.

Shakespeare then gives us the negative example of the headstrong
king, who tries to walk out on his own tragedy. When he can no longer

banish those who cross him, his first impulse is to call for his horses and leave. So he storms off from Goneril's palace to Gloucester's. The impression that he is thereby running away from his problems is underlined by the parallel with Edgar who, more understandably, becomes a runaway at this same time.

King Lear's conduct with Goneril does much to regain credibility for the playwright. The King's virulent curses so far exceed his injuries from Goneril that we can see his earlier outbursts against Cordelia and Kent to have been very much in character, not merely plot contrivances. Contrary to Mack, the shocking 'evil which has nowhere been inwardly accounted for' does not remain 'unaccountable, to characters and the audience alike'. With hindsight we come to see that the King's behaviour in the first scene makes sense, that that is just the way the rash and wrathful King would over-react. The more consistently arbitrary we see the King to be, the less arbitrary in retrospect the playwright seems. Our realization that the King's wrathfulness is a character-trait will shortly be furthered by his own attempt to moderate it. In his dealings with Regan and Cornwall, after an initial outburst he tries to contain his fury by making excuses to himself for their neglect and insults.

At the end of this episode, the King again tries to walk out on his tragedy, calling for his horses and heading off into the storm. This second walk-out is more sympathetic than the first. Its provocation— the attempt by the two daughters to cut his hundred followers to none —is greater. His dawning awareness of his own impotence is more touching (2. 2. 277–87). His withdrawal goes deeper, into madness. And his withdrawal is less voluntary: he tries to resist the onset of madness and, after his headlong departure, the castle doors are shut against him.

Again the example of Kent may help, subliminally, to keep us in the theatre. As the King becomes a more sympathetic figure, for us to leave him in his plight would be an act of desertion. To steadfast Kent in the stocks, the Fool advises: 'Let go thy hold when a great wheel runs down a hill, lest it break thy neck with following.' He knows perfectly well that Kent will not heed this advice; neither for the time does he himself; neither do we.

As Goneril and Regan show more and more of their true colours, we begin to see the justice of the initial revulsion from the two expressed by Cordelia and the Fool. Like those of Hamlet, their antipathies prove prophetic. Before the play is over, Goneril and Regan more than deserve them. In little, the pattern of apparent excess vindicated is very clear in Kent's denunciation of Oswald (2. 2. 13–22). At the time

Kent seems to go too far (he calls the steward 'the son *and heir* of a *mongrel* bitch'); yet such vilification is not far from what Oswald eventually becomes: he does end up a 'bawd in way of good service'. The pattern of vindication extends even to the King's excoriations of his elder daughters. Does not the pattern extend to the playwright as well? He too may have seemed to the audience to have let himself be carried away by his 'own too much'.

From now on, the outrages for which the playwright will be answerable will be perpetrated *upon* the King and Gloucester. Those against the King are carefully graduated. Even the paring of his hundred followers is done in the name of hospitality; Goneril asks:

> What need you five and twenty, ten, or five,
> To follow in a house where twice so many
> Have a command to tend you?   (2. 2. 435–7)

Regan adds: 'what need one?'

Was there ever anything so mannerly as the decision to close the gates against Lear in the storm? Notice the delicacy with which Cornwall and Regan move to their decision, each backing up the other and then moving one small step further: 'It's going to storm. We should go in. 'This house is little. The old man and 's people / Cannot be *well* bestowed.' He's doing it to himself, after all. If he comes back, we'll take him in, but none of his followers. (By no means ask him to stay, Goneril puts in.) It's best to 'give him way'. It will teach him a lesson. Cornwall concludes like an adroit administrator, passing the buck back down; he tells Gloucester: 'Shut up your doors, my lord. 'Tis a wild night. / My Regan counsels well. Come out o'th' storm.'

In the storm the King's wrath reaches cosmic scope. He calls on the elements to 'Crack nature's moulds, all germens spill at once / That makes ingrateful man' (3. 2. 8–9). He flashes out at Kent in a way that recalls the first scene, 'Death, traitor!' (3. 4. 66). His maledictions are even more excessive and unprovoked than before. But they are merely verbal and without potency, symptoms of his madness. For the audience, it is the storm that is fearsome and the wrath of Cornwall, 'the fiery duke'. The King is now a fugitive, whose life has been threatened (3. 4. 153). Gloucester, at the risk of his own life, joins Kent and the Fool in their adherence to the King. Earlier, Kent gave his service to the King's masterful 'authority' (1. 4. 30); now Gloucester sees his succour to his 'old master' as an act of 'charity' (3. 3. 15). The difference between the two reflects the changing basis of the audience's own adherence to the King.

At this point, the Fool drops out of the play. His attachment to the

King had never been strong. When the King left Goneril's palace, the Fool did not follow until she ordered him to do so (1. 4. 294). In the storm he had counselled: 'Good nuncle, in, ask thy daughters blessing' (3. 2. 11–12). In the Quarto but not the Folio something causes Kent to say, presumably to the Fool, 'Come, help to bear thy master. / Thou must not stay behind' (Scene 13. 93–4). Has the Fool been hanging back? At any rate in neither version do we see him again.

Lear's progressive loss of his wits is in one respect another of his afflictions. Yet in another respect it is a mode of escape from his tormenting sense of betrayal. The same may be said of Edgar, not only because his disguise as mad Tom allows him to avoid capture but because his gibberish—which exceeds his need for disguise—expresses the disorientation caused by his father's inexplicable enmity. Their madness, real and assumed, may also serve as a relief for the audience, transposing into fantasy the play's exposé of human inhumanity. Gloucester later describes this very process:

> Better I were distraught,
> So should my thoughts be severed from my griefs,
> *Drum afar off*
> And woes by wrong imaginations lose
> The knowledge of themselves.   (4. 5. 281–4)

Such relief is especially welcome as we watch the interpolated short scenes depicting the coldly 'sane' machinations of Edmond against Gloucester.

The blinding of Gloucester is one of the most outrageous acts performed in Shakespeare's plays, exceeded only by the barbarities of *Titus Andronicus*. The audience's confidence that Shakespeare had won back after his initial outrages is here strained even further. He leads up to it by the remarkable display of fine feeling shown in Edmond's betrayal of his father to Cornwall. Edmond worries: 'How, my lord, I may be censured, that nature thus gives way to loyalty, something fears me to think of' (3. 5. 2–4). Cornwall is no less concerned with proprieties; he tells Edmond, 'Keep you our sister company. The revenges we are bound to take upon your traitorous father are not fit for your beholding' (3. 7. 5–7). Not only does Shakespeare write about violence as naturally as does Bond; he writes about manners as naturally as does Jane Austen; and he knows how to put the two together.

At the beginning of 3. 7, when Cornwall orders, 'Seek out the traitor Gloucester', Regan explodes, 'Hang him instantly', as does Goneril:

'Pluck out his eyes.' Their velvet gloves are off, and their words shift the play shockingly into a new gear of cruelty.

It is Regan, whom the King had thought 'tender-hafted', who is fiercest of the three. Cornwall shows some restraint. Although he vows to give vent to 'our wrath', he—unlike his wife—holds back from Gloucester's death, which would require 'the forms of justice'. When he orders Cornwall bound, it is Regan who insists, 'Hard, hard'. It is she who tauntingly plucks Gloucester's white beard, who refers to her father as 'the lunatic King', who urges, after one of Gloucester's eyes had been blinded, 'th'other, too', who kills the servant who fights with Cornwall, who tells Gloucester that his betrayer was Edmond 'that hates thee', who orders: 'Go thrust him out at gates, and let him smell / His way to Dover.'

Regan's burst of ferocity is not a complete surprise for the audience. Like that of Goneril, her conduct has been less and less justifiable as the play has developed. Her order to shut the doors against her father is reprehensible, but nothing has prepared us for the sadistic pleasure she takes in Gloucester's pain, physical and psychological. Nor has she previously so strongly taken the initiative. Before this, she has largely followed the lead of her older sister, although often outdoing her.

Not content with shocking the audience with the thrust of Regan's fury, Shakespeare makes several ironic twists of the knife. He has Gloucester unwittingly forecast his own fate (telling Regan that he helped the King escape 'Because I would not see thy cruel nails / Pluck out his poor old eyes' (ll. 54–5). And he has the dying servant tell Gloucester 'you have one eye left / To see some mischief on him' (ll. 78–9), which incites Cornwall's 'Lest it see more, prevent it. Out, vile jelly!'

The servant's resistance does something to mitigate the outrages done the audience's sense of justice. And we learn later that although he did not save Gloucester he did hurt the Duke fatally. Yet note even here the contagiousness of anger. What begins as an act of service and loyalty on the servant's part, escalates to an exchange of insults with Regan, and ends as an angry challenge to his lord: 'Nay then, come on, and take the chance of anger.'

In the Quarto, but not in the Folio, two servants provide an epilogue to the atrocity. They make explicit the infectiousness of evil, and foresee with horror the contaminating influence of the continued life of Cornwall and Regan. They then turn to caring for Gloucester. In the Folio such concern is confined to the Old Man, a tenant of

Gloucester's and of his father before him, who—as in the Quarto—offers his help. As Poor Tom, Edgar then takes his father in his care.

Further assurance that the playwright's heart is after all in the right place is provided in the next scene by Albany's denunciation:

> O Goneril,
> You are not worth the dust which the rude wind
> Blows in your face.   (4. 2. 30–2)

In the Quarto, he continues in the same vein for some thirty lines, including not only his wife but Regan, calling them 'tigers, not daughters' (Scene 16. 40). In the Folio, these additional lines do not appear. As with its omission of the servants who minister to Gloucester, the Folio at this point seems less concerned than is the Quarto with mitigating the play's enormities.

If the blinding of Gloucester outrages our feelings of common decency, it is chiefly our common sense that is outraged by what Tolstoy called 'Gloucester's jump'. To G. Wilson Knight the episode represents the ultimate of 'the comedy of the grotesque' which he finds in the whole play:

Gloucester has planned a spectacular end for himself. We are given these noble descriptive and philosophical speeches to tune our minds to a noble, tragic sacrifice. And what happens? The old man falls from his kneeling posture a few inches, flat, face foremost. Instead of the dizzy circling to crash and spill his life on the rocks below—just this. The grotesque merged into the ridiculous reaches a consummation in this bathos of comedy: it is the furthest, most exaggerated, reach of the poet's towering fantasticality . . .[8]

In performance the 'comedy' of the situation is not the primary effect—there is nothing in the text to indicate that Gloucester should fall 'flat, face foremost'; it is not bathos but pathos that is dominant.

Still, the element of the ludicrous is present. The sequence from the blinding of Gloucester to his 'leap' is similar to that in *Titus Andronicus*, when, left with his severed hand and the heads of his two sons, Titus starts off the stage, accompanied by his devoted brother Marcus and daughter Lavinia, who has previously been raped, her tongue torn out, and her hands cut off:

> Come, brother, take a head,
> And in this hand the other will I bear.
> And, Lavinia, thou shalt be employed.
> Bear thou my hand, sweet wench, between thine arms. (3. 1. 278–81)

In both plays, as Edgar puts it, 'the worst returns to laughter'. But in

---

[8] G. Wilson Knight, *The Wheel of Fire* (London, 1965), 171.

Titus Andronicus the audience is prepared for what is ludicrous in Titus's procession by Titus's own reaction to the atrocities he has suffered. Instead of storming with grief, as Marcus expects, Titus is silent and then breaks out in laughter because he has 'not another tear to shed'. In *King Lear* Shakespeare gives his audience no such transition.

Indeed, our distress at the outlandishness of Gloucester's leap is further compounded by something like outrage that Edgar should persist in his disguise and instead of revealing his true identity to his father put him through this bizarre charade.

Why do we not walk out? Partly because we are carried through the moment by our knowledge of Gloucester's previous credulity and his tendencies towards self-dramatizing. We have also seen the same traits in Edgar, and have had an inkling of the well-meaning insensitivity he shows here when as Poor Tom on the heath he continued his antics even when he should have been able to see that he was helping to drive the King mad. His unremitting sententiousness—he has a moral comment at hand to improve almost every occasion—may have prepared us to believe that he would indeed try to concoct such a 'miracle' in order to teach his father a lesson. He himself recognizes what is objectionable in his conduct. When he first undertakes as Poor Tom to lead his blind father, he has the aside: 'Bad is the trade that must play fool to sorrow, / Ang'ring itself and others.' And in this scene he seeks to justify to us what he is doing: 'Why I do trifle thus with his despair / Is done to cure it.'

Even so, we still have, as before, a sense of Shakespeare intruding, with his 'poet's fantasticality'. It is only as we know more of Edgar that the responsibility for this episode shifts decisively from Shakespeare to him. We observe the further lengths to which he is prepared to extend his father's ordeal; we sit through the elaborate trial by combat he devises in order to fight with his brother and kill him; and we hear the iron moralism with which he sums up his father's life-experience: he tells dying Edmond, 'The dark and vicious place where thee he got / Cost him his eyes.' On the other hand, Edgar's conduct is partly vindicated by the fact that when he finally does reveal his true identity to his father, the experience is too much for Gloucester and his flawed heart—too weak to support the conflict of joy and grief—'burst smilingly'.

Furthermore, Edgar's fabricated 'miracle' does serve his purpose—at least to a degree. If it does not inspire Gloucester to embrace life, it does bring him to give up actively seeking death:

> Henceforth I'll bear
> Affliction till it do cry out itself
> 'Enough, enough,' and die.   (4. 5. 75–7)

For if he only could, Gloucester would gladly walk out on his own tragedy. Physically, he has sought to escape his tormentors (who become his pursuers) by having Poor Tom lead him towards Dover. He wishes for madness as a way of severing his thoughts from his griefs (4. 6. 281–4). But chiefly, even after the 'miracle', he hopes for death.

Shakespeare wrings some macabre humour out of his longing for death. At Gloucester's 'resurrection', rising from presumed death, Edgar says: 'Feel you your legs? You stand.' Gloucester's dry response is 'Too well, too well'. A little later, he prays:

> You ever gentle gods, take my breath from·me.
> Let not my worser spirit tempt me again
> To die before you please.   (4. 5. 215–17)

When Oswald then appears proclaiming 'the sword is out / That must destroy thee', Gloucester welcomes him like the answer to his prayer: 'Now let thy friendly hand / Put strength enough to't.'

It is in this part of the play that the patient endurance of suffering is most strongly invoked. Earlier the King prayed for patience (2. 2. 445); in the storm, he vowed 'I will be the pattern of all patience' (3. 2. 37) and 'I will endure' (3. 4. 18)—note his use of the future tense. Now, he tells Gloucester:

> Thou must be patient. We came crying hither.
> Thou know'st the first time that we smell the air
> We waul and cry.   (4. 5. 174–6)

Edgar is the other character who makes repeated comments on the subject, again directed towards Gloucester. He urges his father to 'Bear free and patient thoughts' (4. 5. 79) and when Gloucester relapses into 'ill thoughts' he maintains:

> Men must endure
> Their going hence even as their coming hither.
> Ripeness is all.   (5. 2. 9–11)

The King and Gloucester are, to put it mildly, reluctant exemplars of patient endurance. (The King tries to run away from the shame of confronting Cordelia.) It is Kent, Edgar, and Cordelia who best practise this virtue. Is the audience's endurance of the play analogous to theirs? Does not Shakespeare the theatre-poet invite us to participate in his play's bitter 'ripeness'?

If so, our patience seems to be rewarded by the reunion and reconciliation of the King and Cordelia. The playwright appears vindicated for the sufferings inflicted on the two and on us by the wisdom they have gained from the experience, as the King acknowledges and seeks to atone for the wrong he has done his daughter and she—with more generosity of spirit than she showed in the first scene—responds 'No cause, no cause'.

In the last act, however, the playwright not only disappoints our hopes for a happy ending (they were realized in *King Leir*) but does so in a particularly painful way. Again and again, he raises our expectations of desirable events and then dashes them, immediately. It is bad enough for Cordelia's forces to be defeated in battle; Shakespeare points our disappointment by having Edgar promise Gloucester, 'If I ever return to you again, / I'll bring you comfort' (5. 2. 3–4), only to return with cold comfort indeed: 'King Lear hath lost, he and his daughter ta'en' (5. 2. 6–7). When Edmond orders their imprisonment, he appears to have changed his earlier resolve to do away with them before Albany can pardon them (5. 1. 56–60):

> Some officers take them away. Good guard
> Until their greater pleasures first be known
> That are to censure them.   (5. 3. 1–3)

In the following lines, we may even be reconciled to their imprisonment. The King seems to welcome it! No sooner have they been taken away, however, than Edmond gives a charge to the captain that plainly means them no good. None the less, the falling out between Goneril and Regan, Edmond's defeat by Edgar in the trial by combat, and their exchange of forgiveness—all seem to give the audience grounds for renewed hopes. These hopes, too, are of course soon dashed, and in a particularly cruel way.

The death of Cordelia is so outrageous that it led Dr Johnson to confess that 'I was many years ago so shocked by Cordelia's death that I know not whether I ever endured to read again the last scenes of the play till I undertook to revise them as an editor'.[9] It led A. C. Bradley to take 'his courage in both his hands and say boldly' that as a stageplay he prefers Tate's happy ending.[10] It is outrageous in so many ways that it may be unnecessary to count them all.

To begin with, it is contrary to history. According to all other accounts Cordelia's forces should have won the final battle and

---

[9] *Dr. Johnson on Shakespeare*, ed. W. K. Wimsatt (Harmondsworth, 1969), 126.
[10] A. C. Bradley, *Shakespearean Tragedy* (London, 1951), 252.

restored King Lear to the throne. Those in Shakespeare's first audience who did not know the chronicle accounts might well have seen the anonymous *King Leir*, which followed the chronicle pattern. Or they might have had a sense of what Leo Salingar calls 'exemplary romance' and has shown to be characteristic of medieval romances and early Elizabethan plays: in it 'a family is divided; one of its members, cut off from civilized security and exposed to hazard, suffers with constancy and devotion; at last he or she is redeemed by an unexpected turn of Fortune, and the life of the family begins afresh.'[11]

But most of all it is the inner logic of the play itself that again and again promises a happy resolution. Even at the very last minute the playwright holds out hopes, with Edmond's death-bed conversion, the rush to prevent execution of his command for the hanging of Cordelia, and Albany's prayer, 'The gods defend!'—only to have Lear enter 'with Cordelia in his arms'.

To make matters worse, we can in retrospect see that the playwright went out of his way to make her death gratuitous. Far from being tragically inevitable, it has resulted from a bit of group absent-mindedness. All present have been so preoccupied by the winding down of the Gloucester family story that it was not until Kent arrived that anyone thought to look to the safety of Lear and Cordelia. Albany cried: 'Great thing of us forgot!' Worst of all, Shakespeare has so packed this part of the play with incident that we too may have been party to this disastrous preoccupation. Not without cause, we may feel that the playwright has added insult to injury in a way not unlike Gloucester's vision of divine perversity: 'As flies to wanton boys are we to th' gods; / They kill us for their sport' (4. 1. 37–8).

Does the rest of the play, as before, vindicate the playwright for this ultimate outrage, bring us to see the rightness of his mysterious ways? As so often, Shakespeare presents options for both enactment and response.

As if they were characters in *King Lear*, interpreting critics have often over-reacted to the finale. Judah Stampfer sees in the ending the culmination of the audience's fear that we inhabit an 'imbecile world', characterized by 'neither grace nor the balance of law, but malignity, intransigence or chaos'.[12] Surely this is too bleak an account, as exaggerated as is Kent's 'All's cheerless, dark, and deadly'

[11] Leo Salingar, *Shakespeare and the Traditions of Comedy* (Cambridge, 1974), 30.

[12] Judah Stampfer, 'The Catharsis of *King Lear*', *Shakespeare Survey*, 13 (Cambridge, 1960), 10.

(l. 266). After all, the conclusion of *King Lear* is only a notch or two more catastrophic than is normal in Shakespeare's tragedies. Reassuringly, he as always shows the final defeat of the evil-doers; as usual (Iago is the disturbing exception) he shows their dead bodies as well. It is true, however, that the moral satisfaction of seeing the wicked punished is not as large a factor in *King Lear* as in his earlier tragedies because it is essentially accomplished before the very ending of the play. The bodies of Goneril and Regan remain on the stage, their deaths are mentioned to the King, and Edmond's death is reported; but the predominant final focus is on the suffering and death of the virtuous.

The waste of the good, as Bradley puts it, is also a general characteristic of Shakespearian tragedy. In *King Lear* this waste is particularly painful because it repeatedly seems to have been averted. Imagine that Othello had realized the error of his ways and that his love with Desdemona had been briefly restored, only then for her to be somehow killed anyway. Such a reversal of an apparent reprieve is the special anguish of Cordelia's death.

As is usual in Shakespeare's tragic finales, there are a few sympathetic survivors, and a secondary figure who assumes the rule of the state. As compared with other such rulers, Albany during his brief period of authority is alarmingly inept, first proposing to restore the far-gone King to his throne and then (in a way all too reminiscent of 1. 1) to abdicate and divide the rule between Kent and Edgar. About Edgar, however, there are more grounds for hope. He has not learned all he has to learn about human relations. But he has come to see that it was a 'fault' to withhold his identity from his father until he was the knight in shining armour he wanted to be seen to be. Perhaps through him some of the hard-won gains of the other relationships can provide a beginning for a new era.

As usual, Shakespeare allows his tragic hero to gain some degree of wisdom from his suffering. To H. S. Wilson, indeed, the king 'has forgotten his wrongs, or any thoughts of retribution; and, as he joins Cordelia in death, his love has been made perfect through suffering'.[13] Wilson goes on to celebrate 'the calm, solemn, serene mood in which the play ends for us', concluding: 'the value of life is vindicated, triumphantly and securely.' Surely this is too comforting an account of the ending, almost as given to wishful thinking as is King Lear himself when he thinks that Cordelia still lives. For example, Wilson writes of the King: 'In the end he has forgotten the ingratitude of

[13] Harold S. Wilson, *On the Design of Shakespearian Tragedy* (Toronto, 1957), 204.

Goneril and Regan; all hatred has been transcended through his love.'
Yet the only mention of Goneril and Regan in this last part is the
following passage:

KENT
 Your eldest daughters have fordone themselves,
 And desperately are dead.
LEAR   Ay, so think I.
ALBANY
 He knows not what he says; and vain is it
 That we present us to him.
      Enter a Messenger
EDGAR   Very bootless.

This is scarcely a transcendence of hatred through love. Elsewhere
Lear curses those around him: 'A plague upon you, murderers, traitors
all.' Wilson himself mentions the 'savagery' of 'I killed the slave that
was a-hanging thee.'

   Wilson follows the Folio in having the King die happy, in his belief
that Cordelia lives. Lear's joy is deeply undercut by the fact that it is
deluded. It is true that other Shakespearian tragic protagonists die into
their dreams. Richard II's last words assert once again his belief in his
own divine royalty: 'Mount, mount, my soul; thy seat is up on high, /
Whilst my gross flesh sinks downward, here to die' (*Richard II*,
5. 5. 111–12). Cleopatra sees her suicide as a sensuous reunion with
her lover: 'As sweet as balm, as soft as air, as gentle. O Antony!' But at
least their dreams are based on the fact of their own deaths. King
Lear's belief that Cordelia's lips move is completely out of touch with
reality. The Quarto version, in which the King realizes in the end that
Cordelia is dead, is still less affirmative; his last words are, 'Break,
heart, I prithee break.'

   Within the limits of excessive negation and affirmation represented
by Stampfer and Wilson is a considerable range for varying interpretations. They will differ in the relative weight they give such
positive and negative factors as I have cited. As just mentioned, the
Folio and Quarto versions themselves vary the factors to be included
in the final balance, the Folio being the more hopeful. It not only
allows the King to die happy but assigns the last speech to Edgar; the
Quarto assigns it to Albany.

   Short of utter despair or utter exaltation, spectators may well differ
markedly yet validly in their responses. How glad should we be that
the King recognizes Kent or how sad that he doesn't realize that Kent
was Caius? How cold is our comfort in reflecting (with Kent) that the

King is out of his misery? How do we answer Kent's question, 'Is this the promis'd end?' Our responses to such questions, and the importance we give them, will vary with our temperaments and with the extent to which we, like Edgar, have been conditioned by the play to endure what we think is the worst—and then endure some more.

Because of these differences, individual spectators may see the playwright as vindicated for contradictory reasons. Those inclined to look on the dark side of the finale will see the playwright as facing up bravely to the awful truth; those inclined to look for silver linings will see him as providing compensating values.

No one, though, can feel that the playwright has broken his tragic news to us gently or without raising false hopes. The Cordelias in the audience may feel that none the less there is 'no cause, no cause' for complaint. Others may direct towards the playwright some of Lear's protest at Cordelia's death: 'Why should a dog, a horse, a rat have life, / And thou no breath at all?' Yet Shakespeare knows where to draw the line so that we do not walk out, even at this late point. He might, for example, have had Lear lead Cordelia in, like Lavinia, ravished and mutilated. Instead, in dead Cordelia he presents a *fait accompli*, absolute and final. The sight of Lear bearing his daughter is an occasion for awe and sorrow, not protest.

As theatre-poet Shakespeare has thus given himself extraordinary licence as playwright to present the 'tough world' of *King Lear* to the audience in as tough a way as would a character in it. Yet he does not allow his playwrighting to become too tough. Instead he creates a rhythm of outrage and vindication by which he (as theatre-poet) brings us to play Kent to his Lear (as playwright), Gloucester to his wanton gods. By so doing, the theatre-poet dares to present the same supreme challenge to the audience as to the value of his art that the playwright presents to his characters as to the value of life: in the face of such cruel and unusual punishment are they worth it? By not walking out but enduring the play's outrages to the bitter end, we would seem to conclude with the characters that, on balance, they are.

12

Shakespeare's Theatre-Poetry: Some Conclusions

HOWEVER inclusive it may aspire to be, every address to Shakespeare's text, whether on-stage or off, ends as a study in fractions, and this book is no exception. My method has been to look in an analytical way at the workings of the implied performance-ensemble and especially at how Shakespeare the theatre-poet relates to participants in it. I have deliberately emphasized variety in my choice of plays, seeking the most salient examples of the feature under analysis, with an eye as well to adding something fresh to the body of commentary on the play concerned.

The next step would be to bring such analytical approaches together and apply them in a comprehensive and integrated way to individual plays. As with *Hamlet* in Chapter 6, one would start with a careful determination of the playwright's share in the text, beginning with the plot and choreography, moving to large features of the dialogue, then to the characters and themes. One would then 'rehearse' the interpretative latitudes and limits Shakespeare gives his performers, not just for short passages (as in Chapters 7 and 8) but for key parts of the whole play. As with the BBC television *Measure for Measure* and Zeffirelli's *Taming of the Shrew* in Chapter 9, one should then consider some actual productions and place them in relation to the range of choices surveyed in the 'rehearsal' section. The responses of the audience to the imagined world of the play would then be considered, responses both to the main outlines of the playwright's share and to the principal options left open to his interpreters (as with *Macbeth* in Chapter 10 and *King Lear* in Chapter 11). From these analyses of the participants in the performance-ensemble, one would then be in a position to see how Shakespeare the theatre-poet guides their interactions. Such interactions are sketched for *Henry V* and *A Midsummer Night's Dream* in Chapter 2, for *Hamlet* at the end of Chapter 6, and for *Othello* at the beginning of Chapter 8.

These sketches illustrate how radically Shakespeare's theatre-poetry varies from one play to another. Each text inspires a unique rapport among the members of the performance-ensemble. As discussed in Chapter 2, whereas *Henry V* exhorts all concerned to put their imaginary forces to work, it is a spirit of play that animates *A Midsummer Night's Dream*, a spirit that can be so free as to be freakish.

As protean as it is, Shakespeare's theatre-poetry shows certain common traits. By way of summation, I should like to review these traits and illustrate them, indicating in parentheses the pages above in which the examples were given more detailed discussion.

Considered as rehearsal guides for actors, Shakespeare's texts consistently demand that each character be given his or her due. This is borne out again and again in the imaginary rehearsals. The characters themselves may well want to have things all their own way, but for a production to let any one of them actually do so is to slacken the tension and interest that due regard for their differences will sustain. Such tension among opposing forces is a very large part of what makes Shakespeare dramatic. Of course, his characters often do dominate those around them, but not to the degree that star actors playing Hamlet or Rosalind or Henry V have done.

Typically, Shakespeare makes it very clear to his actors what happens in his plots. As to when it happens, however, he allows much more latitude. When exactly is Macbeth persuaded by Lady Macbeth to kill Duncan (pp. 156–8)? When does Iago succeed in convincing Othello of Desdemona's guilt (pp. 187–95)? When is Angelo smitten by Isabella (pp. 206–7)? And when does she understand the purport of his propositions to her (pp. 207–9)? Within limits, Shakespeare provides his performers with a range of possible answers to these questions, each with its distinctive—sometimes crucial—resonances.

Shakespeare can give an actor very definite pointers as to the emotion a character is feeling. Sometimes he labels the emotion as such—as with King Lear's wrath or Othello's jealousy or Laertes' desire for revenge. Less overtly, he leaves no doubt, through striking changes in Romeo's modes of speech and action, that news of Juliet's death and his own resolve to die at her side make a profound alteration in his whole being (pp. 72–3, 85). On the other hand, Shakespeare can deliberately be so cryptic—as when Banquo feels that Macbeth 'seems to fear' the Sisters' first prophecies—that no one can be reliably sure what Macbeth's reaction is, including Macbeth himself (pp. 64–6). More often than in either of these extremes, the text will suggest a mix of emotions that allows the actor considerable discretion in weighting them. The performer of Celia, for example, can decide how teasing her disparagement of Orlando to Rosalind should be: is she sharing her friend's new joy or feeling left out by it?

Even when Shakespeare is most clear about what a character is feeling, he still leaves the performer options about how strong the feeling is and how overtly it is to be expressed. As was discussed in the rehearsal of the play-within-a-play passage in *Hamlet*, the actor of Claudius is given many opportunities to choose exactly how much alarm he is feeling at Hamlet's incitements and how much of this alarm he allows to show (pp. 168–72). Hamlet's successive soliloquies, beginning "'Tis now the very witching time of night' and 'Now might I do it pat', allow his performer to adjust precisely the degree of ferocity he brings to the scene with his mother (p. 182). 'Fine-tuning' passages such as these are frequent in Shakespeare. Sometimes they are confined to single speeches. So the performer of Shylock, by varying the emphasis he places on the beginning and the end of his 'Hath not a Jew eyes?' speech, can strike just the balance he wants between Shylock's humanity and his vengefulness (p. 77). So Rosalind's 'Come woo me' speech can reflect the desired amount of coaxing that Orlando needs and she wishes to give (pp. 136–7). How determined is Macbeth when he tells his wife 'We will proceed no further in this business'? Depending on how they are read, the rest of the lines in his speech invite the actor to qualify this assertion as he sees fit (pp. 153–4).

Sometimes such fine-tuning goes on in a single sentence. Sir John (Falstaff) muses about repenting to Russell (Bardolph):

I was virtuously given as a gentleman need to be: virtuous enough; swore little; diced not—above seven times a week; went to a bawdy-house not—above once in a quarter—of an hour; paid money that I borrowed—three or four times; lived well, and in good compass. And now I live out of all order, out of all compass. (*1 Henry IV*, 3. 3. 13–19)

Most editors punctuate the passage without the dashes that in the quoted edition help to bring out the potential for humour that such pauses can afford. (The 1598 Quarto indicates no such pauses, the 1623 Folio only the last, putting a comma after 'borrowed'.) Making or not making the pauses allows the actor to give Falstaff just the degree of mock self-righteousness he sees fit. He might, for example, add further pauses thus: 'swore little; diced not—above seven times—a week; went to a bawdy-house not—above once—in a quarter—of an hour . . .' This variability also allows the actor of Falstaff to play off the reactions of a sceptical Bardolph, progressively reducing his claims to virtue until Bardolph can grudgingly accept them. Further, the pauses allow the actor of Falstaff to adjust to the relative responsiveness of his off-stage audience. If it has been quick to catch his humour, he might milk the passage for every possible laugh by making every possible pause. In that case the text encourages the actor to catch us in the audience by surprise. After two pauses about dicing, we might expect the next joke to be complete after 'went to a bawdy-house not—above once—in a quarter'. When Falstaff then adds 'of an hour' our surprise can add to the humour of his (claimed) sexual prowess. We may expect the next joke to go even further in the same direction, but no, Falstaff, after one last pause, shifts into another vein and rhythm. On the other hand, when such by-play doesn't suit a given Falstaff or his relation to Bardolph and the audience, the pauses can be omitted altogether.

When Shakespeare's texts are regarded as sets of cues for audience-response, one finds many of the same traits as when they are seen as guides for actors. Again he can be quite definite about the challenges he presents to his audiences and sometimes banks the whole success of his plays on our readiness to rise to them: to credit—or at least suspend our disbelief in—so miraculous a victory as that at Agincourt or so magical a moon-struck wood as that near Athens and to enter— at least a little—into their inclinations to dream impossible dreams, whether heroic or fantastic.

Egeus has no such inclination. His rigid and tradition-bound authoritanianism is the very reverse of the invitation *A Midsummer Night's Dream* extends to its audience to welcome strangeness. Ancient Pistol's braggadocio and chauvinism define for the audience precisely what *Henry V's* aspirations towards nobility and community are not. The two serve as 'bad examples' to a member of the audience who wishes to enter into the spirit of their respective plays. On the other hand, Kent sets the audience of *King Lear* a good example of that loyal endurance under outrageous injury that keeps us in the theatre during its performance.

Each of Shakespeare's plays encourages its audience to share the unique set of values best suited to its fullest appreciation. During a play we undergo a process of acculturation. The characters play a key part in this process, comprising a spectrum of attitudes that mirror and condition our own responses. Hamlet's theory holds that the purpose of playing is to show virtue her own feature, scorn her own image. Shakespeare's practice is less abstract and more immediate. Through his characters he shows to us in the audience images of our own attitude towards the play in progress. For instance, any sadistic thrill we may derive from the blinding of Gloucester is objectified for us in the person of Regan, and through that process her monstrosity rebukes our own. The 'themes' of a play also figure in our acculturation, spotlighting some of the very issues that we must deal with in our direct responses to the play's imagined world. So the constant talk about proper conduct in *Hamlet* focuses our own concern with the ethics of what is done or not done in Elsinore (p. 121).

Although Shakespeare may thus depend upon his audience's accepting a necessary minimum of a play's special values, he does not demand that our acceptance be complete. The spectrum of characters suggests various degrees and kinds of involvement on our part. For *Macbeth* to have its full effect some susceptibility to evil is necessary; Edward the Confessor would not make its most sympathetic spectator. But we need not be as susceptible to evil as is Macbeth himself or like his wife actively invoke it. We may be more like Banquo who is only gradually attracted towards it, or at the very least like Macduff, who shows a very wide tolerance for the sins Malcolm alleges against himself.

As with his players, Shakespeare may specify for his playgoers what responses he expects yet leave options as to when exactly they occur. He makes sure that his audience turns against the deposition of Richard II but leaves it to individual spectators whether the turn comes as early as the Bishop of Carlisle's denunciation, as late as Henry IV's remorseful final speech, or at some point between (p. 218). Shakespeare the theatre-poet often drives with loose reins yet he does move his playgoers and players along in definite directions, with a firm yet supple hand.

As discussed in Chapters 5 and 6, this same kind of flexible control is evident in Shakespeare's work as playwright, where he leaves little room for doubt about his plots but much room for choice in his characterization. The problem for his interpreters, of course, is to tell when he means to be firm and when flexible. His own practice as playwright is remarkably responsive to the distinctive world he is imagining. He becomes so immersed in his own make-believe that his style reflects that world. Like the characters in *1 Henry IV* who 'make history' to their own liking, he, for his own purposes, changes his chronicle sources to make Hotspur and Prince Hal of an age. At key times, his rendering of *King Lear* is abrupt where in *Hamlet* and *Troilus and Cressida* it is halting and in *Macbeth* it is wickedly tantalizing.

As theatre-poet he is concerned that all the members of the performance-ensemble achieve a rapport that enhances the world they are imagining. He not only makes his actors and audiences complicit in the evil-doings of Richard III, Iago, and Macbeth but—as playwright—himself contrives coincidences that further their plots. In

A Midsummer Night's Dream all concerned are encouraged to treat its fond pageant fondly, as in *King Lear* all concerned are challenged to endure its tough world toughly.

In every respect, his art is very much of a piece. After all, to distinguish between Shakespeare the playwright and Shakespeare the theatre-poet is only a manner of speaking, a way of calling attention to differing functions or aspects of what was for Shakespeare doubtless a single creative impulse, in which he all at the same time imagined a make-believe world and its enactment and reception. Lacking his genius, one has difficulty enough—after the fact and with the resulting text at hand—piecing together this controlling conception, where so much was going on at the same time, let alone trying to imagine the original act of conception. Yet certain moments in his plays do give readier access than others to Shakespeare's mind at the moment of their creation. The period during and immediately after the assassination of Duncan is one such moment. Lady Macbeth, then Macbeth, their performers, and the audience are intently listening and vividly 'seeing' the invisible murder scene in their mind's eye. In creating this moment, Shakespeare too must have been under the same spell. We are all 'rapt' and all give a start at the first knocking at the gate. Another such moment is the end of 'The Murder of Gonzago' in which we in the audience intently watch the members of the on-stage audience watch a play and—more importantly—watch one another. In creating this moment, Shakespeare must have been the most attentive watcher of all, for he was aware of all of the watchers, off-stage as well as on. At such times, the rapport that Shakespeare's theatre-poetry creates among the members of the performance-ensemble is so close as to be a unison. Creation, enactment, reception—all merge, and in perfect tune and timing with the world being imagined. It is at such moments that the presence of Shakespeare the theatre-poet is most powerfully felt.

Index of Names, Key Terms, and Subjects

Index